UNIVERSITIES AND COLLEGES AS ECONOMIC DRIVERS

SUNY SERIES, CRITICAL ISSUES IN HIGHER EDUCATION
Jason E. Lane and D. Bruce Johnstone

Universities and Colleges as Economic Drivers

Measuring Higher Education's Role in Economic Development

Edited by
Jason E. Lane and D. Bruce Johnstone

Foreword by Nancy L. Zimpher

Published by State University of New York Press, Albany

© 2012 State University of New York

For information, contact State University of New York Press, Albany, NY
www.sunypress.edu

Production by Ryan Morris
Marketing by Michael Campochiaro

Library of Congress Cataloging-in-Publication Data
Universities and colleges as economic drivers: Measuring Higher Education's Role
in Economic Development / edited by Jason E. Lane and D. Bruce Johnstone.
  p. cm. — (SUNY series, critical issues in higher education)
  Includes bibliographical references and index.
  ISBN 978-1-4384-4500-7 (pbk. : alk. paper)—ISBN 978-1-4384-4501-4 (hard-
cover : alk. paper)
  1. Education, Higher—Economic aspects. 2. Academic-industrial collaboration.
3. Economic development—Effect of education on. I. Lane, Jason E.
II. Johnstone, D. Bruce (Donald Bruce), 1941–
  LC67.6.U55 2012
  338.4'3378—dc23
                                                            2012003678

10 9 8 7 6 5 4 3 2 1

CONTENTS

ILLUSTRATIONS

FOREWORD

In late spring 2009 I arrived in New York State, the new chancellor of The State University of New York, by way of Ohio, where I had just concluded six years as president of the University of Cincinnati. In the handful of years between 2003 and 2009, my time as UC's head, the United States had undergone remarkable change, much of which, current zeitgeist tells us, was not for the better.

A consensus of decline is especially evident when it comes to discussion of the nation's economy. In 2003 it began to look as though the country was overcoming the short but intense downturn spurred by the burst of the Dot-com bubble and compounded in an unprecedented way by the terrorist attacks of September 11, 2001, both of which served to define those shaky first years of the new millennium. By 2003, though, the economic forecast seemed, by many indicators, to be brighter—but by 2009 the word recession had reentered our daily vocabulary with a vengeance. In 2003 consumer spending was up; in 2009 consumer confidence charted abysmally low. In 2003 the GDP surged upward at its fastest pace in nearly two decades; in 2009 it bottomed out at its lowest point in almost thirty years. In 2003 the national unemployment rate hovered around 6 percent; by June 2009, when I came to New York, national unemployment had climbed to 9.5 percent—the highest it had been since the early 1980s.

It was a grim picture, indeed. And this is not to say that 2003 was an economic paradise lost or that any one thing went calamitously wrong in 2009 to sink the GDP, kill millions of jobs, and shake the country's confidence to its core. Rather, it was a long, crooked road to the edge of a precipice—and it is there that we find ourselves to-day as the economy, while it makes some modest gains, continues to struggle. Life on the edge is uncertain and unsustainable. So, facing our future, the questions we need to answer can be framed as such: Do the solutions to our very serious economic challenges lie behind us, on the road from whence we came? Or are they to be found on the other side of a chasm? And if so, how do we build the bridge to get there?

I am a firm believer that the path to our economic vitality and sustainability does not lie behind us, but that it is ahead of us, on the far side of the divide. And I am equally convinced that institutions and systems of higher education—America's universities, colleges, and community colleges—will build the bridge to get us there. They, as the creators of new knowledge and understanding, as vibrant and reliable anchor institutions in our communities, and as both provid-ers and creators of a vast spectrum of jobs, are in an unmatched position to serve as the most powerful engines for our economic revi-talization. The expert authors who contributed to this volume agree.

It is not the purpose of this work to point fingers or surmise how we came to find ourselves clinging to the edge of a crumbling econ-omy. Rather, it is our entirely constructive aim to offer a means of pulling ourselves up and moving forward toward building a brighter, better, and more prosperous future for New York, the country, and the world. The State University of New York is designating itself as a thought leader on this front, driving the national conversation about higher education's role in revitalizing the country's economy. One way to develop the dialogue is through convening meetings of experts on the subject matter; another way is to publish and further disseminate that work. Here, with the release of this volume, we have done both.

Colleges and Universities as Economic Drivers is the first volume in what will be a series of works entitled *Critical Issues in Higher Education*, after SUNY's conference series of the same name. Not a typical publication of proceedings from our inaugural conference, "Universities as Economic Drivers: Measuring and Building Suc-cess," held in Buffalo, New York, on September 26 and 27, 2011, *Colleges and Universities as Economic Drivers* should be viewed as a continuation of the dialogue sparked there and a tool to extend the reach of those discussions well beyond the conference room walls.

The Buffalo meeting was an outstanding success. SUNY brought together more than four hundred education experts, business and industry professionals, community partners, and others from within our own SUNY system, as well as from twenty-eight states, and Canada and France. The intention of this book is the same as that of the conference—to cultivate greater understanding among elected officials, business representatives, policymakers, academics, and other concerned parties about the central roles universities and colleges play in national, state, and local economies. Each chapter, in its own right, provides a meaningful contribution to the field by providing an update to some of the foundational work in the field or providing cutting-edge and thought-provoking analysis. We are proud to say that this is one of the first book-length volumes to comprehensively examine the role of colleges and universities as economic drivers.

It is worth noting that, overall, 2011 was a momentous year for SUNY, particularly in the economic development arena. The successful organization of the first Critical Issues in Higher Education conference was just one of many important accomplishments toward realizing our goal to continue to provide all New Yorkers with a world-class education at an affordable price while also working toward revitalizing the state's economy. SUNY had the great fortune of finding an invaluable partner in Governor Andrew M. Cuomo, who from the podium has referred to SUNY as a "precious New York asset," and "the great equalizer of the middle class," and has deemed our campuses "centers of excellence, innovation, and job creation." With the governor's support, we also saw the signing of NYSUNY 2020 into law—a plan that not only ensures a fair and rational five-year tuition policy for students and their families, but which will help strengthen SUNY's role as a catalyst for job growth throughout the state, strengthen academic programs at our four university centers, and make New York a more supportive environment for business and industry. In July, the governor appointed me, as SUNY's chancellor, to the statewide Chairman's Committee for his regional economic development councils, and SUNY is playing an active leadership role on each of the ten councils. In 2011 SUNY also orchestrated four Regional Campus Showcases, public events in which campuses from each of New York's ten regions convene to highlight their greatest abilities to help build a stronger economy and a better future for all New Yorkers.

A STATEWIDE TOUR: SURVEYING THE LANDSCAPE, DEVISING A PLAN

When I arrived in New York on June 1, 2009, I hit the ground running, quite literally, having decided that my first act as SUNY's new chancellor would be to undertake a statewide tour of all of the system's sixty-four campuses. Within a week of landing in New York, I was back on the road, crisscrossing the state. This tour took three months, and had never been undertaken by any of SUNY's eleven former chancellors in the university's sixty-year history, much less in such a methodical way. The purpose of the tour was simple: If I were to truly lead this university system, I needed to know it inside and out. I needed to see it for myself; to grasp what made the individual campuses unique and valuable; and to learn what qualities they all shared. At the end of the tour, I wanted to be able to unify and define each campus as a "SUNY school" and as a part of a cohesive system.

The State University of New York is the nation's—and the world's—largest comprehensive public university system. The key word in this distinction is *comprehensive*, meaning that among SUNY's sixty-four campuses, there are twenty-nine state-operated institutions, five statutory colleges, and thirty community colleges. Among those institutions are research universities, liberal arts colleges, specialized and technical colleges, health science centers, and land-grant colleges. SUNY is the only university system in the country to embrace such a wide spectrum of higher education opportunities and environments, and on such a large scale. In 2012, SUNY enrolled more than 467,000 students; employed 88,000 faculty and staff; and counted more than 3 million alumni. The university is embedded in virtually every community in New York State; 93 percent of New Yorkers live within fifteen miles of a SUNY campus, and nearly 100 percent live within thirty miles. In many communities, SUNY is the largest employer.

I knew the numbers and figures before I arrived in New York. What I did not fully understand until I was out in the field during those first one hundred days of my tenure is that this state is breathtakingly diverse: geographically, demographically, politically, and ideologically. The tour opened my eyes to these vicissitudes, and I was as grateful for the experience as I was energized and inspired by it. However, for all of New York's variety—upstate or downstate, mountain or valley, Western or Central or North Country region, metropolis or village or suburb—wherever we went, there was one thing, one thread that weaved its way through every stop and every campus and every conversation we had: a grave concern about the economy and an earnest desire to know what could be done about it.

So, as I toured, I learned the lay of the land, both literally and figuratively, traveling the state and hearing again and again in every corner—it became a kind of drumbeat that accompanied our every move—a persistent, pervasive concern about the economy and questions about what New York could do to protect jobs, to create new jobs, to attract and retain skilled and educated workers, and to stem the tide of graduates who had been leaving the various regions or the state altogether in search of better prospects in other parts of the country.

This listening tour was followed by a series of town meetings, which were organized around the state and featured some of the nation's best minds in innovation, health, education, and other key areas. These events positioned SUNY as a catalyst, convener, and idea generator. Even more important, these two phases yielded the information and emergent themes that ultimately led to the formation of our strategic plan and its central idea: beyond meeting our mission to provide access and opportunity and a world-class education to *all* New Yorkers, more than living up to our motto—*To Learn, To Search, To Serve*—SUNY would become the key driver of economic revitalization and enhanced quality of life for all of New York's communities.

Recognizing this power, we named our strategic plan *The Power of SUNY* and launched it in April 2010. In it we identified what we call our six "Big Ideas": SUNY and the Entrepreneurial Century, SUNY and the Seamless Education Pipeline, SUNY and a Healthier New York, SUNY and an Energy-Smart New York, SUNY and the Vibrant Community, and SUNY and the World. Each of the plan's six tenets support SUNYs role as an engine for New York's economic revitalization.

Moving around the state, I came to know its terrain and the SUNY system better and I began to see SUNY more clearly for the system that it is. In fact, were you to take a map of New York State and superimpose the locations of the SUNY campuses on it, you would see the system as a kind of supporting framework, as an infrastructure.

SUNY, with its ubiquitous presence throughout the state, coupled with its innate power to be the creator of new knowledge and jobs, is uniquely positioned to be the support structure and the economic engine New York needs.

COLLEGES AND UNIVERSITIES AS ECONOMIC ENGINES AND ANCHOR INSTITUTIONS

Higher education is now a major economic driver, and colleges and universities are critical components of national and regional work-force-development strategies and innovation systems. Indeed, over the past several years national policy organizations such as the Association of Public Land-grant Universities (APLU), the Business-Higher Education Forum (BHEF), National Governors Association (NGA), and the National Conference of State Legislators (NCSL) have been calling on higher education leaders, state government officials, and business and industry representatives to align the work of higher education with the economic and social needs of our states and the nation. It is not a surprise then, that higher education's role in economic development emerged as the overarching theme of *The Power of SUNY*, which provides a roadmap for the development of the SUNY system over the next decade, and, we hope, a model for driving regional economic development for public university systems and colleges across the country.

Though the buzz term "anchor institution" is not discussed specifically in the chapters of this book (though the concept of colleges and universities as economy-sustaining community anchors is touched on in chapters 1, 2, and 7), it is a phrase that is never far from our thinking in SUNY. That is because the term astutely defines what we believe is SUNY's greatest strength, describing an indispensable component of the fabric of strong communities everywhere: institutions that are not likely to pick up and move away because of their large size and deep roots in the community. They are, in effect, anchored in place and serve as reliable and powerful forces for economic development and help drive and determine the local quality of life.

Universities and colleges, like hospitals, museums, performing arts centers, sports complexes, and other large cultural institutions, serve as anchor institutions. There is widespread consensus among specialists in economic growth that higher education institutions function as anchors because they (1) are sources of a wide range of jobs, including faculty, administrators, and support staff; (2) act as incubators for new ideas needed to create jobs in a knowledge-driven economy; and (3) help develop a workforce prepared to fill those jobs.

The many economic impacts of universities are specific and sustained. Reliable, annual influxes of new students, many of whom commit to two or four or more years in the area, integrate into and help strengthen host communities by supporting services and businesses. The town-gown relationship is a symbiotic one: campus vibrancy spills over into surrounding communities as universities and colleges attract businesses that cater to students, faculty, staff, and visitors and provide critical jobs and services. Furthermore, the populations of communities that host colleges and universities tend to be younger, better educated, and more diverse. In the most direct terms, educating a diverse population breaks the cycle of poverty and leverages returns to the community over generations. I have yet to hear anyone say it better than *New York Times* columnist David Leonhardt (2009, p. MM22): "[E]ducating more people and educating them better—appears to be the best single bet that a society can make." At SUNY, we could not agree more.

CREATING NEW KNOWLEDGE, MEASURING SUCCESS

While there have been myriad attempts at measuring the economic impact of higher education institutions, until recently there had been almost no research about the full breadth of economic contributions made by colleges and universities. To help confront this shortcoming, SUNY commissioned the Rockefeller Institute of Government (RIG), our esteemed public-policy think tank located at the University at Albany, to conduct a national study of higher education's role in economic development. RIG's results, chronicled in the report *A New Paradigm for Economic Development* (Shaffer & Wright, 2010), painted a colorful picture of the many ways that community colleges, research universities, liberal arts institutions, and regional comprehensive colleges enhance the vitality and competitiveness of their local and regional communities.

With the *New Paradigm* report as a backdrop, RIG, in partnership with the University at Buffalo's Regional Institute, conducted in 2011 what we believe to be one of the most expansive economic-impact reports ever commissioned. The researchers at these two institutes used a variety of qualitative and quantitative methods to capture the full range of economic drivers supported by SUNY's sixty-four campuses. By traveling to nearly every community in the state, the research team was able to see, firsthand, the power of SUNY. The resulting report, *How SUNY Matters: Economic Impacts of the State University of New York*, concluded that "SUNY is an economic anchor and dominant source of educated workers in nearly all regions of the state" and that the university helps "New York succeed in the knowledge-based economy, from educating people in highly specialized skills to assisting employers with the adoption and management of new technologies to transforming new ideas into commercial innovations" (Shaffer, Teaman, & Wright, 2011, p. 110).

In keeping with SUNY's desire and promise to track our economic impact, as well as our progress as an educator, job creator, community partner, and generator of boundary-breaking research, we created a new SUNY report card series in 2011. In May, we released a baseline-setting report card, which was followed in September with the first progress-tracking report. The report card measures the system's performance in areas corresponding to what we believe are New York's greatest social and economic needs, such as growing the state's involvement in the green energy market. The report card, which we plan to release annually each September, has been instrumental in demonstrating the economic contributions of the SUNY system, and will continue to be even more helpful as our "work-in-progress" metrics begin to evidence progress.

SUNY is just one of many excellent examples of the power and potential of universities as anchor institutions and economic drivers. To further develop the intellectual inquiry related to this topic, we knew that we needed to bring experts to the table. Hence, we developed the *Critical Issues in Higher Education* conference and the subsequent publication of this volume.

At its heart, the purpose of this book is to bring greater attention to the critical role that higher education plays in economic development. The intention here is not to put these economic development functions of colleges and universities on a pedestal above teaching, research, and community engagement. However, the conference and these essays emerge from the fact that many elected officials, institutional leaders, and other policymakers are recognizing the importance of these economic functions. This book is meant to bring greater clarity to the different ways in which colleges and universities contribute economically to their communities, and to challenge those engaged in measuring such contributions to do so in an academically rigorous fashion.

The first two chapters present a broad backdrop for the rest of the book. In chapter 1, Jason Lane explains some of the arguments underlying the widely held belief about higher education's important role in fostering a nation's economic competitiveness. Lane shows how this belief is driving development in some nations and highlights how few institutions in the United States discuss this aspect of economic development. The chapter concludes with a discussion of how governments, higher education institutions, and business can collaborate on economic development strategies. In the second chapter, Tom Gais and David Wright, drawing on the Rockefeller Institute reports discussed previously, present a typology of economic development activities engaged in by colleges and universities and discuss the obstacles that these different activities present for establishing appropriate metrics.

The third chapter discusses varied methodological problems with existing economic development reports produced by higher education institutions systems. In this follow-up to their earlier article in the *Economics of Education Review*, Peter McHenry, Allen R. Sanderson, and John J. Siegfried discuss how institutions often inflate their overall economic impact, as well as the return that states receive on their investment in public higher education.

Chapters 4 and 5 explore the economic contributions of university-based research centers. Maryann P. Feldman, Allan M. Freyer, and Lauren Lanahan, in chapter 4, argue that research centers that receive long-term funding and a broad mission are much more productive than those with shorter funding streams and a more narrow scope. In chapter 5, Laura Schultz explores the evolution of university-industry-government–sponsored research centers and demonstrates how they fit with the local innovation system.

The next two chapters explore the relationship between higher education and workforce development. Anthony Carnevale and

Stephen Rose, in chapter 6, trace the convergence of postsecondary education and the labor market. They argue that, in an increasingly global market, the United States is losing ground to many other nations in terms of the overall education level of our workforce. In addition, through their data, they demonstrate how the higher education degree has become one of the most significant factors in lifetime earnings. They also show that, despite the high cost of a college degree, it remains one of the most worthwhile investments an individual can make. Taking a more specific focus, Jim Jacobs, in chapter 7, argues the important role of community colleges in retraining displaced workers and provides examples of how some community colleges are partnering with local businesses to respond to the aftermath of the great recession.

In chapter 8, Jason Lane and Taya Owens examine the international dimensions of higher education's economic contributions. They first show how few institutions in the United States attempt to measure, much less acknowledge, these factors in their economic development reports. Then they present data about the expanding international student trade and explore the growing phenomenon of colleges and universities investing their financial and academic capital to own and operate campuses in foreign markets. In chapter 9, Jason Owen-Smith draws on two intense case studies to illustrate how institutional policies can impact—negatively and positively—the development of academic knowledge into economically viable knowledge. This chapter is particularly important for those looking to improve the ways in which an institution can move new inventions from the laboratory into the marketplace.

Finally, D. Bruce Johnstone explores the effect of the Great Recession on public higher education. He argues that many institutions now face an era of great austerity with reduced state funding and calls for institutions to contain costs. Despite these worsening economic conditions, Johnstone argues, public colleges and universities need to find ways to enhance their economic contributions. At the same time, the vital role that these institutions play in a state's economic recovery suggests that policy makers should place high priority on funding their higher education sector.

I want to express my appreciation to the entire staff of the Rockefeller Institute of Government, particularly Thomas Gais, David

Wright, and Michelle Kelafant, for organizing what proved to be an intellectually stimulating and provocative meeting. I also want to extend my deepest thanks to the book's editors, D. Bruce Johnstone, former SUNY chancellor and Distinguished Service Professor emeritus from the University at Buffalo, and Jason E. Lane, Director of Education Studies at the Rockefeller Institute of Government and Associate Professor of Educational Administration and Policy at the University at Albany, for taking up the charge of developing and editing this volume.

In conclusion, as I sat down to write this foreword, my attention was caught by column by Thomas Friedman (2012, p. A23) in the *New York Times*, in which he observed "[t]he globalization side of this [technology] revolution is integrating more and more . . . people into ecosystems, where they can innovate and manufacture more products and services that make people's lives more healthy, educated, entertained, productive and comfortable. The best of these ecosystems will be cities and towns that combine a university, an educated populace, a dynamic business community and the fastest broadband connections on earth. These will be the job factories of the future."

In those few lines, Friedman is describing the power of universities and colleges as anchor institutions, and the power of institutions of higher education as economic drivers and sustainers and determiners of quality of life. It is my great hope that this idea catches on to the point of becoming a new paradigm, an unshakable, culture-defining, and enhancing meme. But to make that happen, and to reap all the benefits of higher education and its vital institutions, we need to keep the conversation going and spread it far and wide. The call for states and higher education institutions to work more collaboratively is an important one and undergirds the entire SUNY Critical Issues in Higher Education series. In 2012, we will continue the dialogue and explore the important role that state systems play in improving access, controlling costs, and enhancing the productivity of higher education institutions. We at SUNY sincerely hope that you will join the conversation.

Nancy L. Zimpher, Chancellor
State University of New York
January 11, 2012

REFERENCES

Collins, J., & Porras, J. I. (2002). *Built to last: Successful habits of visionary companies* (3rd Edition). New York: Harper Collins.

Friedman, T. L. (2012, Jan. 3). So much fun. So irrelevant. *New York Times*, A23.

Leonhardt, D. (2009, Jan. 27), The big fix. *New York Times*, MM22.

Shaffer, D. F., Teaman, R. M., & Wright, D. J. (2011). *How SUNY matters: Economic impacts of the State University of New York*. Albany, NY: The Nelson A. Rockefeller Institute of Government and the University at Buffalo Regional Institute.

Shaffer, D. F., & Wright, D. J. (2010). *A new paradigm for economic development: How higher education institutions are working to revitalize their regional and state economies*. Report. Albany, NY: Rockefeller Institute of Government.

ACKNOWLEDGMENTS

This book emerged as part of the planning for the SUNY Critical Issues conference, *Universities as Economic Drivers*, which was held in Buffalo, N.Y., in September 2011. We are grateful to all who attended that meeting. Our own understanding of the role of higher education and economic development benefited greatly from the workshops and discussions in which we engaged during our time in Buffalo.

We are indebted to many people for their assistance in preparing this volume. While we are sure to inadvertently leave some people out, there are a handful of folks that deserve special recognition. David Wright and Tom Gais provided intellectual support as we conceptualized the scope and purpose of the book. Patti Cadrette and Taya Owens were critical for dealing with the administrative aspects of organizing the project. Jessica Neidl provided much needed support, despite pressing timelines. To the many wonderful authors who made this volume possible, we greatly value your hard work, dedication, and willingness to work under short timelines. In addition we give our appreciation to SUNY Chancellor Nancy Zimpher for her support of our endeavor to further the scholarly inquiry into the study of higher education's role in economic development.

Finally, we extend our personal thanks to Kari Lane for her patience, understanding, and insight that made this project possible.

Jason E. Lane
Albany, N.Y.

D. Bruce Johnstone
Buffalo, N.Y.

1

HIGHER EDUCATION AND ECONOMIC COMPETITIVENESS

JASON E. LANE

ABSTRACT

Higher education plays an increasingly critical role in the economic competitiveness of local, state, and national economies. The factors driving the World Economic Forum's Global Competitiveness Index are examined to illustrate how higher education has come to be viewed as a driver of economic growth. Then, by examining institutional economic development reports and national economic competitiveness plans, this chapter lays out the growing global interest and import of economic competitiveness and the ways in which governments are seeking to harness the power of higher education to support their own competitiveness. It concludes with a discussion of how governments, businesses, and higher education institutions could collaborate to develop public agendas to guide, among other things, the economic contributions of colleges and universities.

INTRODUCTION

> We are just now perceiving that the university's invisible product, knowledge, may be the most powerful single element in our culture, affecting the rise and fall of professions and even of social classes, or regions, and even nations.
>
> —Clark Kerr, *The Uses of the University*

1

Clark Kerr was prescient about the significant role knowledge would come to play globally in terms of economic prosperity and competition. We now live in an age of a knowledge-based economy, in which the creation and transmission of knowledge has come to be a primary impetus for economic development. This has led to a shift in the policies and practices used by many countries to compete economically. In *The Competitive Advantage of Nations*, Porter (1990a) observed that in most of the world, a nation's economic prosperity would no longer be tied to abundant natural resources and cheap labor; rather, their "competitive advantage" would be increasingly based on creative and scientific innovations. This new paradigm of economic development positioned colleges and universities as primary engines of economic growth (see Romer, 1990).

Today, many nations are involved in *the great brain race*, a phrase used by Ben Wildavsky (2010) to describe the increasing competition among nations for new knowledge and innovation. Governments increasingly adopt comprehensive competitiveness strategies designed to improve their economic position in the global economy. Recognizing that an advantage of the great economic powers of the last century was their higher education sectors, many governments are now seeking to expand the capacity and quality of their own sectors. This, at times, includes actively recruiting and retaining students, scholars, programs, and institutions from other nations—particularly those perceived to have strong higher education systems. Some of these nations are using the higher education resources of other nations to decrease the competitive advantage gap between them. In this new environment, governments have begun to realize that higher education institutions are important anchoring tools as they help to attract and retain students and alumni. Governments also recognize that such institutions drive innovation and industry development, and have begun to invest in research institutions, research parks, and research programs.

Beyond the engagement in educating students, much of the economic development contributions derived from higher education come through partnerships with the government as well as the local community and industry. The reality is that while nations posture over competitive advantages, the economic contributions of colleges and universities occur in their local communities. So, it is also important to understand the connection between higher education institutions and the communities where they are located.

The purpose of this book is to cultivate greater understanding among elected officials, business representatives, policymakers, academics, and other concerned parties about the central roles universities and colleges play in national, state, and local economies. Through the varied contributions, it assesses, based on the best available evidence, ideas, and practices from across the United States and around the world, how universities and colleges exert impact on economic growth. Some chapters explore methodologies, metrics, and data sources that may be used to gauge the performance of diverse higher education institutions in improving economic outcomes. Others present typologies of economic development activities and are designed to improve understanding of such initiatives and generate new energy and focus for a national community of scholars and practitioners working to formulate new models for how universities and colleges may lead economic development in their nations, states, and communities while still performing their more traditional and central educational functions.

The intent of this book is not to privilege the economic development functions of higher education institutions above those of teaching, research, and service. These engagements are well documented and discussed throughout the literature—and, rightly so; they are the primary missions of these educational institutions. However, there is now significant interest among policymakers and institutional leaders about the role of colleges and universities as economic drivers. This volume is intended to provide readers with an overview of the economic contributions of higher education institutions and set forth ways for better measuring, studying, and discussing the concept.

This chapter provides a conceptual context for the rest of the book, discussing the rising focus of nations on their economic competitiveness in the global marketplace. The rise of colleges and universities as economic drivers is set against this broad backdrop. Not all readers may agree that knowledge-driven innovation is a primary force behind the competitiveness of countries and—in the case of the United States—the several states. However, the issue of economic competitiveness is frequently discussed among political leaders, media pundits, and policymakers around the globe; and the desire to enhance one's ability to compete economically has spurred many policy decisions. This chapter seeks to frame how higher education is now engaged with the issue of economic competitiveness, drawing on the literature, rankings, and policy documents.

The chapter begins with a discussion of the competitive advantage of nations, highlighting what many believe to be the critical role that higher education plays in advancing the economic condition of countries. I then discuss the ways in which higher education has been incorporated into national and state economic development and competitiveness plans. Then, drawing on economic development reports, the chapter shows how some U.S. institutions now use competitive advantage terminology as a means to strengthen their position among stakeholders. In the final section, I argue that higher education, business, and government leaders could be advantaged to work more collaboratively to develop public agendas that guide, among other things, the economic contributions of colleges and universities.

GLOBAL COMPETITIVENESS AND HIGHER EDUCATION

When Michael Porter (1990a) published the book *The Competitive Advantage of Nations*, his premise was simple: the economic prosperity of a nation in the twenty-first century would be created, not inherited. He posited that a nation's competitive advantage[1] in the global marketplace is based upon its industries' ability to innovate and upgrade. This conclusion challenged classical economic assumptions that the advantage of nations mostly rested on their access to natural resources and labor as well as productive regulation of their economic markets. Instead, Porter (1990a, p. 19) argued that competitiveness in the modern world would favor the innovators. Moreover, innovation would be "created and sustained through a highly localized process," not a standardized model to be adopted by all nations. He noted that differences in "national values, culture, economic structures, institutions, and histories all contribute to competitive success" (Porter, 1990b, p. 3). This premise quickly garnered the attention of leaders around the globe and led many nations and regions to be more strategic about enhancing their global competitiveness as a means for enhancing their economic prosperity.

The economic competitiveness of nations would soon become a competition in its own right. In 2004, the World Economic Forum, located in Switzerland, began producing an annual index of national competitiveness in their Global Competitiveness Report. The rankings are based on several pillars of economic development: public and private institutions, infrastructure, macro economic framework, health and primary education, higher education and training, market efficiency, technological readiness, business sophistication, and innovation. Given the different developmental stages of nations, the report breaks nations into three groups based on the most important factors driving their economic development. The stages of development, beginning with the stage with the least development, are factor-driven, efficiency-driven, and innovation-driven.

As countries move into more advanced economic stages, higher education becomes increasingly important. Countries with factor-driven economies gain competitive advantage based on what is available within the nation, primarily natural resources and unskilled labor. In this stage, the most important factors in the Global Competitive Index are institutions (e.g., government agencies and accountability), infrastructure, macroeconomic framework, health and primary education. Moving into an efficiency-driven economy, wages tend to increase and productive economies need to figure out ways to support the increased wage demands and further improve quality of life. They do this by enhancing the efficiency of the production process and quality of products. The competitive advantage of nations at this stage is driven by quality and accessible higher education institutions, efficient and well-developed markets, and the ability to effectively use technology. The Global Competitiveness Report explains the importance of higher education as nations transition through the various economic stages this way:

> Although less-advanced countries can still improve their productivity by adopting existing technologies or making incremental improvements in other areas, for those that have reached the innovation stage of development, this is no longer sufficient for increasing productivity. Firms in these countries must design and develop cutting-edge products and processes to maintain a competitive edge. This requires an environment that is conducive to innovative activity, supported by both

the public and the private sectors. In particular, it means sufficient investment in research and development (R&D), especially by the private sector; the presence of high quality scientific research institutions; extensive collaboration in research between universities and industry; and the protection of intellectual property. (Schwab, 2011, p. 7)

Moreover, these nations need to develop their workforce to be able to both create and use these new innovations. Moving from an efficiency-driven economy to an innovation-driven economy requires a nation to produce and take advantage of new products. A nation must be able to both create and utilize innovation. This requires a research infrastructure and entrepreneurial culture that can foster innovation as well as an educational infrastructure to support knowledge acquisition, skill development, and critical thinking among the nation's workforce.

Competitive advantage is not just important for being able to foster economic prosperity within a nation. Some now argue that global power is increasingly being tied to economic might. The title of the 2011 book, *The Coming Jobs War*, underscores this concept. The author, Jim Clifton, chairman and CEO of Gallup, one of the leading international polling organizations, argues that the data from the vast array of Gallup's polling suggests that the competition for good jobs and GDP growth is becoming increasingly critical and that in the next three decades, global competition among nations will be led by economic force, political or military power. Thus, if economic might is driving the power struggle among nations, then innovation will likely be one of the keys to long-term success. And, in many nations, higher education institutions are the primary force driving innovation and developing workers for the innovation-driven economy. Indeed, Clifton argues that because of their unique ecosystems, universities are one of the most important institutions in the competition for jobs and, thus, economic power.

The American research university has been often posited as one of the primary drivers of the nation's economic competitiveness. Many have touted its role in producing a high-skilled work force, attracting some of the best minds from other countries, and fostering creative activity and innovation. Of increasing interest is also how these institutions have been able to sustain their global dominance over the past several decades. The University of Virginia economic development plan argues, "Research universities are akin to large firms producing two valuable products that are most efficiently produced in tandem. These firms compete for customers among students and their families, government funding agencies, foundations, and corporations. To each customer, the university provides a different bundle of services" (Knapp & Shobe, 2007, p. 56). America's higher education institutions proved to be significant components for supporting a range of activities from educating the high-skilled laborers to producing the new knowledge that supports an innovation-driven economy.

Recognition of higher education's crucial role in supporting economic competitiveness has changed markedly in the last twenty years. In *The Competitive Advantage of Nations*, discussion of the role of higher education in a nation's competitive advantage is surprisingly minimal. Porter's (1990a) focus at the time was primarily on the role of firms in fostering competitive advantage. He noted that firms are particularly important in shaping the creation of factors that drive the economy and firms can influence the direction of higher education institutions by sponsoring students, helping institutions identify the needs of industry, helping with curriculum planning, hiring graduates, and financially supporting equipment, facilities, scholarship, research, and programs that recognize outstanding teachers and students.

Twenty years later, higher education is understood not just as a means for supporting a nation's competitive advantage, but as a competitive advantage in its own right. Nations such as the United Kingdom and the United States, among others, have a long history of investing significant resources in their higher education sectors. This commitment to higher education has resulted in the development of quite advanced educational systems (see Carnevale & Rose, 2012, chapter 6 of this volume, for a discussion of how this transpired in the United States). These systems are able to provide the nation with highly skilled laborers and support the innovation economy. In addition, as discussed in Lane and Owens (2012—chapter 8 of this volume), higher education is now a highly valuable tradable service. The United States and the UK also hold competitive advantages not just because their higher education institutions are among the leading institutions in the world; they also attracted some of the most capable students from other countries. Many of these students would remain in the country where they studied, contributing to its innovation and economic development, instead of returning home. In many ways, it is the competitive advantage in the higher education sector that allowed these nations to create and sustain their competitive advantage in several industries.

The theory of competitive advantage can be used to understand the development of higher education as a tradable service. The United States' competitive advantage in the area of higher education has resulted in the U.S. successfully exporting its higher education sector to most other nations. Why would nations desire to import higher education services? The United States has already invested significantly in the development of its higher education infrastructure and attained a very strong global reputation. For many nations, the costs of creating a comparable system to educate their students would be unfathomable. As such, it is more efficient to invest their limited resources in other industries and, instead, send their students abroad to study.

The United States relies on this competitive advantage. In fact, the largest proportion of students studying outside of their home country, study in the United States (OECD, 2010). However, many national leaders have begun to recognize the important role of higher education in economic growth. National competitiveness strategies now often include investment in their domestic higher education system as one of the core strategies. In some nations this even includes attracting colleges and universities in foreign countries to set up shop in their borders, resulting in a range of ventures from joint programs to consultancies to international branch campuses (Lane & Kinser, 2011a). This increased international competition can be measured in many ways; but the dramatic drop of the U.S. market share of international students is the most telling. While the total number of international students studying in the United States continues to increase, the overall market share has declined from 26 percent in 2000 to 18.7 percent in 2008 (OECD, 2010). Recognition of the critical role that higher education plays in fostering a nation's broad-based competitive advantage will lead some nations to invest more in higher education and further enhance the international competition for students and scholars.

Of course, competitiveness is not solely a national strategy. Within the United States, individual states seek ways to improve their own competitive advantage. As semi-sovereign political entities that benefit from the productivity of their own markets (e.g., tax dollars, job growth, quality of life, etc.), state governments compete not just with other nations, but with other states for attracting businesses, jobs, and students. Moreover, institutions are now positioning themselves as a backbone of economic competitiveness in order to strengthen their standing among stakeholders. The following sections discuss the intersection of higher education and competitiveness at the national and state levels.

NATIONAL COMPETITIVENESS: HIGHER EDUCATION'S ROLE

It is difficult to determine exactly how higher education emerged as a competitive advantage in the United States. One might point to any myriad of federal policies. For example, the Morrill Land Grant Acts of 1862 and 1890 spurred the development of research into the agricultural and mechanical arts through the funding of new colleges and universities. The Servicemen's Readjustment Act of 1944 (otherwise known as the GI Bill) opened up higher education to the middle and lower classes and helped move the system from elite access to mass access. The National Defense in Education Act (NDEA), prompted by Russia's launch of Sputnik and their beating the United States into space, provided new funding to advance the nation's scientific progress. Many other policies could likely be added to this list, but policies alone did not create and sustain the worldwide success of this particular national strength. A number of institutional, cultural, and historical factors also contributed. Geiger (2004, p. 132) suggests the answer is "the decentralized, competitive structure of the university system, which fostered and rewarded innovative and entrepreneurial behavior." The collective diversity and flexibility of the entire high education sector, with community colleges, liberal arts colleges, comprehensive institutions, and so forth offering multiple educational pathways to a wide range of students surely also helped. But, for the purposes of this section, I am focusing on how national governments incorporate higher education into their competitiveness strategies.

To start, though many now consider its higher education system as the backbone of its economic success over the last century, the United States does not have a comprehensive competitiveness strategy (Porter, 2008). Nor does it have a national plan as to how its higher education institutions could be used or grown to support its economic competitiveness. There are certainly calls for increasing the number of college graduates in the coming years, and some leaders believe that the federal government should support additional research funding, but these are not plans or strategies. This disconnect is partially explained by the fact that education is a public function that is primarily regulated by the state governments, and the role of higher education in the competitive advantage of states is discussed below.

Though the United States may not have a competitiveness strategy, other countries do, and many of those often put a significant emphasis on higher education. From Guyana to Indonesia and the Republic of Georgia to Qatar, national governments are linking higher education to their competitiveness strategies. They are investing new resources into their own educational institutions in order to educate more highly skilled labor. They are building research and science parks to help spur innovation and research. They are also seeking ways to capitalize on the success of other nations by importing higher education. This importing does not simply come through sending students abroad for an education with the hope that they might return, but also through developing joint partnerships, international branch campuses, and educational hubs designed to build local capacity and, for some, recruit students from other countries (Knight, 2011; Lane & Kinser, 2011a; Obst, Kuder, & Banks, 2011).

One of the more direct statements about the importance of education in national competitiveness comes from Ireland's National Competitiveness Council, which reports directly to the nation's prime minister:

Education is central to our ability to improve our quality of life and wellbeing through success in selling goods and services on international markets. The quality of education outcomes is central to national competitiveness. Ireland's education system has been a key contributor to economic growth and improvements in living standards in recent years. We need to have one of the best education and research systems in the world to drive economic recovery. (National Competitiveness Council, 2009)

For many nations, the role of higher education in fostering economic competitiveness is seen primarily as the production of highly skilled labor. For example, the competitiveness reports of such varied nations as Croatia, Malaysia, South Korea, and Guyana all point to the need for more workers for the knowledge-based industries. Guyana (2006) has an entire action item (HR.R5) in its competitiveness report dedicated to reversing "brain drain." South Korea, through the Korea Research Foundation (n.d.), developed the BrainKorea21 (BK21) program designed to nurture world-class graduate schools and to foster research. Croatia places education as one of the foundational building blocks of its national competitiveness and its plan focuses on the need to expand educational access because of the lack of highly skilled labor (National Competitiveness Council, 2009). In the case of Malaysia, the government wanted to stem the significant outflows of students from the nation. Ziguras (2003) estimated that in 1995 Malaysia lost approximately US$800 million due to the very large number of students studying oversees; this does not include the potential loss of productivity occasioned by a large number of those students not returning to the country. To counter this trend of their students studying abroad, the Malaysian government began expanding its domestic capacity, as well as attracting branch campuses from overseas institutions (Lee, 2001; Sirat, 2005).

Governments such as those in China, Qatar, and Malaysia have gone so far as to actively and purposefully align their educational interests with their economic policies. For example, in Qatar, the nation has actively attracted international branch campuses from the United States with the explicit purpose of supporting the key areas of economic growth—areas that the nation desires to develop into a competitive advantage (Lane & Kinser, 2011a). The foreign institutions, such as Carnegie Mellon University, Texas A&M University, and Northwestern University, that set up shop are intended to help build the local education system as well as spur innovation in local industries (Trani & Holsworth, 2010).

One of the more interesting developments in this arena has been the recent focus on the concept of "educational hubs." Still loosely defined, the general premise behind a hub is that one builds an educational infrastructure to reduce the number of students studying abroad and entice international students to study in that country.

There is very little data yet available to measure the success or failure of such endeavors, but it does have great rhetorical panache. Nations such as Bhutan, Sri Lanka, Malaysia, Singapore, Qatar, and the United Arab Emirates have invoked this strategy, though the developmental process has been varied (see www.globalhighered.org for descriptions of emerging educational hubs).

The increasing importance of economic power, particularly as measured through economic competitiveness, has fostered renewed interest by nations in their higher education systems. Many nations seem increasingly less willing to outsource the advanced training of their students to other nations. The corresponding changes will likely mean increased competition for international students; but also new resources for higher education institutions in nations that deem higher education of strategic importance.

HIGHER EDUCATION'S CONTRIBUTION TO STATE ECONOMIC COMPETITIVENESS

Globally, the concept of competitiveness is mostly discussed at the national level, but it is also influencing much activity at the subnational level as well. For example, in the United Arab Emirates, which is a federation of seven states, Dubai and Abu Dhabi, as examples, are both active in increasing their own competitive advantages (Davidson, 2008). In terms of higher education, both have adopted strategies to import higher education and build new domestic institutions to help expand their advantage (Croom, 2010; Kinser et al., 2010; Lane & Kinser, 2011a). They both also compete with each other as with well as other nations in terms of attracting students, workers, and businesses. This section, which focuses mostly on efforts within the United States, discusses the ways in which colleges and universities foster economic activity within subnational governments.

In nations where subnational governments (e.g., states) retain control over higher education, economic development and competitiveness strategies that utilize higher education can be quite varied, but often lead to states competing over businesses, laborers, and other drivers of economic development. Higher education institutions can play an active role in this competition seeking to attract students, faculty, resources, and recognition.

Within the United States, many states now have competitiveness councils and are ranked based on their own economic competitiveness and how business friendly they are.[2] Some states even have their own international trade departments, designed to help market the goods and services of their businesses in overseas markets. As with nations, states (and other subnational governments) have come to recognize the importance of higher education institutions, though many now have been forced to cut back on their support to higher education (Johnstone, 2012—see chapter 10 in this volume). Despite this new economic reality, many higher education institutions in the United States remain substantially linked to their state environment and state stakeholders. As such, many institutions remain committed to valuing their contributions to their state and explaining how they are important for fostering the state's economic competitiveness.

The Rockefeller Institute of Government recently conducted one of the most comprehensive reviews of the role of higher education in economic development within the United States. After interviewing institutional leaders throughout the country, they concluded:

> From Springfield, Massachusetts, where a technical college has converted an abandoned factory into an urban tech park, to Raleigh-Durham, North Carolina, where research universities worked to turn a sleepy backwater into a global powerhouse of innovation and manufacturing, to Sidney, Nebraska, where a community college operates a training academy that has helped keep the headquarters of a growing national company in its rural hometown, communities today recognize that their hopes for the future are tied to higher education. (Shaffer & Wright, 2010, p. 1)

The report, subtitled *How Higher Education Institutions Are Working to Revitalize Their Regional and State Economies*, categorized the state-level economic contributions of U.S. colleges and universities into four groups: (1) Innovation: Building the Economy of the Future; (2) Strengthening Employers for Success and Growth; (3) Community Revitalization; and (4) An Educated Population. This section provides an overview of these four areas and highlights the ways in which higher education institutions are engaged in each (see also Gais and Wright, 2012—chapter 2 in this volume).

As noted above, innovation has become the driver of economic competitiveness. Colleges and universities, particularly those with a significant research infrastructure, have proven to be one of the primary sources of innovation. In fact, Abel and Deitz (2009) found that having a research university in a community is one of the most important contributors to creating an innovation-based economy, as such entities not only produce new knowledge and facilitate knowledge spillover into the local community but their infrastructure is important for retaining and attracting high-skilled laborers into the local population. The research by the Rockefeller Institute revealed that there were two basic strategies for fostering innovation. The first, which was often pursued with a collaboration of government, industry, and private and public higher education institutions, focused on creating a research infrastructure that would allow for building and/ or attracting an industrial cluster. For example, after Austin, Texas, beat out Atlanta, Georgia, for providing the home for a major semiconductor headquarters, Georgia created the Georgia Research Alliance (GRA), headed by a nonprofit board comprised of university presidents and industrial leaders, to better coordinate the state's economic advantages and be more competitive. A primary component of GRA, the Eminent Scholars program, used matching funds from the state and universities to attract highly productive and entrepreneurial scholars. As of 2010, the program had recruited sixty researchers, which had managed to attract $2.6 billion in research funding, generating more than 5,500 new science and research jobs and creating more than 150 new companies. While Georgia was motivated by losing out in a competition, other regions have had to confront the loss of existing industries. For example, after Pfizer, Inc., closed its research facility in Kalamazoo, Michigan, Western Michigan University developed a plan to mitigate the losses, not by attracting one new large business, but by developing an infrastructure to retain Pfizer scientists to start their own businesses. The University, in collaboration with a local economic development organization, was able to attract twenty-two startup companies as of 2010 (Shaffer & Wright, 2010).

A second contribution is the support offered to local businesses. Many colleges and universities host small business development offices, designed to support entrepreneurs and small business owners with creating and building their companies. Community and technical colleges collaborate with business and industry to provide job training initiatives (Jacobs, 2012—chapter 7 in this volume). Some institutions have become even more aggressive in their support, working with government and financial institutions to provide financial support for small businesses.[3] In their most recent economic development report, the University of Connecticut positions itself as a means for "keeping Connecticut Competitive." They partly explain their contribution in terms of aiding Connecticut businesses:

> Employers across Connecticut are gaining an edge over their competition with the help of the School of Business. Customized and open-enrollment finance, business law, and accounting courses offered to professionals through UConn's Executive Education Programs provide the advanced training employees need to adapt quickly to emerging business trends, advancing technology, and global expansion. (University of Connecticut, 2009, p. 20)

Why are higher education institutions interested in providing such support? The efficiency and effectiveness of a business's operations contributes to how well a region can adapt and absorb new technology (Glaeser & Saiz, 2003). While knowledge creation supports innovation, building better businesses helps facilitate the transfer of knowledge and innovation into the local marketplace.

Community revitalization, a third avenue of contribution, also proved to be an important component of the economic impact of colleges and universities. The impetus for such initiatives is twofold. First, higher education leaders recognize the benefit of being located in productive and welcoming communities. The local environment can affect an institution's ability to recruit and retain students, staff, and faculty. Second, local and state leaders are increasingly calling on institutions to invest in the local community. In many places, colleges and universities are among the largest employers and serve as community centers. In addition, despite their growing global engagements, colleges and universities, as anchor institutions, remain inextricably linked to their local communities (Lane & Kinser, 2008). This is very different than corporations, whose headquarters, research labs, and production facilities have become increasingly mobile. Thus, higher education institutions have also increasingly taken the role once filled by private industry in terms of investing directly into public infrastructure and community institutions (Shaffer & Wright, 2010).

One of the most common strategies for community revitalization comes in the form of downtown and neighborhood reclamation. Colleges and universities, from Pomona, California, to Philadelphia, Pennsylvania, and from Fargo, North Dakota, to Phoenix, Arizona, have become actively involved in the redevelopment of their city's downtown and other neighborhoods. The types of endeavors can vary significantly. Institutions such as North Dakota State University, Southeast Missouri State University, and California State Polytechnic University moved some of their programs into reclaimed structures in struggling parts of town. Such efforts can help attract new business and residential investments. Michigan State University, the University of Minnesota, and the University of Georgia offer an array of community "engagement" programs designed to help build local nonprofits, educational groups, and other community-based organizations. The University of Cincinnati and the University of New Orleans are examples of institutions actively involved in improving their local education pipeline, through developing or leading projects designed to improve P-20 educational quality and access.

Finally, higher education produces an educated workforce and citizenry. Despite the discussions of innovation, community engagement, and economic competitiveness, we must not forget the most significant contribution of colleges and universities is providing an educated populace. Long before policymakers and scholars were trying to identify the reasons for economic growth, this fundamental contribution of colleges and universities was at work benefiting their local communities and those to which their graduates migrated. The connection between education and economic growth has long been studied by human capital theorists (Schultz, 1960; Becker, 1964). The basic argument has been that the better educated a person is, the more productive she or he is, and, therefore, the more she or he contributes to economic development of a region. Later, researchers began to explore the externalities associated with the development of higher education institutions (Lucas, 1988). Community colleges, liberal arts colleges, comprehensive institutions, and research universities all benefit their local communities and others through the development of minds.

FRAMING THEIR COMPETITIVE ADVANTAGE: ECONOMIC IMPACT STUDIES

In order to evidence their economic contributions to local stakeholders, colleges and universities commission economic impact reports to show the extent to which they helped foster economic growth.[4] These reports would often receive media attention and, at least early in their development, attracted the interest of policymakers. Over the last five years, these reports have begun to take on a new angle, arguing in favor of the important role that colleges and universities play in fostering competitiveness.

A review of seventy college and university economic impact plans revealed that twenty-five argued that higher education institutions play an important role in the competitiveness of economies, particularly at the state level. As expected after the research from Shaffer and Wright (2010), which showed broad-based engagement by multiple types of higher education institutions, these statements were not limited to the leading research universities. Out of the seventy reports included in this review, twenty-five were from institutions associated with the American Association of Universities (AAU).[5] Only eleven of those institutions discussed their contribution to an economy's competitiveness. Fourteen non-AAU institutions also argued their case for being part of their state's competitiveness. Indeed, while the elite research universities contribute to innovation creation, it is the comprehensive universities and community colleges that have educated most students.

In many cases, the reports were very direct in their claims that higher education is at the center of their state's economic competitiveness. The following are examples from the reports.[6]

California's economic future is largely tied to the competitiveness of its knowledge-based industries. Consequently, all Californians share a common interest in the foundations that make these industries strong. There is no element of that foundation that is more important than the state's public university systems. Because the California State University provides more well-educated, job-ready graduates to California's knowledge-based industries than any other institution of higher education in the state, it has a strategic role at the absolute center of California's economy. (ICF International, 2010, p. vii)

Universities lie at the heart of successful economies across our nation, and Eastern Kentucky University's impact on Kentucky and, in particular, its 21-county service area reaches to the core of our communities' economic vitality and competitive ability. Eastern is fueling the growth of our region with annual contributions of $518.5 million to the state's economy. That's an almost eight-fold return on the state's investment in the university. EKU is responsible for the addition of almost 6,000 jobs across the state and $192.1 million in household income. Tax bases are broadened as a result of the new business enterprise and new streams of personal and corporate income stimulated by Eastern. (Haywood, 2006, p. 1)

Based on 2008–09 figures, the $109.5 million in annual spending and the equivalent of approximately 730 high-paying jobs in [Montana State University] research would be lost to the state if the University did not exist, and so would the fruits of those research efforts—the patents and inventions, the spinoff of business into the state economy, and the well-trained engineers and scientists that will help keep Montana and the nation competitive into the 21st century. (Montana State University, 2010, p. 11)

Indiana University–Purdue University Indianapolis (IUPUI) has played a fundamental role in its region since it was established in 1969. IUPUI provides central Indiana residents with affordable and convenient access to a range of continuing education, certificate and degree offerings at a premier research university. As a result, IUPUI strengthens the economic competitiveness of the state and increases the earning power of its residents. IUPUI's impact on the state extends beyond its academic mission. The university's budget, the civic engagement of students and staff, and the campus' cultural contributions also bestow many economic benefits to the region. (Indiana Business Research Center, 2008, p. 4).[7]

These four statements are illustrative of the type of overarching description that colleges and universities include in their reports. They exemplify the fact that while they speak of competitiveness, there is almost no discussion of competitive advantage. Above, only Montana State University, which directly mentions patents and inventions, references its contributions to innovation and scientific inquiry. California State University suggests that it provides "job-ready graduates to California's knowledge based industries," and IUPUI states that it provides "affordable and convenient access to . . . education." Other reports make similar claims. Rutgers (2009) provides the education and training necessary for New Jersey workers to "remain competitive" (p. 18). The University of Connecticut's (2009) business schools gives Connecticut's employers "an edge over competition" (p. 20).

This is not to argue that these institutions do not contribute to the competitiveness of their regions. Without these institutions, it is very likely that their regions' ability to attract and grow business and industry would be greatly reduced. But, given the now widely accepted belief that production and use of innovation is the key to long-term competitiveness, it is surprising that more reports do not highlight their role in the innovation-driven economy. Though, it is true, measuring such contributions can be complicated.

The University of New Hampshire actually admits the difficulty in measuring the connection between higher education and a state's economic competitiveness. "UNH's contributions to New Hampshire's competitiveness in high technology and innovation-based economic developments are very hard to quantify." After listing a few pieces of evidence, the report summarizes the issue this way: "UNH's important role in research and business development will continue to be vital in the future as access to its skilled graduates, expertise, and other resources become [*sic*] increasingly crucial in the changing global economy, specifically the state's move to a more innovation-driven economy where the nation's comparative advantage lies" (Gittell, Carter, & Stillwagon, 2009, p. 8).

Not all reports were strictly positive in their discussions about economic competitiveness. Some institutions, particularly in places where government funding is becoming sparse, are arguing that competitive advantage can both rise and fall. Moreover, they assert, the declines in the competitiveness of the institution may be linked to declines in the competitiveness of the state.

The University of Virginia did not mince words in their economic impact report in observing how a loss of institutional competitiveness may directly affect the state's competitiveness.

> Given that many states are now making strong research universities central to their economic development plans, competitive pressures may make it difficult for Virginia's major research universities to maintain their national and international stature. As Virginia government provides a smaller and smaller share of the budgets of the research universities in the state, it is possible that these schools may lose some of their prominence due to the fierce competition among states and schools. This, in turn, would make it more difficult for the state to attract the top students and faculty, with the corresponding reduction in development of knowledge-dependent businesses. (Knapp & Shobe, 2007, p. 14)

A similar conclusion was drawn by the University of California: "Current and potential future reductions in state funding could have profound impacts on the California economy, including reduced economic activity and competitiveness" (Economic and Planning Systems, 2011, p. 2). The report went on state that its purpose was "to frame the state's funding decisions within a broad economic context, revealing that the critical role of the [University of California] within the state" (p. 2).

While the connection between institutional competitiveness and state competitiveness needs to be further researched, the evidence above suggests that institutions are beginning to use "competitiveness" language as a way to further support their claimed economic contribution. However, similar to how McHenry, Sanderson and Seigfried question some of the conclusions drawn by economic impact reports (McHenry, Sanderson, & Siegfried, 2012—see chapter 3 in this volume), it is also important to approach the broad-based assumptions of how individual institutions contribute to economic competitiveness with caution. One of the most important questions to pose is: What would be the impact if an institution did not exist within a state? Would a state still be as competitive? As discussed throughout this chapter, higher education can play a critical role in support competitiveness strategies, but the evidence is not as clear in terms of how specific institutions do so. For example, the reports described above rarely connected competitiveness to innovation, though it is now widely believed that innovation largely drives competitiveness in developed economies. It seems that institutions may want to examine their competitiveness claims and identify ways to measure and evidence such contributions.

ECONOMIC DEVELOPMENT STRATEGIES: BUILDING COLLABORATIONS

The rest of this volume discusses the role that higher education institutions play as economic drivers and the methodological issues associated with measuring those economic contributions. In most cases, those discussions are framed by state and local boundaries. Yet, in addition to considering how colleges and universities contribute to the economic development of states or nations, it is worth also considering how higher education institutions and governments can work collaboratively to advance the overall economic prosperity of their communities. Both Schultz (2012—chapter 5 in this volume) and Feldman, Freyer, and Lanahan (2012—chapter 4 in this volume), argue that some of the most successful examples of producing new knowledge and technologies combined the resources of government, industry, and higher education.

Some prominent theories about fostering economic growth and competitiveness are built, at least in part, on the contributions of higher education institutions. Richard Florida (2003) talks about the need for regions to attract the "creative class"—the innovators and creators of the new economy. Clifton (2011) suggests "super mentors" play an important role in cultivating and growing small businesses. Moreover, industries benefit significantly from the exchange of ideas generated by knowledge spillover (Carlino, 2001). Finally, Etzkowitz and Leydesdorff (2000) argued that successful local innovation systems resemble a triple helix, in which government, industry, and higher education are intertwined. Common among all of these economic development and innovation-fostering strategies is colleges and universities. These institutions are believed to create environments attractive to the creative class, foster super mentors, and fill a critical role in the development of new research and new ideas.

In many cases, it seems that discussions of economic development are one-sided. Institutional leaders, as demonstrated above, often highlight the myriad ways in which their college or university could contribute economically to their state. Government leaders invoke the need for higher education to support their competitiveness agenda, but it seems such plans are often designed with little direct input from academic leaders. Indeed, some elected officials have even recently gone so far as to question the value of institutional activities that are not clearly tied to the economic goals of the state. For example, Florida governor Rick Scott noted in 2011:

> You know, we don't need a lot more anthropologists in the state. It's a great degree if people want to get it, but we don't need them here. I want to spend our dollars giving people science, technology, engineering, and math degrees. That's what our kids need to focus all their time and attention on, those types of degrees, so when they get out of school, they can get a job. (Koebler, 2011)

An economic development plan should not be viewed as a substitute or replacement for an institution's mission or strategic plan. There are many important functions related to research, teaching, and service that are not clearly aligned or connected to economic development goals and strategies. This does not mean they are unimportant. In fact, many of the humanities and social science programs are the core of the American higher education experience and help develop the critical thinkers that create social and product innovations.

There are, however, substantial aspects of the activities of colleges and universities that can and do contribute economically to society. One of the critical connections to remember is that between the institution and the local/regional community. Each region has a different set of historical, cultural, and financial features that will dictate its competitive direction, and, thus, will likely influence the economic development strategies of the related governments. Indeed, Columbia University professor Jeffrey Sachs (2008) has argued that "[e]conomic development is a complex interplay of market forces and public-sector plans and investments" (p. 219).

While the role of higher education institutions in fostering economic development and competitiveness is now widely valued, there is no one common approach to either economic prosperity or higher education's role in developing such. Whether we define an economy by locality, state, or nation, each will likely have a different economic development approach influenced by history and culture as well as industrial and educational strengths. "There is no single trajectory from destitution to development. Iceland, India, and Indonesia are in alphabetical sequence, but their development trajectories could not be more distinct" (Sachs, 2008, p. 219).

Several policy-oriented groups, such as the National Collaborative for Higher Education Policy,[8] National Conference of State Legislators, and the Western Interstate Commission for Higher Education, have expressed the need for states, industries, and higher education to work more collaboratively. These calls are reactions to significant changes in state environments, including the globalization and digitalization of the economy, increased competition for limited state resources, demographic shifts, and greater demand for a highly skilled workforce (and occurred prior to the current economic crisis, which only heighten these concerns). Recognizing the critical role of higher education in this new era, a report from the National Governors Association (2007) calls for the creation of a compact between states and higher education to "better align postsecondary education with . . . economic needs, which will position [the states] to compete in the global economy by producing a highly skilled workforce and by unleashing postsecondary education institutions' power to innovate" (p. 1).

A different National Governors Association (2011) report, entitled "Degrees for What Jobs? Raising Expectations for Universities and Colleges in a Global Economy," suggests that the two primary policy agendas for higher education should be increasing the number of college graduates and aligning degree production with areas with demand for jobs. The emphasis here is that state leaders need to do a better job of aligning higher education outputs with state economic priorities.

What is lost in much of the rhetoric, however, is the need for government leaders and higher education officials to work collaboratively in developing economic development and competitiveness plans and strategies. A government broadly evoking the desire to improve or expand its higher education institutions for the sake of increasing economic development is likely to have minimal effects. Similarly, broad claims by an institution about its role in supporting a state or nation's economic competitiveness often fall on deaf ears. Collaboration between governments and institutions (and sometimes business and industry) can be helpful in identifying and capitalizing on the core strengths of an economy. Moreover, such efforts can help facilitate the alignment of resources to support emerging competitiveness strategies.

Economic development is not the only purpose for higher education, but society is increasingly valuing this role. Globally, it is being argued that power is based on economic might. At home, the ability to sustain quality of life and build successful communities is tied to economic prosperity. Colleges and universities, particularly in the age of the innovation-driven economy, play a critical role in these dynamics.

NOTES

1. Competitive advantage, as discussed by Porter, is often referred to as comparative advantage by economists. Competitive advantage is used throughout this chapter as it has become part of the common vernacular when discussing many of the issues highlighted here.
2. The American Legislative Exchange Council, an open market think tank, now publishes an annual state competitiveness index, and media outlets such as CNBC and business groups such as the U.S. Chamber of Commerce rank the most business-friendly states.
3. The University at Albany, State University of New York, partnered with SEFCU (a credit union) and Empire State Development to provide funding to small business in the Albany, New York, region. More about the program can be found at http://www.albany.edu/news/23644.php.
4. In chapter 3 in this volume, Siegfried et al. raise questions about the veracity of some claims in such reports.
5. The Association of American Universities, founded in 1900, is an invitational membership group for the most productive research universities in the United State and Canada. Currently, 59 of the

group's 61 members are located in the United States. More information about the group can be found at http://www.aau.edu/.

6. Readers are encouraged to read chapter 3 in this volume for analysis about the claims of total impact. I note here that there may be reason to challenge some of the "total impact" claims. These statements are used here not to illustrate the quantitative impact of the institution's activities, but rather to illustrate how institutions invoke competitiveness themes as a means to further evidence their overall economic impact.

7. The same paragraph also appeared in the economic impact report of Indiana University Southeast.

8. The National Collaborative for Higher Education Policy is composed of the Education Commission of the States, the National Center for Higher Education Management Systems, and the National Center for Public Policy and Higher Education.

REFERENCES

Abel, J. R., & Dietz, R. (2009). Do colleges and universities increase their region's human capital? *Staff Report no. 401*. New York: Federal Reserve Bank of New York.

Becker, G. S. (1964). *Human capital: A theoretical and empirical analysis with special reference to education*. Cambridge, MA: National Bureau of Economic Research.

Carlino, G. A. (2001). Knowledge spillovers: Cities' role in the new economy. *Business Review 4*, 17–26.

Carnevale, A. P., and Rose, S. J. (2012). The convergence of post-secondary education and the labor market. In J. E. Lane & D. B. Johnstone (Eds.), *Universities and colleges as economic drivers: Measuring higher education's role in economic development*. Albany: State University of New York Press.

Clifton, J. (2011). *The coming jobs war.* New York: The Gallup Press.

Croom, P. W. (2010). Motivation and aspirations for international branch campuses. In D. W. Chapman & R. Sakamoto (Eds.), *Cross border partnerships in higher education: Strategies and issues* (pp. 45–66). New York: Routledge.

Davidson, C. M. (2008). *Dubai: The vulnerability of success*. New York: Columbia University Press.

Dunning, J. H. (1993). *The globalization of business: The challenge of the 1990s*. London: Routledge.

Economic and Planning Systems. (2011). *The University of California's economic contribution to the State of California*. Berkeley, CA: The University of California, Office of the President.

Etzkowitz, H., & Leydesdorff, L. (2000). The dynamics of innovation: From national systems and "Mode 2" to a Triple Helix of university-industry-government relations. *Research Policy 29*, 109–123.

Florida, R. (2003). *The rise of the creative class: And how it is transforming work, leisure, community and everyday life*. New York: Basic Books.

Geiger, R. L. (2004). *Knowledge and money: American research universities and the paradox of the marketplace*. Palo Alto, CA: Stanford University Press.

Gittell, R., Carter, J. R., & Stillwagon, J. R. (2009). *The University of New Hampshire: A pillar in the New Hampshire economy*. Durham: University of New Hampshire.

Glaeser, E. L., & Saiz, A. (2003) The rise of the skilled city. Discussion Paper No, 2025, Harvard Institute of Economic Research, 44.

Guyana. (2006). Enhancing national competitiveness: A national competitiveness strategy for Guyana. Accessed from http://www.competitiveness.org.gy/NCS_May2006_vII.pdf on November 23, 2011.

Haywood, D. F. (2006). *An economic impact study of Eastern Kentucky University*. Richmond, KY: Eastern Kentucky University.

ICF International. (2010). *Working for California: The impact of the California State University System*. Long Beach, CA: Office of the California State University Chancellor.

Indiana Business Research Center. (2008). *Indiana University–Purdue University Indianapolis: Impact Study 2008*. Indianapolis: Author.

Institute for International Education. (2011). Joint and double degree programs in the global context: Report on an international survey. New York: Author.

Jacobs, J. (2012). The essential role of community colleges in rebuilding the nation's communities and economies. In J. E. Lane & D. B. Johnstone (Eds.), *Universities and colleges as economic drivers: Measuring higher education's role in economic develop-ment*. Albany: State University of New York Press.

Kerr, C. (1963). *The use of the university*. Cambridge: Harvard University Press.

Kinser, K., Levy, D., Casillas, J. C. S., Bernasconi, A., Slantcheva Durst, S., Otieno, W., Lane, J., Praphamontripong, P., Zumeta, W., & LaSota, R. (2010). *The global growth of private higher education*. ASHE Higher Education Report Series. San Francisco: Wiley.

Knapp, J. L., & Shobe, W. M. (2007). *The economic impact of the University of Virginia: How a major research university affects the local and state economies*. Charlottesville: University of Virginia.

Knight, J. (2011). Education hubs: A fad, a brand, an innovation? *Journal for Studies in International Education 15* (3), 221–240.

Koebler, J. (2011, Oct. 13). Florida governor may divert taxes to STEM majors. *U.S. News & World Report*. Retrieved from http://www.usnews.com/news/blogs/stem-education/2011/10/13/florida-governor-may-divert-taxes-to-stem-majors.

Korea Research Foundation. (n.d.). *About BrainKorea21*. Retrieved from http://bnc.krf.or.kr/home/eng/bk21/aboutbk21.jsp.

Lane, J. E., & Kinser, K. (2008). The private nature of cross-border higher education. *International Higher Education 53*, 11.

Lane, J. E., & Kinser, K. (Eds.). (2011a). *Multi-national colleges & universities: Leadership, administration, and governance of international branch campuses*. San Francisco: Jossey-Bass.

Lane, J. E., & Kinser, K. (2011b). Reconsidering privatization in cross-border engagements: The sometimes public nature of private activity. *Higher Education Policy 24*, 255–273.

Lane, J. E., & Owens, T. A. (2012). The international dimensions of higher education's contributions to economic development. In J. E. Lane & D. B. Johnstone (Eds.), *Universities and colleges as economic drivers: Measuring higher education's role in economic development*. Albany: State University of New York Press.

Lee, M. N. N. (2001). Private higher education in Malaysia: Expansion, diversification and consolidation. Paper presented at the Second Regional Seminar on PHE: Its Role in Human Resource Development in a Globalised Knowledge Society, organized by

UNESCO PROAP and SEAMEO RIHED, 20–22 June, Bangkok, Thailand.

Lucas, R. E., Jr. (1988). On the mechanics of economic development. *Journal of Monetary Economics 22*, 3–42.

Milken, M. (2011). Where's Sputnik? *The Milken Institute Review: A Journal of Economic Policy 13* (2), 62–82.

Montana State University. (2010). Economic impact report. Bozeman, MT: Author.

Morrill Act of 1862. (7 U.S.C. § 301 et seq.).

Morrill Act of 1890. (26 Stat. 417, 7 U.S.C. § 321 et seq.).

National Competitiveness Council (Croatia). (2009). 2008 Annual competitiveness report Croatia. Zagreb, Croatia: Author. Retrieved from http://www.konkurentnost.hr/Default.aspx?sec=41.

National Competitiveness Council (Ireland). (2009). Statement on education and training. Retrieved from http://www.competitiveness.ie/publication/nccSearch.jsp?ft=/publications/2009/title,3564,en.php.

National Defense in Education Act of 1958. (P.L. 85-864; 72 Stat. 1580).

National Governors Association. (2007). Innovation America: A compact for Postsecondary Education. Available at http://www.nga.org/files/live/sites/NGA/files/pdf/0707INNOVATIONPOSTSEC.PDF.

National Governors Association. (2011). Degrees for what jobs? Raising expectations for universities and colleges in a global economy. March 22. Available at http://www.nga.org/cms/home/nga-center-for-best-practices/center-publications/page-ehsw-publications/col2-content/main-content-list/degrees-for-what-jobs-raising-ex.html.

Obst, D., Kuder, M., & Banks, C. (2011). *Joint and double degrees programs in global context: Report on an international survey.* New York: Institute for International Education.

OECD. (2010). *Education at a glance 2010: OECD indicators.* Accessed on November 23, 2011, from www.oecd.org/edu/eag2010.

Paulson, K. (2007). Developing public agendas for higher education. In K. M. Shaw & D. E. Heller (Eds.), *State postsecondary education research: New methods to inform policy and practice.* Sterling, VA: Stylus Press.

Porter, M. (1990a). *The competitive advantage of nations*. New York: The Free Press.

Porter, M. (1990b). The competitive advantage of nations. *Harvard Business Review 68* (3), 3.

Porter, M. (2008). Why America needs an economic strategy. *Bloomberg Business Week*. (October 30). Accessed November 29, 2011, from http://www.businessweek.com/magazine/content/08_45/b4107038217112.htm.

Romer, P. (1990). Endogenous technological change. *Journal of Political Economy 98* (5), S71–S102

Rutgers, The State University of New Jersey. (2009). Solutions from Rutgers: New Jersey's partner for a strong economy. New Brunswick, NJ: Rutgers Department of University Relations.

Sachs, J. (2008). *Common wealth: Economics for a crowded planet*. New York: The Penguin Press.

Samuelson, P. (1964). Theoretical notes on trade problems. *The Review of Economics and Statistics 46* (2), 145–154.

Schultz, T. W. (1960). Capital formation by education. *Journal of Political Economy 68*, 571–582.

Schwab, K. (2011). *The global competitiveness report, 2011–2012*. Geneva: World Economic Forum.

Serviceman's Readjustment Act of 1944. (P.L. 78-346, 58 Stat. 284m).

Shaffer, D. F., & Wright, D. J. (2010). *A new paradigm for economic development: How higher education institutions are working to revitalize their regional and state economies*. Report. Albany, NY: Rockefeller Institute of Government.

Sirat, M., (2005). Transnational higher education in Malaysia: Balancing benefits and concerns through regulations. National Higher Education Research Institute (Malaysia) working paper. Accessed from at http://www.usm.my/ipptn/fileup/TNHE_Malaysia.pdf on September 15, 2008.

Trani, E. P., & Holsworth, R. D. (2010). *The indispensable university: Higher education, economic development, and the knowledge economy*. Lanham, MD: Rowman & Littlefield.

University of Connecticut. (2009). *UCONNOMY: Contributing to the economic health of Connecticut*. Storrs, CT: Author.

Wildavsky, B. (2010). *The great brain race: How global universities are reshaping the world*. Princeton: Princeton University Press.

World Economic Forum. (2011). *The Africa competitiveness report 2011*. Geneva: Author.

Ziguras, C. (2003). The impact of the GATS on transnational tertiary education: Comparing experiences of New Zealand, Australia, Singapore and Malaysia. *The Australian Educational Researcher 30* (3), 89–109.

2

The Diversity of University Economic Development Activities and Issues of Impact Measurement

Thomas Gais and David Wright

ABSTRACT

Drawing on a national scan of higher education economic development activities as well as a state-level study of the economic roles of campuses in a large public university system, this chapter describes the many ways in which colleges and universities promote and foster economic development. Higher education economic development activities are diverse, involving many different economic processes. The chapter describes how 1) these activities are often combined in complex combinations; 2) the activities interact with and are contingent on each campus' environment; and 3) the activities and their probable impacts may change over time. These characteristics pose challenges for measuring the effects of higher education institutions on their surrounding economies. The challenges suggest the value of using a combination of methodologies, including program evaluation techniques, comparative site analyses, expanded import-export analyses, and careful comparative studies of the coevolution of campus activities and their surrounding economies and communities.

INTRODUCTION

Higher education's traditional role and strengths lie in educating students and producing new knowledge. Increasingly, though, higher education institutions apply these functions, and take on additional roles, to generate economic growth and prosperity in the institutions' communities, regions, nations, and, in some cases, other countries. In part, this transformation has been fostered by a growing recognition of the economic realities associated with a "flat world," where the global location of production, income, and economic growth is determined by competitive advantage (Friedman, 2005). In this flattened world, innovation has become one of the driving forces behind a nation's economic competitiveness; as such, higher education has, in itself, become a competitive advantage—one that has helped bolster the success of economic giants such as the United States during the last half of the twentieth century (Lane, 2012; Carnevale & Rose, 2012—chapters 1 and 6 in this volume). As Joseph Stiglitz (2010) put it, "The [nation's] long-run competitive advantage lies in America's higher-education institutions and the advances in technology that derive from the advantages that those institutions provide" (p. 194).

Despite the growing awareness of higher education's role in economic development activities, the resulting impacts are not easy to assess and many attempts to do so have been fraught with problems (McHenry, Sanderson, & Siegfried, 2012—chapter 3 this volume). Many economic impact studies focus on summing the spending and re-spending of dollars. However, such studies do not capture the full scope of an institution's economic engagements. Indeed, these activities are often complex and sometimes nonlinear, and their effects may be contingent on local context, the cumulative effects of prior actions, and technological timing. To better understand the economic roles performed by universities and colleges necessitates a mixed-methods approach to trace their processes and products.

The purpose of this chapter is to provide an overview of the myriad ways in which colleges and universities serve as economic drivers and the obstacles associated with some of these activities. First, we describe the several ways in which colleges and universities promote and foster economic development. Second, using this broad picture as a backdrop, we consider some of the methodological and theoretical issues involved in measuring the effects of the university or college on their surrounding economies.

A TYPOLOGY OF COLLEGE AND UNIVERSITY ECONOMIC ACTIVITY

Higher education's engagement with economic development comes in myriad forms and fashions. In this section, we present a typology of the economic development activities of colleges and universities. Our perspective on the range of economic development activities undertaken by institutions of higher education was influenced by two studies commissioned by the State University of New York (SUNY) and conducted by the Rockefeller Institute of Government. The purpose of the studies was to inform SUNY's strategic planning process and its efforts to strengthen the role that public higher education plays in fostering New York State's economy—an issue that became particularly salient following the onset of the Great Recession (see Johnstone, 2012—chapter 10 this volume).

The first study focused on assessing the different ways that higher education institutions and systems around the country contributed to economic development in their region. The Institute assembled data on higher education and research programs in all fifty states, reviewed the literature in the field of universities' economic development impacts, and conducted case studies of programs and projects in about a dozen states. Some of the case studies drew on field visits. In *A New Paradigm for Economic Development* (Shaffer & Wright, 2010), we reported that the importance of innovation in the knowledge economy was driving the development of a new model for state economic development programs, where the priority is to leverage new ideas, technologies, processes, and skills as the way to boost economic growth—and not to emphasize the traditional packages of tax breaks, real estate deals, site infrastructure, and other financial incentives. In this setting, higher education institutions and systems are a primary source of the new knowledge needed to produce high-paying jobs in the innovation economy, and they are essential to developing a workforce prepared to take those jobs. Across the country, we found that higher education is putting its research and educational power to work by developing new ideas, deploying inventions for commercial use, educating potential entrepreneurs, and helping businesses prepare workers for advanced tasks.

Infused with examples from around the nation, a second study was conducted to take a more in-depth look at the ways in which a comprehensive, public higher education system contributed to the economic growth and vitality of a state. The Rockefeller Institute and the University at Buffalo's Regional Institute joined in a study focusing on the economic development impact of the sixty-four-campus State University of New York. Combining qualitative and quantitative techniques, *How SUNY Matters* (Rockefeller Institute & Regional Institute, 2011) provides benchmark estimates of the economic impacts of SUNY's campuses on their regions and the system's overall economic impact on the state. Toward a goal of describing, understanding, and strengthening the efforts of individual campuses and the SUNY system to promote economic growth in New York, the study also provides survey data on campus support for innovation and business assistance programming, and structured field observations of cases where SUNY institutions have encouraged economic development in their surrounding communities and regions.

Drawing from our findings, we classify economic activity by universities and colleges among five broad categories, observing higher education institutions as: (1) economic units, (2) developers of human capital, (3) engines of innovation in research and development, (4) sources of business assistance, and (5) resources for community vitality.

THE INSTITUTION AS AN ECONOMIC UNIT: SPENDER AND CONSUMER

At perhaps their most elemental level, higher education institutions are economic actors that receive and expend resources in exchange for goods and services. Universities and colleges offer services to students and parents, who in turn bring resources to the institution through tuition payments, living expenses, visits, and other economic activities. Most also receive grants from other public and private sources, such as research grants from the federal government, private foundations, or corporations. These resources are then spent by the institution on faculty and staff salaries, scientific equipment and other items essential to research, construction, vendors, service contracts, and other factors. In turn, these expenditures are re-spent, as university employees buy food, shelter, and other items, or as construction companies purchase supplies. And they circulate farther as those who work for businesses supported by higher education institutions spend their income. As these cycles of spending and re-spending continue, depending on their origins and destinations as well as on the spatial boundary of analysis, a dollar imported by a university is seen as producing a multiplier effect on the local economy—at least to the extent that the spending and re-spending remains within the local economy.

Studies seeking to take into account the "import-export" nature of higher education in these terms are common. However, as discussed later in this chapter and detailed by McHenry, Sanderson, and Siegfried (2012) in chapter 3 of this volume, these studies are frequently limited by methodological challenges. There is considerable debate about assumptions made concerning multipliers and whether certain elements of activity—spending by retirees, alumni, university associations, foundations, and partner companies at university-affiliated facilities, for instance—should be included in such analyses. Moreover, perceiving higher education institutions in this limited role as spenders and consumers omits economic impacts generated by the content of what it is that universities and colleges *do,* such as the impacts of an educated population or basic research that makes technological innovations feasible, new businesses spun off by university research activities, productivity gains by businesses benefiting from workforce training and entrepreneurial services, or businesses attracted to a community because of university presence.

Higher education institutions are not akin to large retail stores, whose impact can be summed from their roles as employers and purchasers of goods. In addition to their direct effect on local spending and re-spending, we found that universities and colleges are performing several other general functions, among them, creating and transferring knowledge as an active resource for businesses and communities.

DEVELOPING HUMAN CAPITAL

Universities' and colleges' primary mission is to disseminate knowledge and increase society's human capital through teaching and learning. Important as they may be, all other activities undertaken by universities to foster economic growth and innovation are dwarfed by the impact of their core mission of educating students. For instance, higher rates of college degree completion among residents in a local area are associated with higher wages and levels of gross domestic product per capita (Abel & Gabe, 2011; Moretti, 2004). However, the extent to which local universities' "production" of degrees raises local human capital levels is affected by how many students leave the area after graduation (Faggian & McCann, 2009; Abel & Dietz, 2009 rev. 2011).

We found that SUNY's human capital development role in New York is immense. As of 2008–2009, 1.6 million alumni still lived in New York and made up a large part of the state's highly educated workforce. SUNY alumni from nearby institutions constituted large shares of college graduates in most regions in the state, from 73 percent of all college graduates in the fairly rural North Country and Mohawk Valley regions, to 64 percent of graduates in Western New York, but still as high as 45 percent in the populous Long Island area. Only in New York City—where SUNY institutions are small and specialized—did SUNY alumni make up less than one-third of all local college graduates (only 4 percent). But even in New York City, SUNY's role is significant, as its Fashion Institute of Technology is one of the garment industry's most important sources of skilled workers.

Complementing the traditional curricula, higher education institutions have developed a wide variety of educational programs to support particular industries and businesses. Worker training programs are the most widespread, and arguably the most important, way in which higher education institutions help support the competitiveness and growth of employers in their communities. These are of several types:

1. *Job-specific training in the form of noncredit courses that are developed outside of normal academic guidelines, often to meet the needs of a specific employer for workers with a specific set of skills.* For instance, each of North Carolina's fifty-eight community colleges can access funds to design and deliver training tailored to the specific needs of a company—without charge to the company. The training program is developed at the local college, in concert with the employer. To be eligible a company must demonstrate that

it is making an appreciable capital investment, deploying new technology, creating new jobs or expanding an existing workforce, and/or enhancing productivity.

For new employers or existing companies that are increasing employment or upgrading plant and equipment in Georgia, Quick Start—an arm of the state's technical college system—assigns analysts to dig into the process or workflow in question. It then develops a customized training program, complete with handbooks, presentations, online lessons, or other training materials. Quick Start will even prescreen potential hires for the company, using the knowledge it acquired of the production system to match candidates with the needed skills. Training is then deployed at the company's location, at one or more of the state's technical colleges, or at one of five Quick Start facilities located around Georgia—all at no cost to the employer.

2. *Training designed for a type of job or a career ladder to be shared by multiple employers in a community or region.* Erie Community College has partnered with fifteen area businesses to form the Machining and Manufacturing Alliance, which offers a thirty-two-credit precision machining credential for employment and a stepping stone for students seeking an associate's degree in Industrial Technology. Suffolk County Community College (SCCC) partnered with Good Samaritan Hospital Medical Center to help address a critical shortage of nurses on Long Island. The hospital prescreens student applicants and commits to hiring them after their training at SCCC. Leveraging this multiyear contract with the hospital, Suffolk hired more faculty and leased space in a distressed downtown neighborhood for training. Suffolk built on this model with six other healthcare facilities. Now Suffolk's nursing program is the largest such campus-based effort in New York—and the ninth largest in the nation.

3. *Credit-bearing courses tailored by community and technical colleges to respond to forecasted needs of the local economy.* For instance, anticipating the workforce required for a $4.6 billion chip-fab plant under construction and other industry attracted to the region by the burgeoning

nano complex in Albany, SUNY's Hudson Valley Community College launched TEC-SMART, the Training and Education Center for Semiconductor Manufacturing and Alternative and Renewable Technologies. A joint initiative between the college and the New York State Energy Research and Development Authority, TEC-SMART features state-of-the-art classrooms and laboratories for semiconductor manufacturing and green technologies, including photovoltaic, and also for home energy efficiency, geothermal, alternative fuels, and wind energy.

Universities and colleges have thus shown their capacity to fashion training programs responsive to the particular needs of local employers. Yet, there are failures: efforts to provide training that do not meet the specific needs of businesses, or at the scale required, or within time frames needed. But the flexibility and diversity of programs are impressive and suggest one of the strengths of the role of higher education programs: their protean character or capacity to respond to so many different situations.

RESEARCH, DEVELOPMENT, AND INNOVATION

Universities create new knowledge, including basic research as well as activities aimed at producing market innovations, such as commercializing research findings, public-private partnerships to produce marketable research findings, and pulling together researchers from multiple disciplines, different departments and schools, and high technology businesses to create clusters of people and institutions that learn from each other, generate new ideas, and translate them into innovations.

Research activities among institutions of higher education have been found to have significant and consistent economic spillover effects at the local and regional levels, typically through commercial innovation and research (Jaffe, 1989; Anselin, Varga, & Acs, 1997). The Milken Institute found that the key to growing high-tech industry was to foster robust research universities and institutions, a critical factor for economic growth because high-tech industry "is becoming a more important determinant of the relative economic success of metros" (DeVol & Wong, 1999, p. 53). Similar findings came from a study done for the U.S. Department of Commerce by the State Science and Technology Institute (2006), which found that universities generate scientific breakthroughs at a level that few private firms can manage.

Abel and Deitz (2009 rev. 2011, p. 4) found that while higher education levels in the populace are important to state and regional economies, there is a more powerful impact if the local schools are research universities. Because "college graduates are highly mobile," they write, "we find only a small positive relationship between a metropolitan area's production [meaning the number of college students it educates] and stock of human capital." However, "R&D activity tends to be much more geographically concentrated," and because these activities "influence the demand for human capital in a region . . . we find evidence that spillovers from academic R&D play an important role" in *attracting* highly educated workers to a region.

The process of basic research leading to economic development is well illustrated by the Georgia Research Alliance (GRA), covered in some depth in our *New Paradigm* report. State of Georgia officials saw the value of research strengths and commercialization connections after having lost out in the competition to land SEMATECH back in the early 1980s. The State of Georgia and a group of business and higher education leaders were then determined to collaborate and invest in a matching grant program to attract and fuel a series of eminent scholars recruited to Georgia universities. The scholars, along with new laboratory facilities, would upgrade the state's research capacity, which was expected to push research into commercialization. The GRA has attracted more than sixty researchers and invested some $510 million, which it calculates has leveraged another $2.6 billion in federal and private research grants, creating more than 5,500 new science and research jobs, establishing more than 150 new companies, and helping a long list of existing Georgia companies grow.

Yet basic research does not always generate market innovations and eventual sales and revenues (Geiger & Sa, 2008, p. 40). To commercialize research produced by university personnel, universities have adopted several practices designed to generate more innovation and licensing revenue:

*Mechanisms to Transfer University Intellectual Property Rights
to Private Firms*

One key university technology transfer commercialization mechanism involves university patenting and licensing agreements between
the university and private firms (Geiger & Sa, 2009). Critics have
charged that university patenting of research tools and overreach
in intellectual property claims inhibit technology transfer, diminishing the public good of new knowledge. Tech transfer professionals
counter that the public good is served when inventions are licensed
and developed into commercial products. In recent years, universities have reduced their emphasis on patenting and licensing discoveries as a way of encouraging broader dissemination of ideas and the
growth of fast-growing clusters of companies and researchers around
the universities. Nonetheless, technology transfer offices remain important mechanisms for promoting and reaping the benefits of innovation. In 2008–09, SUNY's applied research centers, facilities, and
programs reported 350 invention disclosures with potential commercial impact, seventy-nine patents, and some sixty licenses yielding
revenue for the commercial use of university discoveries.

*Mechanisms to Nurture Creation of "Spin-offs" or "Spin-outs"—
Incubators for New Private Firms to Commercialize University
Intellectual Property*

Many institutions of higher education have created incubators as
special environments in which to nurture start-up businesses. In some
cases these are formed by external companies developing commercial
applications from research or via research facilities of the university—so-called spin-offs. In other cases, these are start-ups formed
by university faculty to advance products from their own research,
known as spin-outs. Some university business incubators help faculty
become entrepreneurs.

To move research into the marketplace, Georgia Research Alliance's principal tool is its VentureLab, which seeks out research
with commercial potential; offers incubator space for startups at one
of the six universities; provides assistance with planning, marketing,
and technology; and—significantly—provides seed money for startup

and development costs in staged doses as a company proves out its potential. An approved VentureLab startup is eligible for $50,000 in state funds to be used demonstrating the potential of the idea. If the recipient nascent company can raise $50,000 in private capital, it is eligible for another $50,000 state grant to develop a business plan. Upon actual launch, it is then eligible for up to $250,000 in low-interest loans from GRA, which in effect operates a state-backed, rotating venture capital fund. Since 2002 the VentureLab program has evaluated more than three hundred discoveries or inventions for commercial potential. It has proceeded to startup with 107 companies, sixty-eight of which are still in business. These firms employ about 450 people and have attracted some $300 million in private equity investment.

Mechanisms to Strengthen Entrepreneurship

Some universities are taking steps to create stronger incentives for faculty to become entrepreneurs and push innovations to market. Universities have offered researchers laboratory or office space for such work, financial support for patent or copyright applications, support for prototype development, and competitive seed or bridge funds. In SUNY, for example, Binghamton University helps faculty and students learn to be entrepreneurs within its Innovative Technologies Complex, a "Start Up Suite" of small offices that serves as a kind of "pre-incubator" for aspiring and start-up companies with roots in faculty research. Binghamton also has a program called Entrepreneurship Across the Curriculum, offering small stipends to help faculty members who want to fold an entrepreneurship component into their existing classes.

Organizational/Institutional Structures to Promote Innovation

The science-based technologies that inform a number of fields with burgeoning commercial application are typically interdisciplinary and not easily assimilated into traditional academic departments. Incorporating these new fields—or new combinations of older fields—into the departmental and curricular structure of universities has been a challenge. Deliberate steps to restructure academic programs on an interdisciplinary basis have become increasingly common and special institutes for science-based technologies have proliferated.

Research Partnerships for Innovation

Rather than trying to commercialize findings from basic research, some universities are highlighting the goal of commercial innovation from the very beginning of the research process. One way of doing this is to establish research partnerships with private corporations. Many corporations are open to these partnerships, as corporate labs have deemphasized fundamental research in recent years and now look to external performers to complement internal R&D. Some universities have thus become more accommodative to research relationships with industry, and some corporations have established long-term partnerships with university units. The federal government has encouraged collaborative research (the National Cooperative Research Act of 1984), research joint ventures involving universities and firms (the U.S. Commerce Department's Advanced Technology Program), and shared use of expertise and laboratory facilities (e.g., the National Science Foundation's Engineering Research Centers, Science and Technology Centers, and Industry-University Cooperative Research Centers).

One of the more notable examples of university research partnerships can be found at the NanoTech Complex of University at Albany. From its beginnings as a project in the basement lab of the physics department in 1988, the College of Nanoscale Science and Engineering (CNSE) has grown into an extensive public-private partnership, hosting more than 2,600 scientists, researchers, engineers and technicians from more than 250 participating organizations. CNSE offers 80,000 square feet of some of the most advanced and up-to-date clean-room facilities and equipment in the world as well as offices, close access to other scientists (typically with a commercial bent, even within the university), and a ready supply of well-trained students.

Perhaps no facility epitomizes the idea of a partnership research center more than Research Triangle Park (RTP), founded by North Carolina State, Duke, and the University of North Carolina at Chapel Hill. The largest research park in the United States, RTP now hosts more employees than the three universities combined, and is credited with transforming the economy of the region. North Carolina has extended its ambitions with Centennial Campus, a new "research park of the future" with nearly $1 billion invested in facilities, 2.7 million square feet occupied by a combination of global and regional leaders in high-tech industries as well as start-up companies in an on-campus incubator, and with plans to grow to 9 million square feet when fully developed.

Hubs for Regional Agglomeration

The consequences of university support for innovation extend out to industrial sectors and regions. Research universities attract highly educated workers to R&D activity in geographically concentrated areas and thus have a big impact on the demand for human capital in a region. Networking activities among researchers and inventors in a region lead to synergistic effects on discoveries, development of techniques and training, and dispersion of skills and ideas. Labor mobility is one mechanism of knowledge spillovers, and a growing literature documents the importance of social interaction, local networks, and personal communication in knowledge transmission (Varga, 2000)—all of which higher education institutions are uniquely suited to house or foster. Institutions of higher education also help retain top-flight scientists in a region, providing local stability during times of disruption and uncertainty in private firms. In a 2008 study for the Brookings Institution, Timothy J. Bartik and George Erickcek (2008, p. 15) found that in addition to direct technology transfer, local businesses also benefit from "a wide variety of formal and informal interactions in which professors, researchers and students at the university interact with nearby businesses, either through formal contracts or more information interaction to help local businesses solve a wide variety of problems."

SUPPORTING BUSINESSES

Even without playing a direct role in conducting research, universities and colleges can support local businesses and communities through subsidies and services, such as access to laboratories, office space,

computing facilities, and incubators. They can also assist their surrounding cities and towns by using campus buildings or other major
projects to improve community life and sustainability, or by assisting
with other projects that spur overall community development.

Business Services/Management Assistance

Higher education institutions can help private firms incorporate new
knowledge into their operations, products, and services through
workforce development, business assistance, and other forms of consultation. University systems around the country help local firms with
everything from business plans to personnel policy to keeping the
books. Business assistance programs may include market research,
financing, licensing, inventions, and networking, and vary with the
nature of the business being helped. Industrial extension programs
provide consulting to existing, often long-established local firms,
with services that include business consulting for competitiveness,
quality, lean manufacturing, environmental compliance, and energy
efficiency.

In North Carolina, the federally funded small business assistance
program is a University of North Carolina system-wide program
managed by North Carolina State University (NCSU). Its network
of seventeen Small Business Development and Technology Centers is
based mostly at business schools in other public colleges across the
state, providing training courses and counseling for small business
owners. The centers have carved out special expertise in providing
technology assistance; in helping small businesses find local sources
of capital; and in offering intensive one-on-one counseling programs
for small business owners. NCSU's small business program has developed specific, separate training programs to help small investors in
the state understand how to set up, operate, and succeed with local
angel capital networks and to train small business owners in how to
find and work with investors.

Iowa State University operates a series of programs that deliver
assistance to Iowa businesses. The Pappajohn Center for Entrepreneurship provides a wide variety of business-related guidance and
assistance, including market research, business plan development,
financing, licensing, inventions, and networking, both for startups

and for existing businesses. Iowa State Research Park is home to some fifty small companies and an Institute for Physical Research and Technology Company Assistance provides no-cost assistance to companies that want to prove out concepts and compete for federal grants in materials-related areas.

SUNY universities and colleges provide a range of direct services tailored to the needs of specific businesses and different regions. A network of Small Business Development Centers operates at more than a score of SUNY campuses across New York, while most of the colleges and universities in the system assist clusters of firms in their region on joint marketing and shared R&D. On Long Island, Farmingdale State College operates an Institute for Research and Technology providing access to specialized equipment and faculty consultation that increases productivity and sustainability of local businesses.

Sometimes assistance to businesses and community organizations is provided through faculty consulting. Such assistance is typically not arranged through the university and is not centrally reported. Yet, it can also be an important and widely used channel by which universities contribute to their local economies.

Student Internships

Scientific apprenticeships and internships constitute another way in which universities and colleges can support local businesses and communities—by providing inexpensive, semi-expert labor. Most SUNY campuses report that they have programs to place students in internships with businesses in the region, including twelve of thirteen university colleges, seven of eight technology colleges, twenty-seven of thirty community colleges and five of the eight university centers. Roughly half report that they have programs or policies that encourage faculty, staff, or students to provide technical assistance to businesses or community organizations in the region. This includes thirteen of twenty-two university colleges and technology colleges, half of the university centers, and twelve out of thirty community colleges. In New York City, SUNY's Fashion Institute of Technology has partnerships with more than four thousand company sponsors and fills over 5,200 internship positions.

FOSTERING COMMUNITY VITALITY

Higher education institutions also contribute indirectly to the economic health of their region by fostering the vitality of their surrounding communities. Universities provide cultural enrichment and recreational resources, serving as a hub for community and regional identity building. Higher education institutions also assist local governments, businesses, and nonprofit organizations in local problem solving, particularly with respect to urban and regional planning, public and environmental health, and needs assessment. And they can use their physical resources in ways that address community needs, such as establishing facilities in locations that may help turn around declining neighborhoods.

The University of Minnesota has an array of community linkages involving youth and education, economic and community development, as well as agriculture and the environment. Within each area, the university provides academic, community, and program resource information, so that area groups or individuals can find the programs or linkages they seek. The Public Engagement Council brings together faculty, staff, students, community members, politicians, and administrators to encourage and develop public engagement at all levels. The Children, Youth, and Family Consortium works with university, community, government organizations, and nonprofits to address early childhood development, continued student development, family relationships, and intergenerational issues.

SUNY also shares expertise and resources with community groups, nonprofits, and government to support problem solving and decision making. The Performing Arts Center at SUNY Purchase College, for example, is a cornerstone of the region's economy and quality of life. Center performances attract hundreds of thousands of attendees and reach tens of thousands of schoolchildren through arts-in-education programs each season, while the facilities provide essential rehearsal and event space for community arts organizations. SUNY Geneseo's Center for Community Business and Social Entrepreneurship assisted in designing and implementing a redevelopment plan for Rochester's South Wedge community. The plan was so successful that the area has become a model for other areas of the city, with increased resident satisfaction, rising property values, and a 90 percent success rate in new business start-ups after three years.

Institutions of higher education also make investment decisions—concerning the location of new academic buildings, student housing and related services, incentives for faculty/employee housing, local-source preferences for goods, services, employees and the like—that (intentionally or unintentionally) have considerable consequences for host communities. The University of Memphis joined with neighborhood and business leaders in maximizing the university's economic and community revitalization impact on its surrounding neighborhoods. Under the University District project, the university built an expanded student residence hall and joined forces with a private developer on a $63 million mixed-use project with more than 230 residential units, 100,000 square feet of retail and restaurant space, along with additional streetlights, sidewalk improvements, and a new parking garage serving the area. This triggered additional private development, including a $13.9 million, eighty-five-unit luxury student housing project, and a forty-unit condominium building. The university relocated its law school to the old Customs House as part of an effort to create a more vibrant waterfront promenade area in downtown Memphis.

CHARACTERISTICS OF ECONOMIC DEVELOPMENT ACTIVITIES AMONG UNIVERSITIES AND COLLEGES

Our review of different types of higher education economic development activities reveals several characteristics that stand out as significant for understanding their impact on local and regional economies.

First, what is most striking is the great *variety* of economic development activities that universities and colleges have developed. Moreover, these activities are not just different methods of producing similar effects; they involve very different economic processes. The economic effects of these diverse activities operate through different causal chains, over different time horizons, and across different geographical areas. For instance, the import-export model—largely fueled by tuition and fees from students and parents from outside the university's locality—moves money through the local economy fairly quickly and with comparatively little uncertainty.

By contrast, the effects of training and education on human capital and productivity are much harder to gauge, as these effects depend on local demand for particular skills relative to other labor markets as well as additional factors affecting the migration of people trained or educated at the college or university. Business services and subsidies (such as entrepreneurial training or free or low-cost physical facilities, as incubators offer) are more certain to go to local firms. Their impacts, however, on the local economy depend on whether and how these factors affect firms' productivity, their ability to find a market niche, or many other firm-level variables related to growth and sustainability. Finally, the economic effects of research or "idea factories" involve very complex and typically long chains of events—often twenty years or longer—running from the generation of discoveries, their dispersion among other researchers or potential entrepreneurs, the application of those ideas to marketable innovations, and the effects of innovations on economic growth (National Research Council, 2006, p. 62).

Second, these activities are often intermingled in efforts to produce economic impacts; that is, the activities are frequently *bundled*. While we have described the various economic activities of universities and colleges as if they are discrete, separate programs, they are often combined in packages of interrelated efforts within a university or college. Although we found some specialization in approaches across campuses—the research universities did more commercialization of discoveries, of course, while community colleges focused more on developing specialized training programs for specific business or industries—we also found a lot of overlap of activities as some universities performed many economic development functions. Combinations of activities were especially common among the larger, more ambitious economic development initiatives, such as those at Research Triangle Park, University at Albany's CNSE, and Georgia Tech. The activities were often combined to reinforce or complement each other as they targeted certain industries or aimed to build up particular scientific and economic capacities. In some cases, complementary programs spanned across institutions, such as SUNY's Hudson Valley Community College's TEC-SMART program, which trained employees for industries involved in the nearby CNSE.

Third, our overview of higher education economic development activities suggests that economic impacts are *contingent* on many factors not controlled by the university. Timing and context—and entrepreneurs who pull these factors together—were important in designing effective economic development efforts. The CNSE's pub-lic-private partnerships are no doubt useful models for other univer-sity initiatives. But its growth surely depended on its timing, on the fact that the university and the state were ready and willing to build the technological infrastructure to conduct nano-scale research pre-cisely when the demand for such facilities was rapidly growing and not fully met. Many economic development activities are not typical "programs," in the sense of a set of activities that can be replicated with the expectation that they will generate similar results in other settings. Effective implementation is more artful—sensitive and re-sponsive to the resources and opportunities available to a university or college at a specific time. One implication of these contingencies is that, if we do find a university or college to have a major impact, it is not necessarily true that what they did would produce similar results if attempted by another institution at another time.

Fourth, we found ways in which academic institutions dealt with the contingencies and managed the uncertainties—sometimes by developing and implementing initiatives in many small and distinct steps, steps that can be adjusted in light of feedback from prior ac-tions. This process of *innovative incrementalism* involves the "stra-tegic decision to move forward in stages, as quickly as funding and demand allowed," thus permitting the projects to show progress to potential funders and clients and avoid overextension and debt. To produce this sustained and cumulative process, an essential ingredi-ent was a "nucleus of committed, persistent people" who "worked within an organizational culture that encouraged and valued entre-preneurship" (Rockefeller Institute & Regional Institute, 2011, p. 29). For instance, new activities and organizations can be brought into a cluster around an academic institution, and new facilities can be built. These in turn create a new ecology of organizations, facili-ties, projects, and people, which in turn offer additional opportunities to bring other activities and organizations on board (for a discussion of the dynamics of clusters, see Braunerhjelm & Feldman, 2006).

One such example was SUNY's Downstate Medical Center, which launched its Biotech Initiative after recognizing two compat-ible and compelling needs: the demand for affordable space among local biotech start-ups and maturing firms, and an interest among faculty and students in working with such companies. The space was not at first available. But leadership at Downstate and among

Brooklyn members of the state legislature led to the creation of a research project, funded by the state and New York City. Private-sector leasing and construction followed quickly, which then led to the construction of a large laboratory. This construction in turn helped draw additional support from New York State, New York City, and the federal government—and eventually to an incubator and space for expanding firms in the refurbished Brooklyn Army Terminal. Downstate Medical Center thus built up an array of organizations step by step until it grew to fill not only an enormous space but also established relationships and interdependencies that helped hold the community together. This incrementalism may often be a necessity at first, but it is also not a bad strategy overall. As Peter Drucker notes, "[E]ven high-tech entrepreneurship need not be 'high risk'" (1985, p. 29). Incrementalism may be a fine way to manage risk—of dealing with the enormous uncertainties regarding any effort to produce big change, by letting experience reveal weaknesses and strengths.

Fifth, as implied by the points already made, higher education economic development activities, if successful, tend to become *less dependent* over time on continued involvement by colleges and universities. Firms are expected to "graduate" from incubators (though many do not, and many do not last long after graduation), and as a cluster of firms, partnerships, and relationships is built up, it may reach a tipping point where it begins to be an attraction to other enterprises and entrepreneurial efforts on its own. As Alain Kaloyeros of University at Albany's CNSE noted, it was like recruiting businesses for a shopping mall: once he and his colleagues got some anchor tenants, the smaller ones came along on their own (Rockefeller Institute & Regional Institute, 2011, p. 20). More generally, as major university initiatives mature and expand, they will almost necessarily be affected by more numerous and diverse economic processes, while the current significance of the university and its actions for the overall economic impact is likely to dwindle.

IMPLICATIONS FOR USING DIFFERENT APPROACHES TO MEASURING ECONOMIC IMPACTS

The diversity, complexity, contingency, and dynamics of university economic development activities all pose challenges for understanding the full economic effects of higher education institutions. Three approaches to the question of impact have dominated the literature to date. Yet none of them encompass the whole range of activities and potential effects of such institutions, nor do they resolve some of the most difficult questions of impact.

First, as already noted, many studies have sought to define the effects of university economic activity as the rippling flow of university revenues and spending within a geographic region. But not only is this import-export approach prone to significant methodological questions as it is typically done, it usually ignores the many economic activities or functions performed by higher education institutions. Universities and colleges are treated largely as any other "firms," with no special role in human capital formation, increasing productivity, or generating innovations.

A second approach views the economic consequence of higher education in terms of the value of attaining a higher education credential—either at the aggregate level, in terms of how the prevalence of such degrees among the population relates to rates of economic growth (Moretti, 2004; Abel & Gabe, 2011), or at the level of the individual, with respect to how the attainment of a higher education degree relates to lifetime earnings (see Carnevale & Rose, 2012—chapter 6 in this volume). But here too, the results are unable to speak to the particulars of many economic activities or strategies deployed by universities or colleges.

A third approach perceives university economic impact in terms of quantifiable indicators of commercialization activity—as a summing up of patents, licenses, and royalties earned through university research. These metrics, however, are generally intermediate outcomes: not measures of changes in the broader economy attributable to the university but indicators of research and commercialization activities and economic returns to the university or research sponsor. Indeed, some critics suggest that a focus on such measures creates a push for royalty-producing, licensable products over other academic pursuits with perhaps more lasting and wide-ranging benefits.

There are, to be sure, efforts now underway to develop and field test a set of metrics that reflect a much broader range of research-related economic activities in which institutions of higher education are involved (Association of Public and Land-grant Universities, 2010; for a discussion of research-related metrics, see Tassey, 2003, pp. 17–24). Nonetheless, though these efforts are a necessary step toward understanding the economic impacts of universities, they are not sufficient, since metrics by themselves do not answer the question: Which economic changes, and how many of those changes, are directly or indirectly attributable to university activities?

What can be done to overcome these weaknesses? Three types of methodologies may be useful, though each also has limitations and may have to be combined in some way to see the overall picture.

Expansion of the Import-Export Model

One way of thinking about how to estimate the impacts of such activities is to extend the import-export model. The basic idea is to expand the boundaries of the university beyond traditional university expenditures (such as faculty salaries, construction, and student spending) and encompass the spending and jobs generated by spin-offs, firms participating in public-private partnerships, companies in (and graduating from) incubators, or companies attracted to a region because of a customized training program.

This approach, however, begs a host of questions, largely regarding the counterfactual. What would the local economy look like in the absence of these activities? The expenditure or import-export model provides little guidance in making such estimates; it only helps in determining how to estimate the economic ramifications of differences between levels of expenditures for different items, spent by different economic actors. We are still left with the need to make judgments about the real impacts of these economic activities. Would a corporation have come to (or remain in) a locality even if it had not received a tailored, subsidized training program? How many companies would have formed within the local area in the absence of an incubator?

There are also "boundary" questions regarding time. How long, and under what circumstances, can a university claim economic credit for, say, a spun-off, incubated, or otherwise assisted firm? The University at Buffalo's (UB) Technology Incubator has housed one hundred companies since it was established in 1988. But can those companies and their economic roles be "counted" in UB's estimate of its economic impact, even if they are still in the Buffalo area? Some of the companies may not have existed without UB's past support. At some point, however, it makes little sense to count a company's jobs and expenditures as a product of a university, when the firm has dealt with decades of competitive pressures, changes in products, and turnovers in management and workers since it last had anything to do with the university.

Also, when we extend the import-export model, as it is usually implemented, to the effects of such complicated processes as the effects of research on the economy, we run the risk of deploying many other inappropriate assumptions. For instance, the model relies heavily on historical input-output data across industries, specifically, "commodity inputs that are used by each industry to produce its output, the commodities produced by each industry, and the use of commodities by final consumers" (Bureau of Economic Analysis, 2009, pp. 1–2). If, however, the university is generating real innovations, the commercial products associated with the innovations may create altogether new relationships between firms, industries, and customers. Some of the better studies use surveys of companies to estimate these new relationships. But many do not, and even surveys may not capture the wide range of unanticipated effects. Again, this is just one more instance of a fundamental problem with extending the traditional model to encompass a wider range of economic activities: by itself, it does not have the capacity to measure complex impacts.

Program Evaluation Models

There are other methodologies available, however, to estimate the impacts of economic interventions, and perhaps these may be used in combination with an extended import-export model. One such tradition is the rich methodology developed around "program evaluation." This approach attempts to compare changes in outcomes produced by a "treatment" with changes observed in a counterfactual situation. The strongest evaluation design uses randomization to estimate the counterfactual. For instance, a customized training program might be offered randomly to applicant firms—and the design could measure changes in the revenues, jobs, productivity, and other economic outcomes of firms that receive the training program

and compare those changes with those observed among firms not offered training.

If the sample of firms is large enough and other conditions are
met (such as ensuring that there is no "contamination," e.g., the
training program is accessible to individuals working in the firms
assigned to the control group and no others), the difference in outcomes or changes in outcomes can be an estimate of the impact of
the economic program. Research designs that do not use randomization can also, under certain circumstances, be strong in the sense of
producing credible estimates of impacts, though they usually require
more extensive data analyses and interpretations to rule out alternative accounts of observed differences between the treatment and
control groups.

For several reasons, this analytical approach is hard to implement in the case of many economic development programs, though
it may work in some cases. Control groups might be used to estimate
the effects of certain services offered to individuals or firms, such
as a university incubator or an employee training program. These
programs can be offered or withheld from a sample of firms; and
a comparison of changes in economic outcomes between businesses
that were served and that were not could then be used to estimate
impacts.

However, many of the other activities of universities—from creating spin-offs, to licensing of patents, public-private partnerships, and
community-building efforts—cannot be selectively offered or withheld as services to firms or individuals. Indeed, agglomeration and
community-building models treat spillover effects as an essential part
of the process by which economic impacts occur. One firm and its
partnership with the university is expected (or hoped) to attract and
encourage participation by other firms until a self-sustaining cluster emerges. In program evaluation terms, those spillovers would be
"contamination," that is, the treatment is in some way experienced
by members of the control group. Yet that process is precisely what
some efforts try to achieve.

Another difficulty in applying the program evaluation research
design to university economic development efforts grows out of the
contingent character of many of the activities. Program evaluations
work well when the treatment is expected to have a similar impact
on all potential recipients. For instance, a tax subsidy program might

be viewed as having a roughly similar effect on a wide variety of corporations. However, certain partnerships, training programs, or many other economic development measures implemented by universities often represent a conjunction between the special capabilities of the university and the specific needs of one or more local businesses. Indeed, selecting the right firms is part of the "treatment." That selectivity means that it is difficult to identify a control group of firms, since they will probably be different in several respects from the firms that were chosen for support. That is not to say that the problem is insurmountable. If there are many firms whose needs fit what the university has to offer, perhaps a control group could be created. One approach might work if the program is oversubscribed: applicant firms with similar qualifications could be randomly assigned to the control and treatment programs (i.e., rejected from or included in the program). But if the criteria for qualification are fairly focused, not many firms would be included in the study, with a consequent loss in statistical power.

Comparative Site Research

Another analytical strategy for estimating the effectiveness of university economic development programs would be to compare sites, that is, campuses and their local economies. For instance, a study could compare economic changes between (1) localities with universities engaged in extensive economic development activities with (2) changes in other localities (the control sites), which might be selected on several grounds, for instance, localities without universities or colleges at all, or localities with universities but without extensive economic development activities, or some other definition of "no treatment."

This approach would allow researchers to capture the overall effects of multiple or bundled economic development activities of a university—which are a challenge for program evaluation methods. It would also recognize the effects of the university in properly selecting the most appropriate firms in targeting its activities. Finally, it could take into account incremental changes in the university's activities over time, though it would be important to measure these changes and compare them with changes in economic outcomes.

Thus, comparing sites may be the best approach when attempting to estimate the effects of large, multifaceted, and lengthy economic development efforts by universities.

Nonetheless, there are challenges here as well. As already suggested, there is some ambiguity about what sites to use for comparisons. For example, Schultz (2011) compared University at Albany's CNSE to other mature nano centers around the country in order to distinguish special characteristics of CNSE. For other purposes, however, such as understanding the full economic effects of CNSE on its regional economy, one might use other comparisons, such as similar metropolitan areas without any nano center, or without any advanced science/commercialization partnerships, or without any major research university. Of course, another weakness is the typically small number of cases in such analyses. To collect good data over time on a large enough number of sites to have significant statistical power can be costly—and in many cases, the comparisons, though suggestive, are just not numerous enough to test for significant differences.

WHAT TO DO?

The diversity of economic development activities, the different economic processes they involve, and the complex workings and probable effects they can have on local economic conditions suggest that a variety of methods may be most appropriate for estimating their impacts. The import-export model may be most appropriate for estimating the economic effects of activities that are clearly driven by the university. Program evaluation study designs may be best when a service or facility is open to a relatively wide range of businesses or individuals—such as involvement in a training program for employees of selected companies, or an entrepreneurship program for certain faculty members. And a comparative site study may be best when there is interest in understanding the effects on a community of a comprehensive array of economic development activities, such as a nano, biotech, or clean energy center that combines basic research, commercialization, partnerships with industry, training programs, and support for new firms and entrepreneurs. Of course, these different approaches can also be used in combination. Both the program evaluation and comparative site approaches could greatly strengthen an expanded import-export analysis.

Seeing the wide range of economic development activities also gives rise to another set of questions: Why are there so many activities? How are they related to one another? How have they evolved within institutions? And how are they distributed across universities and colleges? The usual conceptualization of university economic development activities treats them as exogenous interventions in the economy—as actions that affect their environment but are not much affected by that environment. But our case studies suggest rich and often cumulative interactions over time between universities and their surrounding economies and communities. One set of relationships with an industry may lead to recognition of new needs and adoption of new economic activities, and relationships with additional firms and industries. That is to say, many of the characteristics we noted may be best understood when we view economic activities as endogenous, as evolving in tandem with the university's economic effects on the economy. Of course, this sort of dynamic interaction can be captured to some extent through qualitative analyses over time. But cumulative, comparative, rigorous analysis would require us to trace these histories of the interactions between higher education institutions and their environments—and their mutual shaping of each other—with as much quantitative measurement as possible. Then perhaps we can see that universities' impact is more than a sum of its effects over a short period of time—in some cases, they may be dynamic and forceful components in a complex and evolutionary economic system, one that is constantly changing universities, industries, and communities alike.

REFERENCES

Abel, J. R., & Dietz, R. (2009, rev. 2011). Do colleges and universities increase their region's human capital? *Federal Reserve Bank of New York Staff Reports*, No. 401. New York: Federal Reserve Bank of New York.

Abel, J. R., & Gabe, T. M. (2011). Human capital and economic activity in urban America. *Regional Studies 45*, 1079–1090.

Anselin, L., Varga, A., & Acs, Z. (1997). Local geographic spillovers between university research and high technology innovations. *Journal of Urban Economics 42*, 422–448.

Association of Public and Land-grant Universities. (2010). *Workshop to identify new measures of university contributions to regional economic growth: Report to the National Science Foundation*. Washington, DC: Association of Public and Land-grant Universities.

Bartik, T. J., & Erickcek, G. (2008). *The local economic impact of "eds & meds": How policies to expand universities and hospitals affect metropolitan economies*. Washington, DC: Brookings Institution Metropolitan Policy Program.

Braunerhjelm, P. & Feldman, M. (2006). *Cluster genesis: Technology-based industrial development*. New York, NY: Oxford University Press.

Bureau of Economic Analysis. (2009). *Concepts and methods of the U.S. input-output accounts*. Washington, DC: Bureau of Economic Analysis, U.S. Department of Commerce.

Carnevale, A. P., and Rose, S. J., (2012). The convergence of postsecondary education and the labor market. In J. E. Lane & D. B. Johnstone (Eds.), *Universities and colleges as economic drivers*. Albany: State University of New York Press.

DeVol, R. C., & Wong, P. (1999). *America's high-tech economy: Growth, development, and risks for metropolitan areas*. Santa Monica, CA: Milken Institute.

Drucker, P. F. (1985). *Innovation and entrepreneurship*. New York: Harper.

Faggian, A., & McCann, P. (2009). Universities, agglomerations, and graduate human capital mobility. *Tijdschrift voor Economische en Sociale Geographie 100*, 210–223.

Friedman, T. L. (2005). *The world is flat: A brief history of the 21st century*. New York: Farrar, Straus & Giroux.

Geiger, R. L., & Sa, C. M. (2008). *Tapping the riches of science*. Cambridge: Harvard University Press.

Geiger, R. L., & Sa, C. M. (2009). Technology transfer offices and the commercialization of university research in the United States. In P. Clancy & D. D. Dill (Eds.), *The research mission of the university: Policy reforms and institutional responses* (177–196). Rotterdam, The Netherlands: Sense Publishers.

Jaffe, A. B. (1989). Real effects of academic research. *American Economic Review 79*, 957–970.

Johnstone, D. B. (2012). The impact of the 2008 great recession on college and university contributions to state and regional economic growth. In J. E. Lane & D. B. Johnstone (Eds.), *Universities and colleges as economic drivers* Albany: State University of New York Press.

Lane, J. E. (2012). Higher education and economic competitiveness. In J. E. Lane & D. B. Johnstone (Eds.), *Universities and colleges as economic drivers* Albany: State University of New York Press.

McHenry, P., Sanderson, A. R., & Siegfried, J. J. (2012). Pitfalls of traditional measures of higher education's role in economic development. In J. E. Lane & D. B. Johnstone (Eds.), *Universities and colleges as economic drivers*. Albany: State University of New York Press.

Moretti, E. (2004). Estimating the social return to higher education: Evidence from longitudinal and repeated cross-sectional data. *Journal of Econometrics 121*, 175–212.

National Research Council. (2006). *A matter of size: Triennial review of the nanotechnology initiative.* Washington, DC: National Academies Press.

Rockefeller Institute [University at Albany] and Regional Institute [University at Buffalo]. (2011). *How SUNY matters.* Albany: Rockefeller Institute of Government.

Schultz, L. I. (2011). Nanotechnology's triple helix: A case study of the University at Albany's College of Nanoscale Science and Engineering. *Journal of Technology Transfer 36*, 546–564.

Schultz, L. I. (2012). University industry government collaboration for economic growth. In J. E. Lane & D. B. Johnstone (Eds.), *Universities and colleges as economic drivers*. Albany: State University of New York Press.

Shaffer, D., & Wright, D. (2010). *A new paradigm for economic development: How higher education institutions are working to revitalize their regional and state economies.* Albany: Rockefeller Institute of Government.

State Science and Technology Institute. (2006). *A resource guide for technology-based economic development: Positioning universities as driver, fostering entrepreneurship, increasing access to capital*. Washington, DC: Economic Development Administration, U.S. Department of Commerce.

Stiglitz, J. (2010). *Freefall: America, free markets, and the sinking of the world economy*. New York: Norton.

Tassey, G. (2003). *Planning report 03-01: Methods for assessing the economic impacts of government R&D*. Washington, DC: National Institute of Standards & Technology, U.S. Department of Commerce.

Varga, A. (2000). Local academic knowledge transfers and the concentration of economic activity. *Journal of Regional Science 40*, 280–309.

3

PITFALLS OF TRADITIONAL MEASURES OF HIGHER EDUCATION'S ROLE IN ECONOMIC DEVELOPMENT

PETER McHENRY, ALLEN R. SANDERSON, AND JOHN J. SIEGFRIED

ABSTRACT

This chapter describes methodological approaches and pitfalls common to studies of the economic impact of colleges and universities. Such studies often claim preposterous levels of local benefits that imply annualized rates of return exceeding 100 percent. We address problems in these studies pertaining to the specification of the counterfactual, the definition of the local area, the identification of "new" expenditures, the tendency to double-count economic impacts, the role of local taxes, and the omission of local spillover benefits from enhanced human capital created by higher education, and offer several suggestions for improvement. If these economic impact studies were conducted at the level of accuracy most institutions require of faculty research, their claims of local economic benefits would not be so egregious, and, as a result, trust in and respect for higher education officials would be enhanced.

INTRODUCTION

Colleges and universities often claim they contribute significantly to their local and/or regional economy, in part through job creation and generation of tax revenue. Periodically, they commission, or produce "in house," economic impact reports to bolster these claims. The purpose of many of these studies is to articulate the value of an institution of higher education, including spillover effects, often to help the institution compete for state funding (or resist cutbacks), maintain its threatened tax-exempt status, obtain a subvention, fend off criticism, or as a core plank in some new fundraising initiative.

Concomitant with these efforts, however, are frequent methodological and measurement pitfalls and potholes. The purposes of this chapter are: (1) to describe common approaches, errors, and extensions in many of these impact studies, and (2) to suggest better ways to think about the economic impact of institutions of higher education. It is certainly not our intention to belittle the colleges that conduct or commission studies of their economic impact, but we believe that the fundamental mission of these institutions compels them to apply equally high standards of scholarship, accuracy, and transparency in assessing their own activities as those that they would demand of faculty and others engaged in scholarly research.

The next section provides an overview of popular economic impact studies and the claims in many of them when the subject is higher education. We then dissect the various components common among these studies—the implicit counterfactual or "but for" alternative, definition of the local area, measuring expenditures and avoiding double-counting, the use of appropriate multipliers or indirect effects, local taxes, spillover effects, and ancillary activities. In the concluding section, we offer our conclusions and recommendations for anyone embarking on, or involved in the creation of, an economic impact study of an institution of higher education.

ECONOMIC IMPACT STUDIES

Higher education is just one industry among many that generate estimates of local economic impact. Newspapers are replete with estimates of purported economic benefits due to the opening of a casino, production of a movie, or a national political convention. Some accounts describe negative impacts—damage caused by hundred-year floods or business lost due to new regulation. Claims of enormous economic gain are ubiquitous in the sports world as well. The National Football League estimates the Super Bowl's value to its host city at more than $500 million. Promoters claim that a new minor league baseball park is worth seven figures in dollars and five figures in jobs. In some cases these claims are harmless self-promotion, but in many instances exaggerated impact studies are used to secure public funding that competes with other social agendas, or cause policymakers or private institutions to misallocate resources, and thus cause spending inefficiencies.

Colleges and universities have been commissioning economic impact studies for decades. Many still follow the template codified in Caffrey and Isaacs (1971), although innovations have added to the complexity and breadth of these studies over time. The basic procedure is to sum expenditures of the college community (students, faculty, staff, and visitors) created by the presence of the institution and apply multipliers[1] to reflect the churning of direct expenditures through a local economy (e.g., part of a dollar paid to a local printing press is subsequently paid to a local repair service). The result is an estimated "local economic impact." This common dollar figure often appears in the headline of the report, is invariably in the millions (often reaching billions) of dollars, and is frequently complemented by an estimate of job creation. For example:

> The study found that the University [of Florida's] total economic impact on the state for the 2009–2010 fiscal year was $8.76 billion, and total employment impact was more than 100,000 jobs. (Wells, 2011)

> Combining the impact of spending by the University, its students and visitors, and taking into account the multiplier effect of this combined spending, we estimate that in fiscal year 2008, Tulane accounted for: approximately $694.6 million in economic activity and more than 8,300 FTE jobs in New Orleans. (Tulane University, 2010)

Inputs into a college impact analysis include: direct employment and payroll, minus federal taxes; expenditures for equipment, supplies, and services; construction costs; public and private support of research grants and contracts; spending in the local community by students from outside the local area and by local students who alternatively would have attended college elsewhere; and expenditures by visitors, including alumni, who visit the campus for academic and/or athletic events. Universities with medical centers sometimes include corresponding expenditures at their hospitals. Multipliers are applied to these sums to account for indirect and induced impacts.

Some studies take credit for in-migration of students (from out of state who come for college and remain) as well as incremental lifetime incomes and sales taxes paid to the state. Impacts in the form of innovation and technology transfer are highlighted with lists of local companies that spun off from university research or student initiatives. Colleges claim to enhance the quality of the local work force and promote public service (e.g., "On average, Liberty University students provide approximately 4.3 hours of volunteer service per month or a total of 586,262 hours per year" [Magnum Economic Consulting, 2010]). Colleges also tout their contributions to local culture and the overall quality of life—theater, music performances, museums, and art exhibitions, most of which are open to the public—but they are difficult to quantify ("Texas Tech offers a number of cultural and educational programs, as well as facilities, to the public and thus provides intangible benefits that improve the quality of life of those in the local community" [Ewing, 2010]). Some studies argue that colleges are valuable because they are "stable" components of the economy, less prone to contraction in recessions than other businesses.

There is no comprehensive list of college economic impact studies. In a review completed prior to 1992, Leslie and Slaughter (1992) surveyed about sixty reports. For this chapter, we reviewed the results of another 186 studies done since 1992, covering 617 individual institutions (updating our review in Siegfried, Sanderson, & McHenry, 2007). Some institutions enter the statistics multiple times because they commissioned multiple studies over time or because they were involved in both individual and group impact studies (e.g., "Higher Education in Middle Tennessee"). Because of their reliance on government support, 86 percent of these impact studies are for public colleges and universities.

In addition to Caffrey and Isaacs, and Leslie and Slaughter, other contributions to the college/university economic impact literature include: Beck, Elliott, Meisel, and Wagner (1995), who proposed new methodologies, attempted to account for short- and long-run flows, and gave alternative ways of thinking about geographic regions; Brown and Heaney (1997), who discussed the traditional "economic base" approach; Felsenstein (1996), who used Northwestern as an example of a university's impact on a metropolitan area; and Blackwell, Cobb, and Weinberg (2002), who discussed traditional and human capital impacts, and conducted a case study of Xavier University in Cincinnati.

The complexity of impact studies and their emphasis on persuasion leads to more dispersion in measurements than the diversity among colleges would imply, raising doubt about their accuracy. A recent study for the University of Wisconsin-Madison claimed a $12.4 billion impact on Wisconsin in 2010 (Ward et al., 2011). But a 2002 study by the same contractor claimed that the entire University of Wisconsin System (the Madison campus plus twelve other four-year universities and thirteen two-year colleges) had a smaller impact, equal to $11.5 billion when converted to 2010 dollars (Winters & Strang, 2002). Most of the difference arises because the Madison-only study claimed credit for the UW hospital: a change in methodology adding to dispersion but absent from the sound byte version of a total impact.

Consider some standardized measures of impacts that should vary modestly among colleges. Leslie and Slaughter (1992) standardized economic impacts by dividing "business volume" by the college budget. We interpret business volume as the headline economic impact in dollars and budget as total expenditures. Among seventy-seven of the post-1992 studies we reviewed, the estimated impact divided by budget ranges from 0.61 to 6.18, with a mean of 2.33 and standard deviation of 1.21. In 130 reviewed studies,[2] the estimated employment impact divided by budget (in $ million) ranges from 9 to 271, with mean 38.2 and standard deviation 36.9. The implied multipliers for job impacts[3] in 136 studies range from 1.03 to 10.47. Although colleges and their communities are heterogeneous, the variety is not enough to justify such a large range of estimates.

In the analysis that follows we address common methodological challenges that affect the accuracy and reliability of these estimates.

THE COUNTERFACTUAL

The key consideration for studies assessing the local impact of a college is the extent to which area residents are better off with the institution there than they would be in its absence. "Better off" is usually defined as higher employment, per capita income, or perhaps more controversial, local tax revenue, but it surely should also include the many aspects of life that are not measured in dollars and cents, such as health conditions, social status, personal relationships, security, cultural opportunities, and other living conditions that are difficult to quantify. The proper procedure is to compare economic indicators in the presence of the institution with predictions of those same indicators "but for" the college—that is, compare actual to "counterfactual" outcomes. From this perspective, *that portion of an institution's economic activity that would remain in the local area even if the institution were not there is not a contribution to the local economy.* Or, as an impact study of the College of St. Benedict and St. John's University in Minnesota put it graphically:

> Essentially, one must imagine that some type of giant laser gun suddenly eliminates both the College and University, and all students, faculty and staff are immediately "beamed" elsewhere to "rematerialize" and continue with their work. By measuring the change in economic activity if this happened, we come to the impact that these campuses have on the community. (Edwards & Apoutou, 2010)

Few studies of the local economic impact of colleges and universities explicitly articulate such a counterfactual.

The absence of a clear vision of a realistic alternative elevates the risk of using inconsistent counterfactuals that exaggerate the impact of a single institution. Moreover, a divergence between the area of study and the area appropriate to the multiplier can lead to internally inconsistent estimates.

The extent of relevant activity depends on the scope of the pertinent area, the capacity of alternative local suppliers of services to substitute for those produced by the institution, and the extent to which consumers would accept alternative suppliers. For example, a university that attracts students who otherwise would enroll at other institutions in the same metropolitan area does not draw many new students or dollars to the area if the other local colleges can increase their enrollment. In contrast, an isolated rural college is likely the sole local attraction to its students, and thus reasonably might be credited with virtually all of the impact stimulated by its students' expenditures. The extent to which colleges and universities attract outside money to an area, that is, sell "exports" or induce "import substitution" (revenues from students who live inside the local area who, but for the college, would have attended a college elsewhere), depends on both the origin of their students and what the students would have done if the college had not been there.

Establishing a counterfactual for a college is challenging. First, institutions of higher education do not appear and disappear quickly. Conceptualizing Williamsburg, Virginia, without The College of William and Mary (founded 1693) is difficult. The annual number of colleges opening or closing is modest.[4] Because most colleges start small and grow slowly over time, it is also usually impossible to identify a short period of time over which the difference between the absence and presence of a college on its local area might be discerned. The abrupt closing in 2008 and reopening in 2011 of Antioch College in Yellow Springs, Ohio, is an unusual counterexample that could provide an opportunity to assess the local economic impact of a small college with a natural experiment.

Second, no one cares about the effect of any economic stimulus on a geographic area void of residents. Interest in impact is a concern about people and their standard of living, in which case the precise relevant population must be identified. This is where many studies of the economic impact of colleges and universities collapse methodologically.

Who, precisely, is of concern? Were a college to leave an area, who would stay, and who would leave? If a new campus were opened that might stimulate economic activity, for example, the University of California-Merced, whose welfare should be measured—the 67,000 Merced residents living in the northern part of the San Joachim Valley before anyone thought of locating a university there, the 100,000 permanent residents who might live there in 2020 when the new university operates at planned scale, or the 130,000 residents, including students, who might live there in academic year 2021? If welfare were measured by the difference between one's income and what one could earn in his or her next best alternative, a general increase in local wages and salaries stimulated by locating the newest University of California campus in Merced would benefit the original residents. But those who move to Merced because of the university may or may not find better opportunities there. Similarly, increases in local property values stimulated by the new Merced campus would accrue to those who owned property there when knowledge of the development was released. But these gains would be offset elsewhere in the state to the extent that this new campus attracts students who would alternatively enroll at other California institutions.

As another recent example, similar to the expansion of California's university system, Florida opened its tenth public four-year university in 1997 in Fort Myers, on the southwest Gulf Coast. Florida Gulf Coast University held its first graduation in 1998, awarding eighty-one degrees to transfer students. A dozen years later, in 2009–10, Florida Gulf Coast enrolled slightly over seven thousand students and awarded 1,460 bachelor's degrees, a remarkable rate of growth. The main local economic impact of Florida Gulf Coast is likely its ability to reduce the number of residents in the Fort Myers and Naples area migrating to other regions of the state to attend one of the nine public Florida universities established earlier.[5]

Studies conducted to enhance the political standing of a college naturally promote benefits accruing to local residents who likely would reside in the area even if the college were absent. The institution's in-migrant administrators and faculty already know they are beneficiaries. They either understand that and are loyal allies of the institution already, or expect they would have enjoyed analogous benefits elsewhere. But hardly any economic impact studies separate the effect of the institution on residents attracted to the area by the institution from the effect on those who would have resided there anyway. The effect on those who migrated to take jobs at the institution is only the extent to which those jobs are better than the ones their occupants left behind.

Migration incentives created by a college complicate the identification of local economic impact even further. Imagine a university that "creates" 1,500 new jobs, attracting 1,800 new workers to the local area, three hundred arriving as members of families of faculty and other specialists migrating to work for the institution. The university touts the addition of 1,500 jobs added to the area, while the residents who would live there anyway face three hundred new competitors for other local jobs. While the impact study trumpets additional jobs, those who would have lived there anyway may be worse off, some perhaps newly unemployed, and others employed at wages diluted by an increased labor supply.[6]

On the other hand, it is possible that a college or university attracts ancillary businesses that require a skilled workforce, affording improved employment opportunities to the local residents who would have lived in the area absent the college. Such a favorable outcome, of course, presumes that the local labor force is able to land the skilled jobs at the ancillary businesses, probably an impractical assumption if we contemplate the many chemists, computer scientists, or engineers working for such businesses.

Third, because the impact of *all* the economic activity generated by the institution is compared implicitly to doing nothing, the implied counterfactual in most impact studies is the complete absence of the institution. But few decisions are of such an "all or nothing" nature, particularly in academe, where change occurs slowly. When considering the effect of an expansion or contraction of a college, it is the effect of *incremental* investment that is relevant. The impact implied by "all or nothing" analysis is an average measure, confounding the irrelevant impact of, say, the first ten thousand students with the effect of the last one hundred students to enroll. Diminishing marginal returns can create mischief when an average impact of the entire investment in a college or university is inappropriately interpreted as the relevant effect of an incremental expansion.

Fourth, when a college or university hires faculty and administrators who migrate to the area, the size of the community changes. Most individuals have preferences regarding the population size and density of their environment. Larger communities may create positive externalities such as greater entertainment, recreation, cultural, medical, shopping, and dining opportunities. Unfortunately, they also usually create more congestion, conflict, and pollution.[7] If a college changes the size of its host community (e.g., Iowa City, Iowa), the debate over the local economic impact of the institution should also consider optimal city size (Getz & Huang, 1978).

Even more important than the challenge of articulating a precise and consistent counterfactual implicit for the college or university is the more general issue of the opportunity cost of public or private investment in higher education. A $100 million infusion of tax revenue to the budget of a state university catering to in-state students might have been directed by the legislature instead to K-12 education, crime prevention, road repairs, or even tax relief. There is no reason to expect that the recirculation of dollars spent on teachers, police, or paving contractors has a different, or smaller, indirect effect on the local economy than dollars initially spent on college inputs.

A dollar spent by a college or university may eventually create multiple dollars of local economic activity. But a dollar spent golfing or for a seafood buffet does the same. One difference between colleges and other establishments is the extent to which initial expenditures of colleges and universities attract new money into an area.

Not all colleges and universities are alike in this regard—some attract much new money to an area, while others attract little. Vanderbilt in Tennessee and the University of Wyoming enroll an entire student body destined to attend an out-of-state college if those two institutions did not exist.[8] Other colleges, for example, Colby in Maine or the University of Texas, enroll many students who would attend a different institution in the same state (e.g., Bowdoin or Texas A&M, respectively) if their first choice were not available. Each college or university must be examined closely to determine the extent to which the revenue it collects would remain in the defined local area if the institution did not exist.

Perhaps partially in response to this critique, some colleges in the same area form groups and measure their economic impact collectively. This circumvents the substitutes issue, since there might be no existing substitute for the entire group of existing colleges. The sixteen colleges and universities in Baltimore are an example. Although Towson University might not be able to claim credit for drawing to Baltimore students who otherwise would have attended the University of Baltimore or another college in the city were there no Towson, the group of sixteen has a legitimate claim that they collectively draw out-of-town students to Baltimore.

The absence of a substantial local economic effect of an individual college or university because reasonable substitutes are available does not imply low value for higher education in general. The overall effect of higher education on the economy is quite substantial. For persons age twenty-five and over in 2010, the unemployment rate averaged 5.4 percent for bachelor's degree holders (with no post-graduate degree), in contrast to 9.2 percent for individuals with some college, but no degree, and 10.3 percent for those holding only a high school diploma. For full-time workers in 2010, median annualized earnings averaged $54,000 for bachelor's degree holders, $37,000 for those with some college but no degree, and $32,500 for individuals who ended their formal education with a high school diploma (Bureau of Labor Statistics, 2011). A careful study (Heckman, Lochner, & Todd, 2008) calculates the average private rate of return to an investment in four-year college tuition and fees (but not room and board, because those costs would have been incurred even without investing in higher education) to be over 15 percent. This is far greater than the average expected return on the investment in incremental physical capital or most financial instruments.

DEFINING THE "LOCAL AREA"

To estimate the impact of a college or university on all or some (e.g., those who would have lived there absent the institution) of the residents of a "local area," one must carefully delineate geographic boundaries. Two principles govern the choice of boundaries. First, the area should fit the purpose of the economic impact study. Second, however delineated, the boundaries must remain consistent throughout the analysis.

The appropriate geographic boundary for analyzing local economic impact depends on the question(s) at hand. If a state university wishes to justify a subvention from its legislature, the geographic boundaries should be congruent with the interests of the legislature—for instance, the state's borders. A private college using a study to justify exemption from local property taxes would presumably delineate the area on the basis of the local tax jurisdiction. A research university seeking more media attention might focus on the television reception or newspaper distribution area surrounding it.

Geographic boundaries have two important effects on the analysis. First, only export sales from, or import substitution into, the defined area constitute "new spending" that would have a significant first-round economic impact. Sales that substitute for other purchases by local residents may increase the apparent economic impact of a college or university, but they will generate an offsetting negative effect elsewhere in the area. For example, if a student from New York City enrolls at Columbia instead of her second choice, New York University, and NYU does not replace her with another student, Columbia generates no net economic expenditure in New York City.

In contrast, almost all student expenditures in Boulder by University of Colorado students are either exports or import substitution from the perspective of Boulder because there are no other traditional colleges there. If the area of interest is expanded to the state of Colorado, many UC-Boulder students alternatively would have remained in-state and attended Colorado State University, University of Northern Colorado, or Colorado College. As the relevant area expands, the amount of expenditure that is "new" to it declines. The smaller the area considered, the larger the proportion of total expenditure that is properly treated as exports or import substitution.

Second, the appropriate multiplier grows as the area under consideration expands. In a narrowly defined perimeter, for example, just Boulder, much of the first round of expenditures by the university to purchase goods and services leaves the area immediately.[9] Not only are many of UC-Boulder's vendors located in Denver and Fort Collins, but also many of its employees live and spend much of their disposable income outside Boulder. When UC-Boulder's expenditures recirculate beyond Boulder, they do not expand Boulder's economy. Viewed from the entire state of Colorado, however, many first-round expenditures on vendors and employees who live in Colorado but outside Boulder remain "local." The multiplier is largest in a completely closed economy, devoid of leakages.

It is tempting to define the area narrowly so as to maximize the export and import substitution nature of enrollments and spending, and simultaneously use a multiplier that has been derived by following economic activity through a larger, inconsistently defined, self-contained area. Because many college impact studies use "off the shelf" multipliers not tailored to the particular area under consideration, they are susceptible to such an analytical sleight of hand. In reality, there is always a tradeoff between the extent of export sales and the magnitude of the multiplier.[10] When using off the shelf multipliers, the analysis must necessarily use the same "local area" as was used to compute the multiplier.

MEASURING EXPENDITURES, DOUBLE-COUNTING, AND *CUI BONO*

Some economic impact studies conducted by colleges and universities apply a regional multiplier to *all* expenditures by the institution. Such an approach is *never* valid. It is inconceivable that every dollar of any college's revenues (and corresponding expenditures) is derived from export (or import substitution) sales. Surely some revenue, if only from a resident who purchases lunch at the campus grill rather than a local Olive Garden, does not represent new money attracted from outside the area.

In order to identify the amount of *net* new spending a college or university contributes to a local area, it is necessary to measure funds *that are new to the area* as they pass a particular portal, and *to apply the appropriate multiplier only to the portion of those new-to-the-area funds that are spent in the local area*. Funds that are new to the area include spending on tuition, room and board, and incidentals (e.g., purchases of supplies at a local Wal-Mart, or haircuts at a barber down the street) by students who would not otherwise ("but for" the college) live or attend college locally. This includes revenues from students from inside the area who, absent the college, would have attended a college elsewhere (import substitution).

New spending also includes grants for research projects funded by organizations that would have sent their grant money elsewhere but for the college, gifts and contributions to the college that would have gone elsewhere but for the college, and any other local revenue flows originating outside the area that would not have materialized absent the college, for instance, money spent by visitors attracted by the institution on potential college scouting trips for high school seniors, on journeys to attend college sporting events or visit friends or family attending the institution, money spent by retirees who moved there because of the college, or medical bills paid by patients consuming specialized teaching hospital services that are not available from alternative local medical centers.[11]

The fundamental underlying principle is to count funds new to the area only once. It is improper to add together *all* spending by students *plus* expenditures by the college or university, because (1) some of the spending by students might have occurred in the area but for the college if some students are local residents who, absent

the college, would not have continued their education beyond high
school or would have attended another local college, and (2) the majority of student spending is made *to the college or university,* which,
in turn, spends those same funds to meet its payroll and pay vendors
for goods and services consumed by the college. So, counting tuition
revenue and spending by the college is double-counting.[12]

After new-to-the-area revenue is isolated, multipliers should be
applied to it that reflect the extent to which each portion of the revenue is spent and re-spent within the local boundary. Some college
expenditures immediately leave the area, for example, purchases of
goods or services that are not produced there, and salaries paid to
employees who live and spend most of their income somewhere else.
Also leaving the area immediately are most federal income and payroll taxes. It is more appropriate to use disposable income plus local
(sales, income, and property) taxes to measure first-round expenditures that affect the local area. The multiplier for expenditures that
immediately leave the area is one, or at least very low, since most of
those funds are not re-spent locally. Other expenditures remain in the
area for many rounds of re-spending, for example, payments by the
college to a plumber who repairs a leaky water line and, who, in turn,
spends the money at a neighborhood restaurant that, in its turn, pays
its workers and local produce suppliers, and so on.

If the appropriate criterion for evaluating economic impact is
the welfare effect on residents living in the area were the college or
university not there, then, quite importantly, *none* of the college expenditures made to in-migrants (faculty and specialized staff, such
as librarians and computer specialists) should be counted in the first
round of expenditures, because those in-migrants are not part of the
"but for" population. *However, the second and subsequent rounds
of expenditures passing through these employees and on to individuals who would have lived in the area absent the college should be
counted.*

Colleges and universities have another characteristic that in-
duces double-counting: they sell products and services to their own
employees, or hire their "customers" as student-workers. Colleges
typically sell lunches, books, logo merchandise apparel, supplies, and
athletic tickets to their employees. Universities with hospitals often
self-insure employee medical benefits and create incentives for employees to consume medical services at university facilities. In such

cases, compensation paid to employees overstates expenditures that move on to a second round locally, because a portion of the compensation is spent "internally" within the university, thus constituting revenue for the institution that does not originate from outside the local area. Including such internal transactions may lead to nontrivial double-counting. Similarly, charitable donations from faculty and staff to the institution that employs them should be excluded from first-round expenditures because such donations are transferred back to the employer as revenues.

Construction and other investment spending require special treatment in impact studies. If construction on a state university campus is financed via a capital expenditure budget, and the opportunity cost of building, say, a new student residence hall is the resurfacing of roads in the same geographic area, the construction expenditure is not net new spending. If, on the other hand, investment in educational facilities is financed from outside the area (say, by federal support), reflecting no local opportunity cost, the expenditures should be included because they represent new economic activity for the local area.

Another counting issue arises from the distinction between head counts and what is generally referred to as an "FTE" (full-time equivalent) when it comes to number of students served, jobs created, or another aspect of some activity. For example, estimates of the impact of a Super Bowl game on the local economy invariably count the number of jobs created while ignoring the fact that most of them are temporary and for only a fraction of something akin to full-time employment. If one is hired for, say, twenty hours a week for the four weeks leading up to the game, that's a total of eighty hours a year (or for ten years if the Super Bowl won't return to town again for a decade), or only one-twenty-fifth of a full-time job, defined as working two thousand hours a year (forty hours a week for fifty weeks).

Like the National Football League, some colleges claim their presence is responsible for thousands of jobs without specifying clearly that many of them are temporary and/or part-time jobs. This ambiguity can confound comparisons of the economic impact of a college or university across academic settings. Institutions could state that they have an annual enrollment of twenty thousand, but if each of those students takes one course per semester at one college, but in another college students take a full-time, academic-year load of eight courses, then the former only has five thousand students on an FTE basis. The same is true on the faculty side of things as well. One institution may employ a large number of adjunct instructors who, over the course of a year, may teach only a fraction of what a full-time faculty member would teach. Many hourly employees, such as cafeteria workers, do not work at all—or get paid—in the summer months. When comparing an institution's impact in terms of jobs created, it is important to express results in terms of conventional full-time equivalent units.

MULTIPLIERS

Two approaches are used to convert an injection of first-round expenditures into the total impact of an institution. Both rely on the idea that local expenditures new to an area create income for other firms and individuals, and they, in turn, spend some of their added income locally, thereby "multiplying" the initial infusion. Most economic impact studies commissioned or conducted by colleges and universities (68 percent of the studies we reviewed) make use of a standard "off-the-shelf" regional analysis software model to estimate their local and/or regional economic impact. IMPLAN (IMpact analysis for PLANning) and RIMS (Regional Input-Output Multiplier System) are two of the more popular packages used.

Feeding in data on goods and services flows, as well as employment and compensation levels, these "I/O" models can capture both the direct (or "first-round") and secondary (or indirect or "induced") impacts of tourism, a transportation system, the fishing industry, or a big ticket sporting event such as the Super Bowl. And, of course, the economic impact of an institution of higher education. The I/O models predict local economic activity in two situations: (1) the institution is present and operating, and (2) the institution is absent, so its expenditures did not occur (the "but for" situation). The difference between the predictions is the impact of the institution on the local area.

Some impact studies apply a simpler method that does not require I/O models like IMPLAN. Authors of such studies typically apply a single numeric multiplier to all new expenditures attracted to the area by the institution,[13] in order to capture the subsequent rounds in spending. Thus, an initial expenditure eventually boosts spending more than the initial outlay.[14]

Regional impact models allow researchers to change parameters to suit the circumstances, while simple numeric multipliers are less costly to use. Regional models used to estimate the local impact of new expenditures in an area are calibrated on the basis of the average interactions among all economic agents in the area. They assume that new expenditures are distributed as the average of historical expenditures.

There are several reasons to suspect that the coefficients relating inputs to outputs in a regional economic model may be inappropriate for estimating the local impact of a college or university. First, if the pattern of *incremental* local expenditures differs from the pattern of average local expenditures (perhaps because incremental expenditures contain less infrastructure content than average expenditures) the use of average inter-industry interactions imbedded in a regional economic model will distort the estimate. Second, the outputs of a college or university—individuals with innovative and technical skills, and new technology itself—are intended explicitly to alter a regional economic model's coefficients, thus eventually rendering obsolete the model's estimated relationships between inputs and outputs in the local economy. Third, the coefficients in the model often assume that preferences of residents for purchasing goods and services in a "college town" match those of residents in other areas, which may not be true.

Regional multipliers usually have a magnitude around two (Elliott, Levin, & Meisel, 1988, p. 26). The size of the multiplier varies with the scope of the local area. Among impact studies we reviewed are thirty-four separately reported expenditure multipliers, ranging from 1.34 to 3.25, with a median of 1.7. The upper end of this range is almost certainly too high, since colleges study their impacts on cities and states where plenty of spending leaks out of their economies (say, in the form of federal taxes or Internet purchases).

Some state-supported colleges and universities engage in a sleight of words that exaggerates the multiplier even further. The crafty statement from a 2010 study that "[f]or every $1 invested in the University of Iowa by the state, $15.81 is generated in the state's economy" (Tripp Umbach, 2010) may be accurate, but it is misleading. It implies that every dollar spent on the university causes a return of $15.81 to the state annually, for an annual rate of return on state investment near 1500 percent. When stock returns of just 10 percent bring joy to investors, a 1500 percent annual rate of return sounds too good to be true. And, of course, it is, because it attributes all of the return from the university's myriad activities to the small portion of its budget contributed by the state, and no return to tuition, fees, private donations, or grants and contracts received by the university's faculty. These measures are particularly sensitive to the proportion of an institution's budget that is paid by government, but have little to do with local economic impact.

In seventy-six studies that reported a relationship between state appropriations and economic impact, the multiplier ranges from 1.84 to 26 with a median of 5. Some studies drop the sleight of words and claim explicitly that readers should interpret the state-appropriations-to-impact relationship as causal. For example, "Maine taxpayers realize a more than 800 percent return on their investment of $184.7 million through state appropriation" (Maine's Public Universities, 2007). Such a claim is all too common and also incorrect. This kind of logic has even been applied to state tax revenues, with the implication that the college is a money machine: "For every $1 in state funding allocated to the UW [University of Washington], $1.48 in tax revenue is returned to the state" (Tripp Umbach, 2010). This makes it sound as though the University of Washington is better than a perpetual motion machine. An institution of higher learning should never make such an obviously misleading statement.

LOCAL AND NOT-SO-LOCAL TAXES

As recession-racked cities struggle to balance their budgets . . . a growing number are seeking more money—just don't use the word taxes—from nonprofit institutions that occupy valuable land but by law do not pay property taxes. (Cooper, 2011, p. A1)

Tax considerations regarding colleges and universities may also affect state finances and their surrounding areas in a number of ways. On the one hand, most not-for-profit institutions are exempt from local property taxes and sales taxes. (More than half of the land in the

Greater Boston area is tax exempt.) To the extent that it consumes local public services and replaces otherwise taxpaying property, a college or university creates an added burden on other taxpayers in its area. For example, Pittsburgh has challenged the tax-exempt status of an apartment building Duquesne University purchased in order to use as a dormitory, therefore taking it off local property tax rolls. The conversion would cost the city about $350,000 in lost property taxes annually (CNN, 2004). In November 2004, when Northwestern University purchased an office building, it made payments totaling $2.1 million over three years to the city of Evanston and local school districts; payments it estimated were approximately equal to the amount of real estate taxes that these public units would have received in those years had the university not purchased and converted the property (Bay Area Economics, 2006, p. 16).

Many colleges and universities make "payments in-lieu-of-taxes" (or "Pilots" in common parlance) and provide some private services such as police protection and trash disposal. (Princeton University contributes $1.7 million to its two local political jurisdictions [Cooper, 2011, p. A1].) In 1989, 11 percent of university communities received payments in lieu of taxes from universities; 38 percent of cities with fewer than 25,000 residents received payments in lieu of taxes (Gumprecht 2005, p. 44). To the extent that "in-lieu-of" payments exceed the remaining burden of local public services not provided by the institution (e.g., the University of Chicago police patrol an area larger than just the campus; Davidson College operates a volunteer fire department that also serves the town; and Northwestern University maintains its campus water and sewer lines), tax considerations might, on average, even produce a net financial gain to the surrounding jurisdiction and its residents.

Although the property of nonprofits is normally exempt from local taxes, for a variety of reasons the value of private property surrounding most colleges and universities may well be enhanced relative to its likely value in their absence. (In economic jargon, the institution creates a positive externality.) The additional property taxes collected from this enhanced value help to offset taxes foregone on exempt property. Rising property values are not welcomed by all native residents, however, particularly those who do not own homes.

The net impact of local taxes both paid and avoided, services provided in lieu of taxes, and changes in property values in the local area are complex and often make for contentious town-gown relationships. They are seldom considered in impact studies. One report that did not duck this issue was Northwestern's 2006 study that concluded with a "net fiscal impact" paragraph:

> In fiscal year 2004 the City of Evanston revenues generated by Northwestern University's presence exceeded total costs attributable to the University by $2.9 to $4.4 million. Direct costs to the city were more than offset by taxes and fees paid directly by the University. Northwestern also provided key economic support to Evanston businesses and real estate markets, undergirding the local economy and Evanston's tax base. Though exempt from real estate property and sales taxes, the University generates substantial tax and fee revenues through the expenditures of its students, faculty, staff, and visitors. (Bay Area Economics, 2006, p. 29)

In addition to the local revenue dimensions just discussed, state governments provide varying levels of tax revenue to support the cost of education at public and some private institutions. Public universities, by virtue of their location as well as admission decisions and policies, affect the flow of tax revenues within and across state boundaries. If one takes at face value the assertion that neither in-state nor the higher out-of-state tuition comes close to covering the cost of providing the typical undergraduate with a public college education, then there are clearly subventions for both within-state and out-of-state students to be considered.

Within a given state, higher education activities are not distributed equally, so state appropriations are also likely not to be distributed equally It may be that within a large metropolitan area a number of community colleges and four-year institutions serve largely a local (and mostly commuting) community. In these cases, it is likely that tax dollars paid by the local citizens are going to support local institutions. But when BSU ("Big State University") is located in the stereotypical "college town," where students come from across the state, then some revenues from state sales, income, and/or property taxes are shipped from taxpayers around the state to that campus (or those campuses). In addition to the simple mathematical calculations of those flows, there may also be equity issues at play—the average income (and taxes) of the state resident is likely to be different than the average income of those receiving the transfers.

In addition, for the United States as a whole, 20 percent of college freshmen are enrolled outside of their state of residence. Our nation's capital drew 93.3 percent of its students from outside the District; North Dakota had 44.7 percent of its students from out of state; and Texas, with only 7.7 percent, was at the lower end of this spectrum (Helliker, 2011, p. 1). Although out-of-state tuition is generally much higher than in-state tuition at public colleges and universities, the out-of-state tuition rate does not often cover the cost of educating the typical nonresident. That additional cost is often subsidized through appropriations from the state government where the institution is located. Thus, what may be a *positive* net fiscal impact on the local community comes at the cost of a potentially *negative* net fiscal impact to the state that is funding the college.

We now turn in the following section to complementary aspects of these policies—from financial to population to human capital.

LOCAL SPILLOVER BENEFITS FROM ENHANCED HUMAN CAPITAL

Although colleges produce consumption services, such as entertainment, status, and culture, their basic purpose is to enhance human capital—to create and foster graduates' skills, talents, curiosity, imagination, and creativity. Everything else the same (e.g., new expenditures attracted to the area), one would expect a college that produces human capital to have a larger impact than a sports venue or a manufacturing facility. The remaining question is the extent to which that effect is local.

Economists have long recognized that returns to investments in higher education differ when viewed from the perspective of society than from the narrower self-interest of an individual. One difference is in cost burdens: society typically subsidizes a portion of the investment individuals make in higher education, so investment costs to an individual fall short of total opportunity costs of a college education. A second difference is that dividends from human capital investment may accrue to society and the individual in different ways. For an individual, the primary benefit is a higher future earnings stream. For society, it might be aggregate earnings; but better health, social cohesion, and aggregate growth through technology and ideas might be important effects as well.[15]

Bluestone (1993) argued that incremental future incomes of college graduates who stay in the area should be counted in local impact.[16] *Little of this income, however, would go to people who would have populated the area "but for" the college.* Consequently, earnings of migrant students who join the local labor force after graduation should be excluded. Moreover, only *incremental* earnings of local college graduates should be counted. They would have earned something had they remained in the area with only a high school diploma.

In addition to direct human capital effects, a college may generate indirect human capital impacts by increasing the overall local education level. This may have beneficial indirect effects on those who would have lived in the area without the college present. Possible social benefits of education include the enhancement of productivity and earnings that spill over to local residents who themselves did not attend college, reduced crime, improved public health (and lower medical costs), and greater civic responsibility.

Spillover benefits occur if more highly educated workers enhance the productivity of other workers. Evidence based on cross-section regressions of individual earnings on individual characteristics (including educational attainment) and the average level of education in a local area suggests that this phenomenon is real, at least on a national basis (Rizzo, 2004). Rauch (1993) found that large social benefits of education are capitalized into wages and housing prices. More recent studies attempt to account for the fact that local education levels do not evolve randomly. Moretti (2004) found that a percentage point increase of college graduates in a community's workforce increases wages of local high school dropouts by 1.9 percent, high school graduates by 1.6 percent, and other college graduates by 0.4 percent, for a weighted average effect of 1.3 percent. In contrast, Acemoglu and Angrist (2000) found little evidence of local productivity spillovers from increased education. Iranzo and Peri (2009) argue that college education has much larger positive spillovers than lower levels of education, and this can rationalize different findings in the previous literature. Lange and Topel (2006) concluded in their review of the literature that there may be productivity externalities from the accumulation of local human capital, but they are difficult to quantify.

It is also difficult to quantify the effects of education on crime, health, and civic responsibility, but there is growing evidence that these effects are meaningful. Lochner and Moretti (2004), controlling for feedback effects of crime on education, estimated that differences in educational attainment between black and white men explain 23 percent of the black-white difference in incarceration rates. Breierova and Duflo (2002) and Currie and Moretti (2003) found that higher maternal education improves infant health (although McCrary and Royer, [2011] found that increasing mothers' education at low levels does not significantly improve infant health). Milligan, Moretti, and Oreopoulos (2004) found a strong positive effect of education on voting in the United States, and that more educated adults have better information about election issues.

Spillover benefits that manifest themselves in higher earnings of individuals other than the graduates themselves can be added to direct local economic effects. Groen (2004) estimated that, on average, for students originally from elsewhere, 10 percent are likely to reside in the state where they attended college ten to fifteen years after graduation. Using an estimate of the number of college-educated workers attracted to an area annually by the presence of a college, it would be possible to calculate the cumulative annual percentage increase in the education level of the local workforce caused by the college, if there were no offsetting effects. Offsets, however, are likely. Unless Emory, Spelman, and Georgia Tech graduates who take jobs in Atlanta fill *new* positions created only because of the presence of those particular Atlanta colleges, graduates of, for example, South Carolina, Duke, Auburn, or Florida State would move to Atlanta to occupy the positions otherwise taken by the Emory, Spelman, and Georgia Tech graduates (Brown & Heaney, 1997; Krieg, 1991, p. 72). If employers locate in Atlanta *only because* of the supply of college graduates there, the employers must believe it is difficult to persuade graduates of Atlanta universities to move elsewhere. However, if college graduates are mobile, the net effect of a college on the proportion of the workforce holding a college degree is close to zero, although there will be more Emory, Spelman, and Georgia Tech alumni/ae in Atlanta than would otherwise reside there. The argument that a college or university enhances the education level of the local workforce is cogent only if its presence attracts new *employers* to the local area.[17] Bound, Groen, Kezdi, and Turner (2004) found that the link between a state's production of higher education and its stock of human capital is weak.

It is difficult to determine what metric to multiply by Moretti's estimated effect on wages (1.3 percent per 1-percent increment in the proportion of the workforce with a college degree). The proportion of an institution's graduates who remain in the area surely varies by location—it could not be 10 percent at Cornell because there are not enough jobs in Ithaca, New York, to absorb 10 percent of Cornell's graduates—and the net effect is likely to be much less than 10 percent, on average, because the local college graduates who stay in the area crowd out graduates from other institutions who otherwise would have migrated in. Although spillover effects of education on the productivity and earnings of non-college graduates may be substantial, as Moretti estimated, the effect on local areas is likely modest because college-educated workers would be attracted to the area regardless of their alma mater. Similarly, while spillover benefits of education on crime, health, and civic responsibility may be real and substantial, it is also not likely that they depend critically on the presence of a local college or university.

In addition, there are other important areas and examples where the presence of universities, particularly research universities, undoubtedly plays a role in the local existence of major industries that draw highly educated workers. The Route 128 corridor in Boston (as well as University Park at MIT, a joint Cambridge-MIT venture) and the Stanford Research Park, which spawned much of the Silicon Valley entrepreneurial activity, are two well-known instances. In the "heartland," Madison, Wisconsin, start-ups and the Evanston Research Park in Illinois are two other examples.

> From its founding in 1986, the Research Park attracted and supported many businesses. . . . Most of these businesses were attracted to Evanston by the intellectual capital of Northwestern University, the educated labor force, access to the University's high-speed telecommunications network, and

access to Northwestern's faculty and researchers. (Bay Area Economics, 2006, p. 13)

Similar research agglomerations are scattered around the country, and the presence of research faculty, graduate students, and recent graduates likely keeps them local. However, such examples are the exception rather than the rule in U.S. economic geography, and most colleges and universities do not have the necessary research output to create an agglomeration of high-tech industry where none exists, and this is especially the case with liberal arts colleges and more teaching-oriented (or arts and humanities–focused) universities. The development of vaccines, public policy ideas, literature, and even commercial products makes up an important part of a university's impact. Benefits from such activities quickly accrue to people outside the local area.[18] Universities employing research faculty should advertise positive outcomes of their research. Quantifying them is not easy, however.

ANCILLARY ACTIVITIES, INCLUDING COLLEGE ATHLETICS

For many institutions of higher education, natural "core" activities that complement their missions of the discovery and dissemination of knowledge include: the provision of housing; food services; the operation of art museums and bookstores (though these are now more often than not "outsourced" to a commercial firm that specializes in this activity); maintenance of a medical center and an environment supportive of ancillary start-up research firms and business enterprises that can flourish nearby; and offering their facilities and staff for professional development conferences and summer camps that bring visitors to campus. A number of these initiatives are normally referenced in institutional impact studies.

One high-profile activity, however, conspicuous by its absence in many of these reports is intercollegiate athletics. In college towns across the country, alumni make pilgrimages back to their alma maters to sit with townspeople and students on autumn weekends and winter nights. Think of Ann Arbor, Gainesville, Durham, Lexington, or Provo. It is not simply a matter of the number of bodies crammed into those stadiums and arenas, but the dollar flows (in ticket, logo apparel and broadcast revenues, and donations from wealthy bene-factors and state governments) in such locales are overwhelmingly from outside the immediate area.

Division I athletic powers have certainly not been shy about ex-tolling their virtues and positive impacts on their institutions. Even a former president (Robert Carothers) of Rhode Island University, a place not usually associated with athletic supremacy, once remarked about intercollegiate athletics at his institution: "When the Provi-dence Journal and the Daily News decide to run a physics section ev-ery day, then things will change. Sports get attention. That's how the name of the institution gets out there. There's no question a winning program is a tremendous advantage for a school. (O'Keefe, 2003) ." President of the Ohio State University E. Gordon Gee was quoted in the *New York Times* as having the belief that "even if football revenue represents only one-half of one percent of the total budget [at Ohio State], it also garners 90 percent of the attention" (Bishop, 2011, p. SP1). Yet it takes a careful eye to spot any mention of these activities in economic impact reports. Visitors for sporting events are counted tacitly along with visitors for academic conferences in most studies (although some, e.g., Texas Tech, tout the dollar impact of home football games). Economic impact studies of colleges and uni-versities tend to emphasize a relatively sedate image of applied re-searchers and large construction projects, rather than the more bois-terous environment of college football or basketball games, leaving those images for the athletic and alumni associations to advertise.

CONCLUSION AND RECOMMENDATIONS

This chapter has described the methodological approaches and pit-falls common to studies of the economic impact of colleges and uni-versities. In this concluding section we offer suggestions for reforms in two areas that would make for more transparent and useful col-lege economic impact studies: presentation and substance.

With respect to presentation, impact studies of public universi-ties should stop claiming, "For every $1 the state legislature spends, the university returns $X dollars to the state." At best, such state-ments are meaningless. At worst, they may delude decision makers into thinking (incorrectly) that the marginal return on investment in higher education is several orders of magnitude more than returns on other public investments. If the returns to higher education were as high as these statements imply, states and the private sector would be building universities frantically.

Second, colleges should stop reporting a single impact in two formats so as to mislead readers into thinking benefits are larger than reality. The financial impact and the jobs impact are alternative measures of one concept. The value of economic activity to a local area occurs when that activity employs local residents, who use their income to enhance their welfare. Moreover, expenditures by employees (e.g., on local taxes or for charity) are not additions to the financial impact, but rather are included in payroll. Yet, many studies report them separately, tempting readers to infer that they are additions to the impact generated by applying a multiplier to local spending that includes payroll.

With respect to substance, there are even more opportunities to improve these impact studies. These include:

- Every impact study should articulate the counterfactual it is employing at the outset of the report, and thereafter adhere to it relentlessly. If the study compares economic activity in the area to a prediction of what would have occurred "but for" the college, it should omit the benefits that accrue to in-migrants.
- The reported impact should relate to the issue at hand. For example, if the college or university is asking for a zoning variance to build a new residence hall, the economic effect should relate to the incremental increase in the number of students the hall is planned to accommodate rather than to the entire effect of the college. While the impact of the entire institution may be impressive, and so good for rhetoric, it is disingenuous to use it to justify a policy that accommodates an incremental change.
- The pertinent geographic area should be articulated explicitly, and both the multiplier used and the extent to which revenues reflect exports and import substitution should relate precisely to its boundaries. It is inappropriate to use a small area to identify a large proportion of revenues as

export, and then adopt an off-the-shelf multiplier that has been calibrated on the basis of a larger area that experiences few leakages.

- First-round expenditures should exclude amounts that would have been spent in the local area "but for" the college. (Expenditures at university hospitals are likely the largest of these. Another is money spent by students who otherwise would have attended another college in the same area.)

- The appropriate multiplier must be applied to each type of expenditure. Research expenditures on materials imported into the area have a multiplier of zero. Any multiplier exceeding two for an area less than an entire state is suspect.

- Expenditures should be counted only once. Students' spending on tuition and the college payroll are one and the same thing: students pay tuition so the college can meet its payroll. The payment of tuition has no effect on the local economy until it is used to meet the payroll and buy other local goods and services.

- An institution may take credit for stimulating the local economy through its spillover effects on the general level of productivity, reduced crime, enhanced health, and civic responsibility. However, before these claims are valid, the college or university needs to articulate how its presence created the jobs filled by its graduates. This might be through technology spillovers from research faculty (not students), which, of course, would make it a difficult argument for primarily teaching colleges. New jobs might also arise from lower wages that compensate for attractive amenities that are fostered by the college.

If college impact studies were conducted at the level of accuracy most institutions require of faculty research, we would see fewer preposterous claims like a 2600 percent annual rate of return ("for each dollar of state support, [Michigan] universities collectively generated $26 of economic impact" [SRI International, 2002, p. 3). This would improve public trust in higher education officials.

Most local "economic impact" consists of activity relocated from other places, with little effect on the national aggregate. One community's gain is offset by another's loss. Rearranging resources improves aggregate welfare only to the extent that a new location affords less costly production, say, through the exploitation of agglomeration economies or use of geographically immobile inputs, or tailors the location of output more closely to the geographical distribution of demand. Neither of these situations seems important in higher education.

In contrast, moving resources geographically can improve local welfare. Because a particular community is often the audience of a college impact study, it makes sense to tout local benefits even if they are largely offset by corresponding losses elsewhere. However, the academic mission of colleges compels them to refrain from engaging in rhetoric that places their interests above all other social goals. Implementing our recommendations in economic impact studies would help colleges align their public communication with the mission statements in their charters and increase the trust in, and respect for, higher education officials and their institutions.

NOTES

This chapter is a revised and updated version of an essay by the same authors, originally published as "The Economic Impact of Colleges and Universities," *Economics of Education Review* 26 (2007): 546–558. Portions of the original article are reprinted here by permission of Elsevier, Ltd. The authors gratefully acknowledge financial support from the Andrew W. Mellon Foundation. Malcolm Getz, David Shulenberger, Paula Stephan, and two anonymous referees provided useful comments on the previous version. Morgan Wiener suggested the topic to us. She wrote an undergraduate honors thesis (Wiener, 2003) on it at Vanderbilt University.

1. See the section on "multipliers" for a more extended discussion of this issue.
2. The counts of studies reflected in these statistics vary, because studies do not report all the same information. For example, some studies include an estimate of jobs created but not the "business volume" dollar impact.
3. Some studies submit a multiplier applied to the college's number of employees to estimate the employment impact of the college.

Other studies assume a proportionate relationship between college expenditures and induced local jobs. In both cases, we infer an employment multiplier by dividing the estimated employment impact by the reported number of employees.

4. From 1980 to 1996, the annual number of four-year college openings in the U.S. ranged from 1 to 10 with a mean of 4.6. The rate declines over time. We are grateful to Enrico Moretti for sharing data on college openings.

5. Florida Gulf Coast University's Web site reports that 53 percent of current (2010) students come from the counties holding Ft. Myers and Naples (Lee and Collier) and the three contiguous (mostly rural) counties (Charlotte, Glades, Hendry).

6. However, when a college or university hires a local resident, the position formerly held by the resident may open up additional opportunities for another local resident, and so on. A number of local residents may secure better jobs through such a "vacancy chain" until eventually someone from outside the local area fills a job in the chain or a vacancy goes unfilled (Chase, 1991). To our knowledge, no college or university impact study has addressed this possibility.

7. Only rarely do the studies consider effects of the college on property values or the value of amenities and negative consequences that accompany a large agglomeration of young adults and complementary commercial activities, including bars and football stadiums, in a concentrated area. Gumprecht (2005) catalogues various effects a college has on its host community.

8. This conclusion is based on a survey of Vanderbilt freshmen, and the fact that the University of Wyoming is the only four-year college in that state.

9. See below for a discussion of first-round expenditures and multipliers. Furthermore, the amenities of a college town, such as Eugene, Oregon, or Chapel Hill, North Carolina, may attract high-value residents, including retirees, whose local expenditures serve as exports.

10. For example, an impact study by Duke University applies a spending multiplier of two to estimate its effect on Durham ("Duke University Economic Impact Year 2000 Report," Duke University Office of Public Affairs, 2003). The multiplier was chosen as representative of other studies, but a multiplier of two is more

appropriate for studies focused on larger areas (such as states) than cities (which experience more leakage outside the area, and thus have lower multiplier effects).

11. The revenues and expenditures of university hospitals usually dwarf the rest of the institution. Seldom do medical center expenditures contribute much to local economic development, however. Teaching hospitals usually are surrounded by other acute care medical facilities. In such circumstances, were the university hospital to evaporate, most of the medical services provided by it would be assumed by other local hospitals. Only patients with specialized medical problems would likely turn to hospitals outside the area. Thus, most university hospital expenditures should *not* be included in the first round of expenditures, perhaps an exception being isolated university hospitals that serve broad geographic areas in the Plains and Mountain states.

12. This approach assumes that the college spends exactly the revenues it receives each year. To the extent that the institution spends more than it receives in annual revenues, as is the case nearly everywhere, "export sales" are understated, because the deficit must be covered by drawing on endowment earnings, and the proportion of endowments that represent funds that would have been spent in the local area if they had not been contributed to the college is likely quite small.

13. The multiplier should reflect the ratio of the difference in the predictions of economic activity derived from the regional economic model estimated with and without the college or university included, to direct expenditures new to the area.

14. At the level of the entire economy, the precise value of the multiplier from some fiscal action—a change in spending or taxes—on the part of the federal government is a controversial and hotly contested issue among macroeconomists.

15. The notion that education enhances social cohesion has been in the economics literature since Smith (1994 [1776], Bk. V, Chap. I, Pt. III, Art. II). For examples of the link between aggregate education and growth in the economics literature, see Lucas (1988) for theory and Glaeser, Scheinkman, and Schleifer (1995) for empirics.

16. Several subsequent college impact studies have claimed graduates' future earnings as college impacts. Bluestone studied the

University of Massachusetts, Boston. Impact studies for Arizona State University, University of Maryland system, and Michigan public universities also have included human capital.

17. In a few cases the location of university science or engineering faculty and/or PhD students may attract an employer to a particular area, but these occurrences are few and far between in the universe of about two thousand four-year colleges and universities.

18. However, the Bayh-Dole Act (1980), which allows universities to better capture the intellectual property inherent in the discovery and transmission of knowledge by their faculties and researchers, internalizes some of what one might otherwise consider a spillover. So, universities themselves—in addition to their communities—benefit substantially from commercial applications of their research.

REFERENCES

Acemoglu, D., & Angrist, J. (2000). How large are the social returns to education? Evidence from compulsory schooling laws. In B. S. Bernanke and K. Rogoff (Eds.), *NBER Macroeconomics Annual* (pp. 9–59). Cambridge: MIT Press.

Bay Area Economics. (2006). Northwestern University's economic impact on Evanston, Illinois. Northwestern University, University Relations.

Beck, R., Elliott, D., Meisel, J., & Wagner, M. (1995). Economic impact studies of regional public colleges and universities. *Growth and Change 26* (2), 245–260.

Bishop, Greg. At Ohio State, football scandal rattles a reformer. *New York Times*, August 13, SP1.

Blackwell, M., Cobb, S., & Weinberg, D. (2002). The economic impact of educational institutions: Issues and methodology. *Economic Development Quarterly 16* (1), 88–95.

Bluestone, B. (1993). *UMASS/Boston: An economic impact analysis.* Boston: John W. McCormack Institute of Public Affairs, University of Massachusetts.

Bound, J., Groen, J., Kezdi, G., & Turner, S. (2004). Trade in university training: Cross-state variation in the production and stock of college-educated labor. *Journal of Econometrics 121* (1–2), 143–173.

Breierova, L., & Duflo, E. (2002). The impact of education on fertility and child mortality: Do fathers really matter less than mothers? MIT Working Paper (March).

Brown, K. H., & Heaney, M. T. (1997). A note on measuring the economic impact of institutions of higher education. *Research in Higher Education* 38 (2), 229–240.

Bureau of Labor Statistics, Current Population Survey. (May 4, 2011). Employment projections. Available at http://www.bls.gov/emp/ep_chart_001.htm, consulted July 20, 2011.

Caffrey, J., & Isaacs, H. (1971). *Estimating the impact of a college, or university on the local economy*. Washington, DC: American Council on Education.

Chase, I. D. (1991). Vacancy chains. *Annual Review of Sociology 17*, 133–154.

CNN. (2004). Cities challenging university tax status. March 16. http://www.cnn.com.

Cooper, M. (2011). Squeezed cities seek some relief from nonprofits. *New York Times*, May 12, p. A1.

Currie, J., & Moretti, E. (2003). Mother's education and the intergenerational transmission of human capital: Evidence from college openings. *Quarterly Journal of Economics 118* (4), 1495–1532.

Edwards, M. E., & Apoutou, Y. V. (with assistance from R. A. Magar). (2010). The economic impact of the College of St. Benedict & St. John's University on the City of St. Joseph and Collegeville Township. St. Cloud State University. February.

Elliot, D. S., Levin, S. L., & Meisel, J. B. (1988). Measuring the economic impact of institutions of higher education. *Research in Higher Education 28*, 17–33.

Ewing, B. T. (2010). The economic impacts of Texas Tech University. July. Accessed at http://www.depts.ttu.edu/provost/acadaffairs/docs/Reports/Economic_Impacts_of_TTU.pdf

Felsenstein, D. (1996). The university in the metropolitan arena: Impacts and public policy implications. *Urban Studies 33* (9), 1565–1580.

Getz, M., & Huang, Y. (1978). Consumer revealed preference for environmental goods. *Review of Economics and Statistics 60* (3), 449–458.

Glaeser, E. L., Scheinkman, J. A., & Schleifer, A. (1995). Economic growth in a cross-section of cities. *Journal of Monetary Economics 36* (1), 117–143.

Groen, J. A. (2004). The effect of college location on migration of college-educated labor. *Journal of Econometrics 121*, 125–142.

Gumprecht, B. (2005). Town vs. gown: City-university relations in the American college town. Department of Geography, University of New Hampshire.

Heckman, J. J., Lochner, L. J., and Todd, P. E. (2008). Earnings functions and rates of return. *Journal of Human Capital 2* (1), 1–31.

Helliker, K. (2011). Frigid North Dakota is a hot draw for out-of-state college students. *Wall Street Journal*, July 16–17, p. 1.

IMPLAN. Minnesota IMPLAN Group, Inc. Available at http://www.implan.com/other_links.html/.

Iranzo, S., & Peri, G. (2009). Schooling externalities, technology, and productivity: Theory and evidence from U.S. states. *The Review of Economics and Statistics 91* (2), 420–431.

Krieg, R. G. (1991). Human-capital selectivity in interstate migration. *Growth and Change 22* (1), 69–76.

Lange, F., & Topel, R. (2006). The social value of education and human capital. In E. Hanushek and F. Welch (Eds.), *The Handbook of Education Economics*, Vol. 1. Amsterdam: North Holland Press.

Leslie, L. L., & Slaughter, S. A. (1992). Higher education and regional development. In W. E. Becker and D. R. Lewis (Eds.), *The Economics of American Higher Education*. Dordrecht: Kluwer Academic Publishers.

Lochner, L., & Moretti, E. (2004). The effect of education on criminal activity: Evidence from prison inmates, arrests, and self-reports. *American Economic Review 94* (1), 155–189.

Lucas, R. E. (1988). On the mechanics of economic development. *Journal of Monetary Economics 22*, 3–42.

Magnum Economic Consulting. (2010). Analysis of the economic contribution that Liberty University makes to Region 2000 and Virginia. April. Available at http://www.liberty.edu/index.cfm?PID=18495&MID=17970.

Maine's Public Universities. (2007). Economic impact on the State of Maine: The connection between the University of Maine System and the State of Maine. September.

McCrary, J., & Royer, H. (2011). The effect of female education on fertility and infant health: Evidence from school entry policies using exact date of birth. *American Economic Review 101* (1), 158–195.

Milligan, K., Moretti, E., & Oreopoulos, P. (2004). Does education improve citizenship? Evidence from the United States and the United Kingdom. *Journal of Public Economics 88* (9–10), 1667–1695.

Moretti, E. (2004). Estimating the social return to higher education: Evidence from longitudinal and cross-section data. *Journal of Econometrics 121* (1–2), 175–212.

O'Keefe, M. (2003, March 16). Being held accountable for scandals in sports programs. NYDailyNews. Available at http://articles.nydailynews.com/2003-03-16/sports/18222512_1_college-sports-knight-commission-scandals/2.

Rauch, J. (1993). Productivity gains from geographic concentration in cities. *Journal of Urban Economics 34*, 380–400.

RIMS II. Bureau of Economic Analysis: Regional economic accounts. Available at http://www.bea.doc.gov/bea/regional/rims/.

Rizzo, M. J. (2004). The public interest in higher education. Cornell Higher Education Research Institute Working Paper, WP 56 (November).

Siegfried, J. J., Sanderson, A. R., and McHenry, P. (2007). The economic impact of colleges and universities. *Economics of Education Review 26* (5), 546–558.

Smith, A. (1994 [1776]). *An inquiry into the nature and causes of the wealth of nations*. E. Cannan (Ed.). New York: The Modern Library.

SRI International. (2002). The economic impact of Michigan's public universities. Michigan Economic Development Corporation. May. Available at http://www.michiganadvantage.org/cm/Files/Reports/univimpactreport.pdf.

Tripp Umbach. (2010). The economic and societal impact of the University of Washington: Executive report (FY 08–09). July 7. Available at http://www.washington.edu/externalaffairs/eir/pdfs/fullreport.pdf.

Tripp Umbach. (2010). University of Iowa: Economic impact study. September 30. Available at http://www.uiowa.edu.

Tulane University. (2010). *From recovery to renewal: The economic impact of Tulane University*. New Orleans: Tulane University.

Ward, D. J., Seibold, B. E., Hart, A. J., & Winters, D. K. (2011). The University of Wisconsin-Madison's $12.4 billion impact on the Wisconsin economy. NorthStar Economics, Inc., March.

Wells, Robert H. (2011). Study finds UF has $8.76 billion economic impact on Florida. *University of Florida News*. Available at http://news.ufl.edu/2011/03/30/economic-impact-2011/.

Wiener, M. (2003). A critical analysis of Vanderbilt University's 2001 economic impact study. Unpublished, Vanderbilt University (May).

Winters, D. K., & Strang, W. (2002). The University of Wisconsin System's economic contribution to Wisconsin. NorthStar Economics, September.

4

On the Measurement of University Research Contributions to Economic Growth and Innovation

Maryann P. Feldman, Allan M. Freyer, and Lauren Lanahan

ABSTRACT

The increasing complexity of university scientific research and the increasing pressure for accountability in public expenditures creates a challenging environment for the measurement of scientific productivity. Of course, the choices of metrics employed create different incentives for institutional actors at the federal, state, and university levels. This chapter uses the example of the Center for Environmentally Responsible Solvents and Processes, an NSF-funded science and technology center over its ten-year span to assess economic impact, research outcomes, and public benefit. First, we conduct an economic impact assessment using the IMPLAN methodology for input-output analysis. Next, we analyze conventional knowledge and technology transfer metrics. Our third analysis attempts to consider the social, cultural, and educational public benefits from the research center. Then we employ *ex post* thought experiments to compare the center with other modes of federal research funding. We advocate a broad, holistic, and case-specific approach to the evaluation of multidisciplinary research centers, combining traditional research outcome and knowledge transfer metrics with social, cultural, and educational measures.

INTRODUCTION

The mission of universities has become more complex, encompassing commercialization goals and economic development along with the traditional goals of educational and research excellence. Rather than constituting the model of a single-investigator project, the nature of university research practice has come to encompass a range of organizational forms, such as multidisciplinary and interdisciplinary collaborative research endeavors that span across universities, government labs, and industry (Aboelela et al., 2007). The motivation is that the applications with the greatest potential for economic growth often exist at the intersection of disciplines and require the integration of diverse forms of knowledge (Metzger & Zare, 1999). To increase the practical impact of university research, many state and federal programs require university research projects to involve industrial actors, which may include large firms, industry consortium, and new start-ups firms (Hagedoorn, 2002). Increasing in both scale and scope, the university research enterprise not only supports fundamental research but also delivers results in the form of economic outcomes and societal impacts (Mallon & Bunton, 2005). The result is that the academic research enterprise has evolved substantially to develop new multifaceted capabilities.

Alongside these formative changes, state and federal funding agencies have come to demand greater accountability of the results of public investments in academic research. These demands for accountability to political authority, especially to the U.S. Congress—building on the 1993 Government Performance and Results Act (GPRA)—have remained central over the past decade. The Office of Management and Budget's recent 2009 memorandum, "Increased Emphasis on Program Evaluations," is one recent example of pressure for research evaluation and accountability (Chubin et al., 2009). These requirements, however, present particular challenges for the evaluation of multidisciplinary and interdisciplinary collaborative university research programs (Bozeman & Boardman, 2004).

Traditional measurements of research outcomes have relied on assessments of economic impact, such as the multiplier effects associated with expenditures, or focused on metrics of knowledge creation and technology transfer, such as publications, patents, and spinoff companies. These metrics capture the more tangible outcomes that result from university research; however these measures alone fail to capture the spectrum of results (Cozzens & Melkers, 1997; Ruegg & Feller, 2003; Wagner et al., 2011). A given university research project has the potential to span many years, leveraging additional resources—both public and private, training and education, knowledge generation and transfer, dissemination via publications, technology transfer products, job creation, and greater societal gains. Moreover, traditional performance indicators limited to economic impact assessments and technology transfer may underestimate the total outcomes of the research project (Wagner et al., 2011). This formative change and evolution in university research practices demands new evaluation metrics that look beyond the direct tangible outcomes (Wagner et al., 2011; Kabins, 2011; Chubin et al., 2009).

The choice and use of metrics are critical as they will subsequently influence the conduct of scientific research and define the nature of the research that is undertaken and may even delimit the resulting contributions. A focus on easily measurable outputs may skew attention toward less risky and more immediately realized countable metrics. The nature of large-scale university research projects inherently incorporates learning and adaptation as it proceeds. A lack of immediate results may indicate the identification of new and relevant problems or some intervening serendipity that suggests a new approach. Moreover, the conduct of research, and the search for solutions, often generates significant positive externalities that, while difficult to measure, may be its most significant impact.

To more completely assess a research investment, this chapter compares various methods and suggests a broader scope of analysis to include a greater range of social, cultural, and educational benefits. We present a framework for capturing the totality of the university activity produced by extending beyond immediate and traditional quantifiable benefits to consider and include less quantifiable impacts. To guide our investigation, we trace one university research program, UNC Chapel Hill's Center for Environmentally Responsible Solvents and Processes (CERSP), a National Science Foundation University Research Center (URC), which serves as an exemplar of the emerging organizational form that has come to characterize the evolving university research enterprise (Slaughter & Hearn, 2009; Bozeman & Crow, 1990). Section 2 provides our theoretical framework, highlighting the limits of the traditional methods used to evaluate research outcomes. Section 3 uses CERSP as a case study to show how broadening the evaluation approach to include an economic impact assessment, research metrics, and public benefit analysis allows for a more comprehensive understanding of the university's contributions. In addition to presenting the conventional knowledge and technology transfer metrics and social, cultural, and educational public benefits from the research center, we employ *ex post* thought experiments to compare the center with other modes of federal research funding. We advocate a broad, holistic, and case-specific approach to the evaluation of the evolving university research enterprise by combining traditional research outcome and knowledge transfer metrics with social, cultural, and educational measures. Section 4 concludes by extending this discussion to university research evaluation metrics more generally.

ON THE FOLLY OF REWARDING ECONOMIC OUTCOMES WHILE HOPING FOR PUBLIC BENEFIT

In his influential article "On the Folly of Rewarding A, While Hoping for B," Steven Kerr (1975, p. 769) highlights discrepancies within the reward system that lead to suboptimal outcomes. Using the example of orphanage practices, he argues that directors are often faced with a dilemma between the societal goal of placing children in suitable homes and programmatic budget incentives to maintain enrollment. As Kerr notes, "[T]o the extent that staff size, total budget, and personal prestige are valued by the orphanage's executive personnel, it becomes rational for them to make it difficult for children to be adopted" (p. 772). Thus, what is immediately rewarded may act against society's longer-term interest.

We argue that Kerr's theory may also occur with scientific research and development, if a limited range of concrete, traditional outcome metrics at the expense of the less tangible goals that include broader public benefit drives the university research enterprise. When evaluators measure specific activities they incentivize those activities. While society desires technological progress and economic growth, increasingly there are pressures to celebrate the number of companies started, reward faculty for taking out patents, or count the number of jobs that result from research activities.

This emphasis on economic impact and research metrics, by Kerr's logic, would lead scientists to align their research and results with metrics rather than with the less tangible goal of public benefit. Moreover, by defining the performance indicators by these metrics, a significant portion of the research outcomes important to society may be overlooked. Fundamental research projects are likely to simultaneously serve multiple educational, technical and industrial objectives. Thus, there is a need to calibrate the metrics used in rewarding resources to ensure the integrity of the larger research enterprise. The desired outcomes of economic growth and technological progress will be enhanced if the science policy community and university officials expand their assessment metrics to include social, cultural, and educational measures as well.

One issue is that motivations vary among stakeholders. Given the range of demands, research outcomes are often measured from multiple perspectives using disjointed frameworks. University officials are often most interested in demonstrating the regional economic impact of research, providing a justification for more funding, and satisfying economic development concerns. Moreover, the dollar amount of research funding figures prominently in university rankings. State and local economic development officials have incentives to garner the greatest impact for their jurisdiction, even if nationally the impact is a zero sum. Federal officials, especially at funding agencies, on the other hand, have an interest in broader contributions to education and research, but still face the need to justify their programs. The data available from the Association of University Technology Managers (AUTM) has focused attention on invention disclosures, patents, licenses, and new firms; some academic scholars focused on research productivity have made use of these existing measures while other scholars have taken in-depth qualitative approaches that are not scalable to the assessment of large national funding programs. University research officials, especially those affiliated with state-funded institutions, are asked to provide economic impact statements for research projects similar to those produced for sporting events or a new office park. Nationally, though, the assessment of economic impact should reflect productivity gains in terms of economic and societal outcomes rather than simply reflect distributional impacts. From a national perspective, any incentive to increase funding to any one locality where the largest local impact might be anticipated rather than where the best science could be conducted would result in suboptimal allocation.

It is both possible and necessary to define and measure the productivity of multidisciplinary university research projects in a way that motivates university scientists to seek private gain through publication records and management of intellectual property *and* to maximize societal benefit. Ensuring this range of outcomes, however, demands concerted efforts from researchers themselves, and from the evaluators who define, frame, and assess the central research missions. If we only promote traditional research outcomes, then we overlook the great potential of public benefit that results from university research. Evaluators not only have a role in tracing programmatic impacts, they also serve a guiding role in defining and promoting the range of possible societal outcomes delivered by the university research enterprise.

UNIVERSITY RESEARCH CENTERS

Hailed as the most significant institutional innovation in science policy in the past thirty years (Bozeman & Boardman, 2004), URCs have demonstrated great promise and are believed to promote innovation and technological change. Nevertheless, they are plagued by high levels of uncertainty, long-term horizons, and complex causal paths requiring multiple inputs and integrating industrial actors; this in turn presents difficulties in reconciling with political needs for accountability. In an effort to present a set of evaluation metrics that captures the evolving university enterprise's contributions to academic audiences, economic growth, and public benefit, we trace one university research program, CERSP, as an exemplar.

Broadly defined, URCs extend beyond the boundaries of a single disciplinary department, receive financial support independent of departmental allocations, and demonstrate strong ties to industry and commerce (Miller, 2010). Sustainability is a major concern for these centers due to the absence of tuition revenue; however, centers often enjoy more flexibility in terms of their organizational structures and their research agendas. These features offer a unique research environment for producing outcomes distinct from their departmental counterparts. Specifically, given the multidisciplinary nature of both the topic and research team, centers produce spillover effects across departmental lines and between the university and industry. Regardless of how the research project evolves, the facilitation of communication across disciplines and beyond the bounds of the university has considerable implications for those involved with the URC. If the efforts of a collaborative multidisciplinary team of researchers transform a scientific discipline, we argue that research becomes richer, thus producing public benefits. Each center represents an experiment in the conduct of university research, requiring significant investment but having the potential to generate transformative scientific breakthroughs and broad societal impact.

While URCs are generally time-limited, their contributions extend well into the future. Annual and final reports are only able to account for the short-term contributions, yet studies have found that research continues to have an impact by way of spillover and demonstration effects beyond the term of funding. Mansfield (1998) found in his analysis of seventy-seven industries that there is a time delay of roughly seven years between academic research and industrial practice. Applying this to the maximum ten-year NSF funding period for some of its major centers programs, at most 30 percent of a center's industrial and economic benefits are likely to be realized during its existence. As we proceed in this attempt to account for the total impact of a university research center, it is important to acknowledge the likelihood of as-yet-unrealized future outcomes.

CERSP AS AN EXEMPLAR—BACKGROUND, METHODOLOGY, AND DATA

We examine the Center for Environmentally Responsible Solvents and Processes (CERSP), which completed its tenth year of funding as a National Science Foundation (NSF) Science and Technology Center (STC) in 2009. CERSP was awarded roughly $36 million by NSF for the collaborative effort between The University of North Carolina at Chapel Hill (UNC), North Carolina State University (NCSU), University of Texas at Austin, Georgia Institute of Technology, and North Carolina A&T State University. When awarded in 1998, it was the single largest grant received by researchers in the UNC system.

To robustly assess the performance of CERSP, we employ multiple methodologies. Evaluating a complex center with myriad objectives that span K-12 education, higher education, industry extension, and technology transfer activities—including infrastructure, start-up, and consulting services—provides an interesting and challenging opportunity. Previous efforts to measure outcomes of STCs against their triple mission of knowledge transfer to industrial partners while advancing research frontiers and the quality of science education have been criticized for taking an overly quantitative approach (Fitzsimmons, Grad, & Lal, 1996), though recent work by Chubin et al. (2009) has begun employing a more robust approach.

Arundel asserts that science policy is hampered by "a lack of indicators and analyses that are relevant to policy needs" (2006, p. 11). By using CERSP as a case study, we will illustrate the limits of the traditional outcome metrics and try to show how scholars, university officials, and the public can account for additional educational and cultural impacts. Our approach represents a combination of what Helper (2000) has described as learning "just by watching," and appreciative theorizing, or what Weick (1995, p. 385) has defined as "an interim struggle in which people intentionally inch towards stronger theories." This is in the tradition of Yin (2003), who advocates for the use of field research and case study analysis to question existing theory and empirical findings. Edmondson and McManus (2007) similarly argue that the appropriate methodological fit for a study of this nature, which resides in a relatively nascent field, requires a greater degree of qualitative and observational analysis.

As we attempt to account for the contributions of the evolving university research enterprise, we recognize that this evaluation of CERSP serves as an exercise in exploring possible measures as well as in building a stronger foundation with which to account for university research outcomes. With significant variation among staffing structures, connections to universities, core activities, and funding allocations, it would be unrealistic to implement a one-size-fits-all approach to evaluating the contributions of a center. We argue that it is the unique nature of each URC that presents the primary methodological challenge in defining and evaluating a research program's outcomes. While comparative analysis between two or more centers is one possible method for measuring impact, we argue that the selection of only the most promising centers and the wide variation among centers make this approach generally unworkable. As emphasized by Roessner (2000), URCs, and other competitive university research programs lack a counterfactual, given that they are subject to peer review before being awarded funding. Only the most competitive proposals receive funding, which leads to a selection bias in comparative analyses. Moreover, those that do receive funding vary considerably from one another, thus making it exceptionally difficult to do a comparative analysis.

Ideally, we would employ a comprehensive list of evaluation indicators to capture the totality of a center's impact. However, the unique design of URCs, university research projects more generally, and limitations of standard outcome metrics make this unrealistic. Thus, such an effort to evaluate the contributions of a URC necessitates extensive observation and creativity. Rather than limiting an analysis to the traditional evaluation metrics, we take a slightly different approach. We follow one NSF STC over time, utilizing various methods to assess research outcomes in terms of its economic impact, research outcomes, and public benefit. Then we contextualize the center's performance using a number of *ex post* thought experiments comparing the center with other modes of federal research funding.

The data we use include approximately three thousand pages of documentation, including the original proposal to NSF, the center's annual reports, and its final report. We also have data on formal technology transfer outcomes available from UNC's Office of Technology Development. These data are supplemented with interviews with program participants. Two of the authors attended center meetings, including an NSF site visit, as participant-observers. We reviewed other published and unpublished social science research and journalistic accounts of CERSP's economic impact. In the thought experiments, we use publicly available information on NSF funding patterns, provided by NSF and the Academy of Arts and Sciences.

Dr. Joseph M. DeSimone, William R. Kenan Jr. Distinguished Professor of Chemistry at UNC and Professor of Chemical Engineering at NCSU, served as the PI and director for CERSP. The center's co-director was Dr. Ruben G. Carbonell, now the Frank Hawkins Kenan Distinguished Professor of Chemical Engineering at NCSU and the chairman of the Department of Chemical Engineering. These two researchers led a team of more than six hundred students, staff, and researchers at the five affiliated research universities during a ten-year period. With a vision to "enable a revolution in sustainable technology" and a mission to support multidisciplinary, fundamental research that would yield sustainable processes, products, and broad societal benefit, the researchers affiliated with CERSP deliberately undertook the type of high risk/high reward research that is often avoided by universities and industry (CERSP final report, 2009). It was the unique long-term, high investment structure of the NSF STC program that allowed researchers at the Center flexibility to undertake an endeavor of this magnitude. The potential contribution of the technology was clear from the proposal: the researchers aimed to develop sustainable technology for processes to manufacture high value products based on environmentally friendly solvents. This technology would provide substantial public benefit by developing manufacturing processes that would be more sustainable due to decreased emission of chemicals harmful to human health and greater energy efficiency.

TRADITIONAL METRICS AND BROADER BENEFITS

Accurately capturing the impact of a university research center requires a holistic approach in order to identify the full range of outcomes created and to measure the spillover effects in the local community and beyond. In this chapter, we use a set of mixed and varied methods to capture the total set of impacts. First, we conduct an economic impact assessment using the IMPLAN methodology for input-output analysis. We then analyze conventional knowledge and technology transfer metrics. Our third analysis considers social, cultural, and educational public benefits from the research center. Using calculations from the center's final report, Table 4.1 presents a comprehensive list of the economic impacts, research metrics, and public benefits. We review the metrics and discuss the results of each analysis in turn.

Table 4.1. Evaluation of the Center for Environmental Solvents and Processes (CERSP)

Outcome	Economic impact	Research metrics	Public benefit
Jobs created	66/year		—
Income effect	$3.35M/year, in constant 2007 dollars		—
Impact on NC state industries	$13.51M/year, in constant 2007 dollars		—
Research investment	$30M in research; $6 M in education		—
Licenses	14	—	—
Start up firms	8	—	—
Leveraged funding	$145M in supplemental funds reported by all PIs	—	—
Start up centers	5 new centers[a] and an additional $310M budgeted by state of NC	—	—
Patents and applications	—	90	—
Networks: PI external collaboration	—	297 total (110 with universities, 20 with government, 67 with industry)	—
Networks: Students co-authoring with researchers outside of CERSP		208 total (8 undergraduates, 143 graduates, 57 postdocs)	—
Students supported via CERSP		554 total (235 undergraduates, 235 graduates, 84 postdocs) 345 students were from underrepresented groups	—

Table 4.1. (*continued*)

Outcome	Economic impact	Research metrics	Public benefit
Students recruited to industry and research institutes		26 postdocs and 41 graduate students	—
Conference presentations		750 total (330 invited lectures and 200 abroad)	—
Student conference presentations		266 students gave 431 presentations	—
Publications		511 peer reviewed papers, 54 chapter, 1 textbook	—
Citations		—	—
Workshops		—	—
K-12 education contribution to teachers			11,000 teachers trained with environmental science laboratory workbooks
K-12 education contributions to students			1.2M students in grades 7–12 reached in classrooms via certified workbooks and CERSP trained teachers, mentoring program for high risk students, two kits used by more than 25,000 K–12 students
CERSP students who continued academic training			141 undergraduates, 45 graduates, 3 postdocs

Table 4.1. (*continued*)

Outcome	Economic impact	Research metrics	Public benefit
Student outreach			200 students involved with K–12 outreach
K–12 education diversity			Reached 20,000 K–12 students in underrepresented groups via demos and presentations, reached 1M grade 7–12 students in underrepresented groups via workbooks
Cultural shifts in research practice			Shift from disciplinary research practices towards more diverse interdisciplinary and translational research environment, demonstration effect
CERSP Web site			More than 2M hits

Note: Dashes represent metrics that are applicable in the holistic assessment model where data are unavailable or not reported. Blank cells represent metrics that are not applicable.

[a]Triangle National Lithography Center at North Carolina State University (NC State), Clean room and 600 MHz NMR facilities at University of North Carolina (UNC), $35M for Engineering Research Centers at NC State and North Carolina Agricultural and Technical State University, and $55M for University of Texas and UNC for Energy Frontiers.

ECONOMIC IMPACT ASSESSMENT

Economic impact assessments frequently use input-output analyses to estimate the impacts of specified economic events. This technique examines the repeated rounds of spending among industries, households, and governmental institutions that result from specific events within a specified study region. In this case, we studied these interactions using IMPLAN Professional Software, an input-output modeling program. Input-output analysis examines business-to-business and business-to-consumer relationships, capturing market transactions for a given period of time (Minnesota IMPLAN Group, Inc., 2004). We estimated the projected effects of CERSP as an exogenous increase in demand from the infusion of federal funds into the state of North Carolina.

IMPLAN software constructs the two key models used in input-output analysis—the descriptive model and the predictive model. As its name suggests, the descriptive model provides information about local economic interactions in the form of regional economic accounts. These tables describe a local economy in terms of the flow of dollars from purchasers to producers within the region, while also including information about trade flows—the movement of goods and services within a region and between the region and the outside world. Along with these purely economic elements of input-output analysis, IMPLAN also permits the incorporation of *social accounting* into the descriptive model, a method that allows the analyst to examine nonindustrial transactions within the region, including the payment of taxes by households and businesses and transfer payments from government to households and businesses. For its predictive model, IMPLAN uses the regional economic accounts to construct local-level multipliers, which describe the response of the economy—defined by the descriptive model—to some exogenous change in demand or production.

The implicit assumption in any economic impact assessment is that the direct, indirect, and induced spending attributable to the project would not have occurred without the event of interest.[1] This is the "but for" assumption on which all impact assessments are based and is more applicable for planning purposes and evaluating the impact of alternative investments. The simplifying assumption is that all revenues generated by the university research center are new

Table 4.2. IMPLAN Estimates of Annual Economic Impacts for the CERSP

Type of impact	Direct	Indirect	Induced	Total
Increased industry output (millions of 2007 dollars)	7.97	3.45	2.10	13.51
Increased employment (IMPLAN calculations of job-years)	29	17	20	66
Increased labor income (millions of 2007 dollars)	1.81	0.88	0.65	3.35

Note. Sum of components may not add up to totals due to rounding.

to the area and are not substitutes for existing research or technology commercialization efforts.

Economic impact studies separate out spending related to the center's operations, direct NSF funding, and education programming, and model each according to the multipliers associated with that economic activity. We assume that the $36 million in total funding received from NSF was distributed evenly over the center's ten-year existence.[2] Adjusted to 2007 dollars, we estimated that $3.347 million per year were spent on research, $335,000 on operations, and $335,000 on education programming.

The results of the IMPLAN analysis are summarized in the economic impact section of Table 4.1. Table 4.2 provides a breakdown of estimated direct, indirect, and induced effects. We estimate the total impact on North Carolina's economy at $135 million over ten years, an average of $13.51 million per year. We estimate that CERSP has generated $33.5M in additional income for North Carolina workers and business owners over ten years, an average of $3.35 million per year. These estimates are consistent with the creation of sixty-six person-jobs over the course of the center's existence.

These results represent a significant impact on the state, with the start-up company Liquidia providing the largest share. Due to the region's strong presence in biotechnology and medical product development, the center's activities (including Liquidia) have produced significant economic synergies along these supply and value chains, producing a multiplier of 1.7. A recent review of 138 university economic development studies found that they used multipliers ranging from 1.34 to 2.54, with a median of 1.7 (Siegfried, Sanderson, &

McHenry, 2007). In practice this means that for every dollar invested into the state's economy by the center's activities, IMPLAN's calculations estimate that those activities yield another 1.7 dollars in return. This analysis indicates a significant and positive impact on the state's economy.

In performing this analysis, we encountered several limitations. First, the static nature of the software's modeling introduces a certain level of uncertainty into our efforts to address a dynamic, inherently temporal economic process covering ten years using a single-year model. Second, the difficulty in translating the additional events specified above (licensing, research networking, educational programs, etc.) into concrete investment values or jobs created ensured that while the analysis captures a majority of the center's economic impact, it does not capture everything. Taken together, these limitations introduce a degree of uncertainty into our results. Even those events we can model successfully involve the significant application of assumptions.

More sophisticated economic impact analysts will doubtless point out that we could potentially avoid these shortcomings with refinements to our existing model, the use of more advanced software or the use of a different assessment technique altogether. Indeed, Drucker and Goldstein (2007) provide four refinements to the economic impact modeling of university research activities, noting that each requires subjectivity. It is indeed paradoxical that economic impact models require very subjective assumptions that undermine the motivation for comparable, objective metrics in the first place. If the quest for clearly defined outcomes is intended to replace subjectivity with concrete, comparable metrics, then by their very nature, economic impact assessments cannot provide them. Moreover, the incentives to demonstrate the largest economic impacts allow for overly optimist assumptions.

TECHNOLOGY AND KNOWLEDGE METRICS

In addition to quantifying the economic impact of a project, there are a number of other outcomes that are simply unaccounted for in an economic impact analysis. Thus, we additionally quantify the center's contributions in terms of technology and knowledge for industrial development, future university research, and science education. As Laursen and Salter (2004) highlight in their paper on university influences on industrial innovation, many studies are finding a deepening relationship between university basic research and industrial development, which is not exclusively attributable to an economic relationship. Using the Carnegie Mellon Survey of 1,500 R&D managers representing multiple sectors, Cohen and his colleagues (1998) found that university research contributes to industrial R&D by producing new ideas for research projects, facilitating the execution of existing R&D projects, and serving as a source of information for competitors, thus stimulating further research. Quantifying this relationship in a comprehensive way, however, presents quite a challenge. Patents, publications, citations, university-initiated start-ups, and licenses are among the most common metrics used to quantify basic research output. While these are relatively straightforward to compute, many scholars argue that they do not accurately capture the total knowledge or technology gained from research. A number of more recent studies on the impact of university research on industry have examined additional factors: informal information exchange, public meetings and conferences, recently hired graduates, joint or cooperative ventures, contract research, consulting, and temporary personnel exchanges (Cohen, Nelson, & Walsh, 2002; Agrawal & Henderson, 2002; Agrawal, 2001; Salter & Martin, 2001). While it is easy to quantify metrics such as the number of recently hired graduates, it is more difficult to evaluate other metrics, such as identifying and evaluating the nature of informal information exchanges. We use a combination of these research measures to provide a comprehensive analysis of impact.

The center has an ambitious vision focused on enabling a revolution in sustainable technology by integrating interdisciplinary and translational research practices. While analyzing some of these outputs presents empirical challenges, it is nonetheless critical to consider the multiple dimensions to provide a comprehensive assessment of the research project.

Patents, university-initiated start-ups, and licenses are among the most prominent metrics used for directly measuring technology transfer between the university and industry (Jaffe, 1989; Henderson, Jaffe, & Trajtenberg, 1998; Jensen & Thursby, 1998; Mowery et al., 2001). Over its ten-year lifespan, CERSP produced ninety patents and patent applications, fourteen technology licenses, and eight startup firms. While these values do not exhaustively account for the total technological contributions made by the center, these data suggests that the center has been extremely active and has made considerable contributions to industry.

In addition to these technology transfer channels, there are other more indirect channels that facilitate knowledge transfer between the university and industry. These measures are presented in the research outcomes section of Table 4.1. Knowledge and technology transfer measures both suggest that contributions to the academic community and to industry are substantial. The exact nature of these contributions, however, is difficult to determine. For example, while affiliates of CERSP may have presented at more than 750 conferences, we are unable to determine the extent to which those presentations have directly influenced subsequent university research and/or industrial development. Although bibliometric analyses that measure the quality of knowledge outputs are well established within the literature (Wagner et al., 2011), we did not have access to these data for this analysis. Despite the challenge of measuring the precise impact associated with these various knowledge channels, the data nonetheless reflect a significant degree of output produced by the center.

PUBLIC BENEFITS

While many studies (Neal, Smith, & McCormick, 2008) include economic impact assessments, research metrics, or some combination of the two, surprisingly few have addressed public benefit as an outcome (Sarewitz, 1996). In his highly influential report, which served as the impetus for the creation of the National Science Foundation, Bush (1945) highlighted the critical link between basic research and public welfare. Although the path may be circuitous, Bush argued that basic research provides the foundation for applied research, which in turn leads to the development of products and, more importantly, to public benefit. Scholars and policy officials, however, have struggled over defining metrics to account for public benefit. Even though they have not been able to devise a comprehensive methodological toolkit for evaluating this outcome, its importance should not be understated. In light of this obstacle, the common practice used to capture this outcome often takes the form of anecdotes and individual case studies that highlight the impact of a certain scientific discovery. As a step toward developing a framework for evaluating public benefit, we broadly define the public benefit to include widespread educational, cultural, or societal factors. We would be naive to assume that each of these public benefit factors takes on a definitive form: thus, we use this construct as a guiding tool for recognizing these contributions as we evaluate outcomes.

Much of this discussion has focused on CERSP's contributions to industry and the greater academic research community. However, CERSP has also had an educational impact through improvements in K–12 science teaching, science outreach programs, and higher education. These impacts are summarized in the public benefit section of Table 4.1. CERSP has improved K–12 education in North Carolina, Georgia, and Texas. For example, as a result of the serendipitous adoption of a requirement for all North Carolina schools to teach environmental science, CERSP developed environmental science laboratory workbooks that have been widely disseminated to more than 1.2 million seventh through twelfth grade students. The CERSP research team was also able to provide materials for teacher training. Since that time, over 4,100 teachers have participated in CERSP workshops and received certification. More than seven thousand additional teachers are estimated to have used the CERSP workbooks. All of these numbers reflect calculations as of 2009; however, it is likely that these numbers will continue to grow. While these data do not provide a comprehensive account of the total impact that this center has had on secondary education, they do suggest that the program has made considerable contributions both to scientific pedagogy and to the next generation of scientists and researchers.

Moreover, more than two hundred university students were involved in K–12 outreach activities and viewed these activities as a major benefit of participating in the center's programs (DeSimone and Roberts, 2009). Not only did they view this activity as a critical social responsibility, but they also found the challenge of explaining complex concepts to fifth graders to be exceptionally valuable.

CERSP has also made significant contributions to education programs for UNC, NC State, University of Texas at Austin, Georgia Institute of Technology, and North Carolina A&T State University, including scholarship support at all levels of higher education. Thirty departments (up from the original ten) among the five partner institutions were actively involved in the various interdisciplinary activities and programs affiliated with the center. Exemplifying faculty-student collaboration and mentoring, 8 undergraduates, 143 graduates, and 57 post-doctoral associates co-authored 535 peer-reviewed papers or book chapters with 55 faculty members. In addition, two hundred researchers outside CERSP took part in collaborative work with these students and faculty. These numbers alone illustrate the center's success in promoting interdisciplinary and translational research. Over the past ten years, hundreds of faculty, staff, and students have been exposed to a more progressive interdisciplinary and translational approach for conducting research. This likely has contributed to a shift in the educational culture and general practice of research. Arguably, there has also been a demonstration effect, through which CERSP has served as a model for other university researchers to initiate interdisciplinary and translational research projects. These efforts have strengthened the connection between the affiliated universities and their surrounding communities.

In light of the discussion above, we argue that CERSP not only contributed to the training of students but also to larger cultural and social shifts. This is reflected in an emerging educational environment that promotes interdisciplinary and translational research practices.

CERSP—AN ALTERNATIVE METHOD: WHAT IF . . .? A THOUGHT EXPERIMENT

While the commonly used metrics help to quantify CERSP's impact, we would like to shift our focus and consider what the *potential* implications might be if CERSP had been funded by an NSF program other than the STC program. As noted above, comparing the impact of CERSP to another research project presents a number of issues given the diverse and unique characteristics of large university research centers. It would be unrealistic to compare this ten-year, multi-institution, multidisciplinary center to other research activities, given the vast disparities in size, structure, and topical focus. In light of this, we have chosen to present several *ex-post* thought experiments in an effort to contextualize and compare this center with other forms of federal investment in university science. We argue that investment in the ten-year, interdisciplinary, multimillion dollar, multi-university center was more effective and productive for CERSP than a comparable investment in multiple smaller NSF centers or in standard awards. The rest of this section explores this notion in greater detail by considering two scenarios: (1) one STC center versus multiple smaller projects; and (2) a flexible program versus a more structured research program.

One STC Center vs. Multiple NSF Projects

While one might presume that $36 M invested in an STC produces a similar level of output as investment in multiple projects, say, twelve $3M awards (totaling $36M); we suggest that this is not the case. We argue that one large center is able to optimize its productivity to a greater degree than can the aggregate of multiple projects. In essence, the total is greater than the sum of its parts. Given that researchers affiliated with one large center are not subject to the same financial and time constraints as those affiliated with smaller and limited duration projects, they are able to focus more of their efforts on the actual research project. Researchers affiliated with shorter-term projects, on the other hand, are subject to the pressures of securing future funding, which consumes considerable time and resources and serves as a distraction from the active project.

THOUGHT EXPERIMENT 1: ALTERNATIVE NSF FUNDING SOURCES

To highlight this point, we compare CERSP, an MPS (NSF Directorate for Mathematics and Physical Sciences) STC, with other NSF programs that support similar fields of research. In particular, we consider the following programs: standard awards in the chemistry division, Phase I Centers for Chemical Innovation (CCI), and Nanoscale Science and Engineering Centers (NSEC). Table 4.3 highlights the average time span and funding allocations for all chemistry awards made in 2008, all active CCIs and NSECs, and CERSP. While all of these programs support basic research in the physical sciences, specifically chemistry and nanotechnology, these data illustrate the wide variety of MPS programmatic support in terms of funding expenditures and project lengths.

Table 4.3. Comparison of NSF Chemistry Grants (I)

Program	Time span	Annual allocation ($)	Total allocation ($)
Chemistry standard awards (FY08)	3.1 years	$145,000	$449,500
CCI (Phase I)	3 years	$486,000	$1,460,000
NSEC	5 years	$2,387,000	$11,540,000
CERSP (STC)	10 years	$3,612,000	$36,117,733

The data for CCI (Phase I) and NSEC awards were compiled from the NSF award search database: http://www.nsf.gov/awardsearch/. The data on the Chemistry standard awards was retrieved from AAAS Report (XXXIII).

As already noted, in 1999 UNC, NCSU, University of Texas Austin, Georgia Tech, and North Carolina A&T State University were jointly awarded a ten-year grant of $36,117,733 to support CERSP. How might things have been different if that same amount of money was awarded as multiple chemistry standard grants, CCIs, or NSECS? In that case, the university would have been awarded approximately eighty standard awards, twenty-five CCIs, or three NSECS (Table 4.4, Column I). The cumulative time spent drafting eighty, twenty-five, or even three proposals far outweigh the time spent drafting one proposal for the STC. Thus, if the university had received the same amount of funding for multiple projects, greater administrative time would have been devoted to drafting and submitting proposals, rather than in conducting the research. Compared to the eighty different standard projects that might have been awarded, CERSP was in fact able to fund 139 separate projects with roughly forty active on an annual basis. This far exceeds the amount of research that would have been conducted via the standard grant mechanism and is partially reflective of time not wasted in securing additional funding.

THOUGHT EXPERIMENT 2: FUNDING SUCCESS RATES

What if the *same* group of CERSP investigators conducted research through one of the other three avenues? Over the course of ten years, at best the investigators would only be able to conduct research for three standard awards, three CCIs, or two NSECs (Table 4.4,

Column II). As noted above, in each of these scenarios, the research-ers would have needed to spend additional time drafting proposals for funds that would not come close to the $36M allocated for the STC. Furthermore, with the funding rate as low as 26 percent (Scott & Smith, 2008), the chances that the same researcher could secure constant support over the course of a ten-year period are slim. CER-SP's NSF funding expired in 2010, however, the center's investigators were able to secure more than $430M in supplemental funds for the continuation of various projects that began under the STC grant. While we make no claims regarding the ideal length of time needed to conduct research and secure additional funding, we do suggest that the ten-year period allowed the investigators sufficient time to focus on conducting research and producing results, which helped them secure future funds. We suggest that three to five years would not have been sufficient for the investigators to conduct the research and sustain the project.

Thought Experiment 3: Time to Conduct Research under Multiple Programs

On another note, what if the *same* group of researchers conducted $36M worth of research through these three different programs? Considering the time-span data in Table 4.4, Column III, it would take the research team 250 years to conduct $36M worth of research via standard grants, seventy-five years via CCI, or sixteen years via NSECs. Only the third scenario is plausible, and even in this case it would take an additional six years to conduct research with the same level of investment. These numbers highlight the large scale of CERSP and the limits of securing this level of funding through other NSF programmatic avenues.

Basic research clearly takes a variety of forms, ranging from lab-based experiments to computer-simulated analyses, and these differ-ent projects require various modes of support. For a multi-university, interdisciplinary, physical science center, however, we suggest that the ten-year $36M allocation was much more effective than other pos-sible modes of funding available through the MPS Directorate. STCs are surely not optimal programs for all avenues of basic research, but we argue that CERSP's productivity was optimized through being funded as an STC.

Table 4.4. Comparison of NSF Chemistry Programs (II)

Program	(I) No. of awards > $36M	(II) No. of projects completed in ten year period	(III) No. of years for one research team to conduct $36M worth of research
Chemistry standard awards (FY08)	80	3	250
CCI (Phase I)	25	3	75
NSEC	3	2	16
CERSP (STC)	1	1	10

Research Program: Flexible vs. More Structured

CERSP's overarching aims to revolutionize sustainable technology and support multidisciplinary fundamental research for broad societal benefit remained integral components of CERSP, the center's objective, goals, domains, and/or performance measures evolved over the decade and reflected a number of significant shifts in the investigators' research directions. CERSP benefited from its unique structure as an STC through a greater degree of flexibility compared with other more structured and inflexible programs. Moreover, we suggest that the ten-year, multi-university, multidisciplinary center afforded the participating universities a research environment conducive to significant and surprisingly unexpected returns. We explore this in greater detail by highlighting the evolution of the research objectives over the tenure of the center and by noting the subsequent shifts in the internal funding allocations.

In 1999, CERSP focused 100 percent of its research efforts on fundamentals and microelectronics related to CO_2 processes. As noted in their final 2009 report, this trend of research continued over the first few years of the project when the investigators focused much of their attention on surfactants, polymerization, and reaction kinetics and mechanisms in both continuous and batch regimes. They predicted that this research would lead toward improved techniques in the fermentation processes and possible transformative discoveries in biotechnology. By 2004, however, they realized that industry giants were too heavily invested in existing technologies to support the revolutionary research to which CERSP aspired. Even if the CO_2 processes continued to evolve from the research, the underlying technology and existing manufacturing facilities were too firmly embedded to allow for much change (CERSP final report, 2009). Thus, in 2005 with the approval of NSF, CERSP broadened its research from microelectronics to include CO_2-related areas on nanostructures. Figure 4.1 highlights this shift in research focus by tracing the number of new, active, and total projects over the ten-year period. In 2005, we notice a significant shift in the number of new projects, which reflects a redirection of research from fundamentals and microelectronics toward nanotechnology. Furthermore, Figure 4.2 illustrates the distribution of funds by project over the formative, transition, and legacy phases of the project. Research on fundamentals and microelectronics was a priority for the first half of the project. However, the redistribution of funds toward energy and nanotechnology reflects a substantial shift in research priorities for the second half. By refocusing their efforts on freeing nanostructures from silicon wafers, the investigators were able to cultivate new industrial affiliations and become more active in entrepreneurial activities. Given the inherent time lag in realizing benefits from academic work, the benefits of the center's research is likely to be realized only in the coming years (Mansfield, 1998).

Had CERSP not had the flexibility to evolve and redirect its research over the span of the project, we suggest that its contributions would have been significantly curtailed. The unique structure of a multi-university interdisciplinary research environment afforded CERSP's investigators a fortuitous environment to explore new avenues of research. If the center had been more narrowly focused on one specific discipline or field, or if the length of the project had been limited to the standard three to five years, we suggest that these discoveries in nanostructures would not have been realized.

This shift in research focus illustrates that the investigators were able to adhere to the strategic plan yet remain flexible in its implementation. As the investigators noted in their final report, the ultimate distribution of funds and research priorities were not what they had envisioned. Although they did not originally anticipate this shift in research, they describe a cross-disciplinary migration of technology that may have contributed to greater creativity and productivity. We argue that less significant advances would have been made had the research been conducted through a more structured program, namely, one that was either shorter in length or more restricted by

Figure 4.1. CERSP New and Active Research Projects, 2000–2009

These data were compiled from CERSP annual reports.

Figure 4.2. Distribution of CERSP Funds by Project over the Formative, Transition, and Legacy Phases

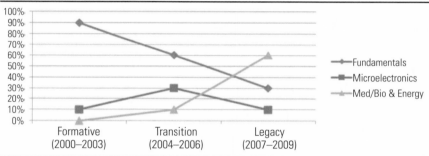

These data were compiled from CERSP annual reports.

a certain field of research. It was the unique structure of the STC that allowed considerable new discoveries and technology to come to fruition.

CONCLUSIONS

Economic impact assessments frequently use input-output analyses to derive the estimated impacts of specified economic events. This technique examines the repeated rounds of spending among industries, households, and government that result from a specified event within a study region considering direct, indirect, and induced effects.

Limitations include reliance on a host of embedded subjective assumptions and a tendency to characterize distributional effects as productivity gains. While more sophisticated input-output models might overcome these techniques, we would continue to produce answers that may disguise complex assumptions under a simplistic veneer of objectivity. If the quest for clearly defined outcomes is intended to replace subjectivity with concrete, comparable metrics, then even the most sophisticated economic impact assessments fail to deliver.

We therefore propose a broader array of metrics to measure the impacts of complex interdisciplinary research. Research outcome measures, augmented by emerging bibliometric, social network, and geospatial analysis techniques, will continue to play an important role in the assessment of these projects. However, we argue for advancing the boundaries of assessment farther into the realm of public benefit to encompass holistically the full impact of research in social, cultural educational progress.

ACKNOWLEDGMENTS

This material is based upon work supported by the Science and Technology Centers (STC) Program of the National Science Foundation under Agreement No. CHE-9876674. Additional funding was provided by the U.S. National Science Foundation SciSIP 0947814. Authors are at the University of North Carolina, Chapel Hill, and are listed alphabetically. The authors acknowledge Jennifer Miller's research assistance.

NOTES

1. Direct effects represent the changes for a given industry resulting from the increase in final demand for that same industry on, for example, payroll; indirect effects include the impacts on all local industries resulting from industries purchasing from industries

in multiple iterations as a consequence of this increase in final demand; and induced effects result from the increases in spending by households that were caused by both the direct and indirect effects. The total effect of the new investments from the proposed projects is represented by the sum of all three of these effects.

2. $145M in additional research funds leveraged by principal investigators (see Table 4.1) are not included in this analysis.

REFERENCES

Aboelela, S. W., Merrill, J. A., Carley, K. M., & Larson, E. (2007). Social network analysis to evaluate an interdisciplinary research center. *Journal of Research Administration 38* (2), 97–108.

Agrawal, A. (2001). University-to-industry knowledge transfer: Literature review and unanswered questions. *International Journal of Management Reviews 3* (4), 285–302.

Agrawal, A., & Henderson, R. (2002). Putting patents in context: Exploring knowledge transfer from MIT. *Management Science 48* (1), 44–60.

Arundel, A. (2006). *Innovation survey indicators: any progress since 1996?*. Paper for the G20 at the Leader's level Workshop (L20 Workshop), Maastricht, The Netherlands.

Bozeman, B., & Boardman, P. C. (2004). The NSF Engineering Research Centers and the university-industry research revolution: A brief history featuring an interview with Erich Bloch. *The Journal of Technology Transfer 29* (3), 365–375.

Bozeman, B., & Crow, M. (1990). The environment of U.S. R&D laboratories: Political and market influences. *Policy Sciences 23* (1), 25–56.

Bush, V. (1945). Science, the endless frontier. *Transactions of the Kansas Academy of Science 48* (3), 231–264.

Chubin, D. E., Derrick, E., Feller, I., & Phatiyal, P. (2009). AAAS review of the NSF Science and Technology Centers integrative partnerships (STC), 2000–2009. Report supported by NSF Grant: 0949599.

Cohen, W. M., Florida, R., Randazzese, L., & Walsch, J. (1998). Industry and the academy: Uneasy partners in the cause of technological advance. In R. Noll (Ed.), *Challenge to the university* (pp. 171–199). Washington, DC: Brookings Institution Press.

Cohen, W. M., Nelson, R. R., & Walsh, J. P. (2002). Links and impacts: The influence of public research on industrial R&D. *Management Science 48*, 1–23.

Cozzens, S. E., & Melkers, J. E. (1997). Use and usefulness of performance measurement in state science and technology programs. *Journal of Policy Studies 25* (3), 425–435.

DeSimone, J., & Roberts, G.W.. (2009). Final report for Center for Environmentally Responsible Solvents and Processes. NSF Grant STC-9876674.

Drucker, J., & Goldstein, H. (2007). Assessing the regional economic development impacts of universities: A review of current approaches. *International Regional Science Review 30* (1), 20–46.

Edmondson, A., & McManus, S. (2007). Methodological fit in management field research. *Academy of Management Review 32*, 1155–1179.

Fitzsimmons, S. J., Grad, O., & Lal, B. (1996). An evaluation of the NSF Science and Technology (STC) program. OSTI Report 95-22582. Available at http://128.150.4.107/od/oia/programs/stc/reports/abt.pdf.

Georghiou, L., & Roessner, D. (2000). Evaluating technology programs: Tools and methods. *Research Policy 29*, 657–678.

Hagedoorn, J. (2002). Inter-firm R&D partnerships: An overview of major trends and patterns since 1960. *Research Policy 31* (4), 477–492.

Helper, S. (2000). Economists and field research: "You can observe a lot just by watching." *American Economic Review 90*, 228–232.

Henderson, R., Jaffe, A. B., & Trajtenberg, M. (1998). Universities as a source of commercial technology: A detailed analysis of university patenting, 1965–1988. *Review of Economics and Statistics 80* (1), 119–127.

Jaffe, A. B. (1989). Real effects of academic research. *The American Economic Review 79* (5), 957–970.

Jensen, R., & Thursby, M. (1998). Proofs and prototypes for sale: The tale of university licensing. *National Bureau of Economic Review.* Available at http://www.nber.org/papers/w6698.pdf?new_window=1.

Kabins, S. (2011). Evaluating outcomes of different types of university-industry collaboration in computer science. Presented at the 2011 Academy of Management Annual Meeting.

Kerr, S. (1975). On the folly of rewarding A, while hoping for B. *The Academy of Management Journal 18* (4), 769–783.

Laursen, K., & Salter, A. (2004). Searching low and high: What types of firms use universities as a source of innovation? *Research Policy 33*, 1201–1215.

Mallon, W. T., & Bunton, S. A. (2005). Research centers and institutes in US medical schools: A descriptive analysis. *Academic Medicine 80* (11), 1005–1011.

Mansfield, E. (1998). Academic research and industrial innovation: An update of empirical findings. *Research Policy 26*, 773–776.

Metzger, N., & Zare, R. N. (1999). Interdisciplinary research: From belief to reality. *Science 28* (5402), 642–643.

Miller, J. M. (2010). Universities, industries, and government in collaboration: A review of the literature on research centers. *Tomorrow's Technology Transfer 2* (1), 69–85.

Minnesota IMPLAN Group, Inc. (2004). *IMPLAN pro user's guide, analysis guide, data guide.* Stillwater, MN.

Mowery, D. C., Nelson, R. R., Sampat, B. N., & Ziedonis, A. A. (2001). The growth of patenting and licensing by U.S. universities: an assessment of the effects of the Bayh-Dole act of 1980. *Research Policy 30* (1), 99–119.

Neal, H. A., Smith, T., & McCormick, J. B. (2008). *Beyond Sputnik: U.S. science policy in the 21st century.* Ann Arbor, MI: University of Michigan Press.

Roessner, D. (2000). Quantitative and qualitative methods and measures in the evaluation of research. *Research Evaluation 9* (2), 125–132.

Ruegg, R., & Feller, I. (2003). *A toolkit for evaluating public R&D investment.* Gaithersburg, MD: National Institute of Standards and Technology, NIST GCP 03-857. Available at http://www.atp.nist.gov/eao/gcr03-857/contents.htm.

Salter, A. J., & Martin, B. R. (2001). The economic benefits of publicly funded basic research: A critical review. *Research Policy 30* (3), 509–532.

Scott, A. & Smith, T. (2008). National Science Foundation in the FY 2009 budget. In Intersociety Working Group. (Ed.). *AAAS*

Report XXXIII Research & Development FY 2009. Washington, D.C.: American Association for the Advancement of Science.

Sarewitz, D. (1996). *Frontiers of an illusion: Science, technology and the politics of progress*. Philadelphia: Temple University Press.

Siegfried, J. J., Sanderson, A. R., & McHenry, P. (2007). The economic impact of colleges and universities. *Economics of Education Review 26* (5), 546–558.

Slaughter, S., & Hearn, J. C. (2009). Final report for centers, university, and the scientific innovation ecology: A workshop. NSF Grant BCS-0907827.

Wagner, C. S., Roessner, J. D., Bobb, K., Thompson Klein, J., Boyack, K. W., Keyton, J., Rafols, I., & Borner, K. (2011). Approaches to understanding and measuring interdisciplinary scientific research (IDR): A review of the literature. *Journal of Infometrics 165*, 14–26.

Weick, K. E. (1995). *Sensemaking in organizations*. London: Sage.

Yin, R. K. (2003). *Case study research: Design and methods*, 3rd ed. Applied Social Research Methods Series no. 5. Thousand Oaks, CA: Sage Publications.

5

University Industry Government Collaboration for Economic Growth

LAURA I. SCHULTZ

ABSTRACT

Higher education, industry, and government have been increasingly collaborating through the development of research centers. University-industry-government (UIG) research centers provide environments in which actors from multiple sectors of the innovation system come together to share the costs and risks associated with research, organic development and technology commercialization. The development of UIG research centers is part of a three-decade trend that includes multiple forms of university-based collaboration designed to foster economic development, including industrial research parks where firms can receive university support, startup incubators to foster and develop new businesses, and university-housed industrial consortia. These research centers garner the attention of academic researchers and policymakers for their potential to expedite the development and commercialization of new technologies, improve national competitiveness, and spur regional economic growth. This chapter explores the specific phenomenon of UIG research centers, focusing on their role as public policy instruments and their impacts on regional economic growth. The frameworks and key examples of UIG research centers, research parks, and incubators are described and the channels through which they generate economic impact are identified. The chapter concludes with suggestions for measures that can be used to assess the impact of these centers on their field of science and their regional economies.

INTRODUCTION

University-industry-government (UIG) research centers are environments in which researchers from multiple sectors of the innovation system come together to share the costs and risks associated with research and development (R&D). Over the past three decades many forms of research centers have evolved, including cutting-edge research facilities designed to enable multisector collaboration, industrial research parks where firms receive support to commercialize university technologies, startup incubators, and university-housed industrial consortia. UIG research centers garner the attention of academic researchers and policymakers for their potential to expedite the development and commercialization of new technologies, improve national competitiveness, and spur regional economic growth.

This chapter explores the phenomenon of UIG collaboration through research centers and their impacts on regional economic growth. Section 2 traces the history of research centers as public policy instruments. The importance of multisector research centers was first broadly acknowledged when researchers observed the important role local universities played in the development of the high-tech industrial centers of Silicon Valley and Boston's Route 128 corridor (Saxenian, 1994). These observations led to the development of formal theories of cluster development as well as federal and state level programs to support such development. Section 3 highlights the different forms of UIG centers. The structures of collaborative research centers, research parks, and incubators are described and key examples are highlighted. The channels through which these research centers generate a regional economic impact are explained in section 4. Understanding these channels and their relative effectiveness allows policymakers to design UIG research centers to support regional economic environment. Section 5 details the metrics that have been used to measure the impact of UIG centers on their field of science and the regional economy.

HISTORY OF UNIVERSITY RESEARCH CENTERS

Universities have long played an important role of providing research support and workforce training for local industries. In 1888,

Massachusetts Institute of Technology initiated the first four-year bachelor program in chemical engineering to meet the emerging demands of local industry. In 1929, the University of Washington established one of the first aeronautical engineering programs in the country to support the growing aerospace industry in the Seattle area. These are just two early examples of higher education institutions responding to the demands of the local economy; however, it was not until recently that the phenomenon has attracted the attention of academic researchers and policymakers.

Universities now play a critical role in generating knowledge and trained labor that support emerging high-tech fields. For example, high-tech entrepreneurs were attracted to regions with a concentration of industry-friendly higher education institutions such as Boston and Silicon Valley. The co-location with universities allowed entrepreneurs access to a support network that included university scholars and research facilities, a uniquely trained labor force, and a critical mass of like-minded entrepreneurs. The result was a hub of innovation and industrial activity growing around the university. It was not until after the clusters formed that scholars began to observe the important connections between higher education, industry development, and regional economic growth.

This section chronicles the development of UIGs. The first phase in the development of UIG research centers as public policy tools was the recognition that in certain parts of the country, universities, industry, and government were working together to support the growth of regional industry. In the second phase, federal agencies such as the National Science Foundation (NSF) and the Department of Defense supported the development of industry-university collaborative research centers with the goals of expediting technology development and transfer. In the latest phase, local and state governments emerged as more active players through the support of UIG collaborations, primarily driven by the desire to spur regional economic development.

Phase 1: The Role of the University in Technology Growth and Economic Development

The earliest industrial clusters formed organically in locations where there was a substantial concentration of higher education institutions and related firms. These clusters self-organized in the mid-twentieth century in areas such as Silicon Valley and the Route 128 corridor in Boston, Massachusetts, with little direct involvement from local or state governments. The clusters were hot spots for innovation, generating a large number of technical advancements and enabling successful commercialization of the new technologies by local entrepreneurs. These technical advancements were accompanied by significant regional economic growth. New companies were forming, venture capital was flowing, employment opportunities were abundant, and growth was being experienced in many sectors of the regional economy. Thirty years after they began, these phenomena were noted by a number of academic researchers who wanted to identify the factors that contributed to the clustering of high-tech industry and the resulting high levels of growth.

Michael Porter (1990) was among the first to formalize the link between cluster formation and industrial competitiveness. Porter (1998) defined clusters as "geographic concentrations of interconnected companies and institutions in a particular field . . . that encompass an array of linked industries and other entities important to competition" (p. 197). He maintained that industrial clusters lead to higher rates of economic productivity, innovation, new business formation, and economic growth. After the positive benefits associated with clusters were identified, additional research observed the important role universities play in cluster formation. Local universities supply the skilled human capital critical for the survival of the cluster and perform research that provides innovations integral for the local industry's continued development and the creation of startup companies. Porter (2000) and subsequent researchers (Braunerhjelm & Feldman, 2006; Saxenian, 1994) focusing on specific clusters often recognized research universities as a key factor in the development of high-tech clusters such as Silicon Valley and the Route 128 corridor.

Concurrently, Rosenberg and Nelson (1994) observed an evolution in the academic-industrial relationships for the purpose of developing new technologies. They noted two trends: the growing share of academic R&D funded by industry; and the emergence of university-based centers designed to foster effective research links between academic scientists and local firms. While industrial influence was growing more prominent in university research, the authors noted the continued dominance of the university in the development of emerging technologies, such as biotech. Rosenberg and Nelson proposed that the university plays a critical role in the advancement of technologies for which no formal industrial R&D infrastructure had yet developed. These findings suggested that university research could be used to attract firms interested in the development of emergent technologies.

It was these initial studies about the role of university research in technology development and regional industry growth that drew the attention of policymakers. The innovative capabilities of universities could be harnessed with local industry to power an engine of economic growth. The academic work studying the formation of clusters lead to the establishment of university-industry research centers as engines for technology advancement and economic growth. The frameworks for these research centers were being developed concurrently in a series of federal investment programs that comprise Phase 2.

Phase 2: Federal Engagement in Developing Research Centers for the Advancement of Emerging Technologies

While, in Phase 1, research centers and clusters manifested due to the serendipity of geographic proximity, in Phase 2 the federal government began supporting collaborative research centers to actively foster the development of emerging technologies. The primary goal of federal investment in the earliest UIG collaborative research centers was the advancement of new fields of science and engineering. The first formal initiative to create research centers was the National Science Foundation's Industry/University Cooperative Research Centers (I/UCRCs) program which was established in the 1980s. The I/UCRC program provided seed funding to universities to enable cooperative research in emerging fields. NSF funding was leveraged by the host institution to gain additional support from other universities, industrial partners, and state and local governments. The NSF has built on this framework through the establishment of similar programs such as Science and Technology Centers and Engineering Research Centers. These programs fund collaborative research centers that span multiple universities with dozens of investigators from a range of disciplines. The research concentration of these centers must be multidisciplinary, focusing on the development of fundamental knowledge with broad industrial implications. NSF requires I/UCRCs to distribute their knowledge through two channels. The first is educational outreach. These centers are required to offer research opportunities for both graduate and undergraduate students. In addition, centers often engage in K–12 outreach programs and develop widely available curriculum materials that can be adopted by teachers. The centers must also engage industry in order to promote the transfer of the technologies developed from the center laboratories into the commercial sectors. NSF has sponsored more than eighty Science and Technology Centers and Engineering Research Centers over the past twenty-five years. Other agencies including the Department of Defense, Defense Advanced Research Projects Agency, National Institutes of Health, and National Institute of Standards and Technology have all supported CRCs to address research topics relevant to agency missions. (Bozeman & Boardman, 2004; Chubin et al., 2010; Feller, Ailes, & Roessner, 2002; Gray & Walters, 1998). In chapter 4 of this volume, Feldman, Freyer, and Lanahan (2012) provide more details on the formation of these federally funded research centers and focus on the impacts the NSF-funded Center for Environmentally Responsible Solvents and Processes has had on economic growth and innovation.

These research centers have been recognized for their potential to expedite the development, transfer, and commercialization of emerging technologies. One key factor in their success is regular engagement with industry partners (Chubin et al., 2010). Industry involvement comes in a variety of forms. Centers invite industrial partners to serve on external advisory committees that provide feedback on the centers' missions and approaches. NSF research centers use government funding to leverage financial support from industrial partners. Centers provide an alternative atmosphere where researchers from different institutions can work beyond the traditional academic department–based laboratory. This shared workspace may encourage collaborations that would not occur within departments. The encouragement of university-industry engagement has been successful. The American Academy for the Advancement of Science recently surveyed center faculty and found that faculty affiliated with NSF

Science and Technology Centers interacted more frequently with industry than the nonaffiliated members of their departments (Chubin et al., 2010). The survey also revealed that 88 percent of center-based students credited center affiliation for enabling and encouraging their interactions with industry. This frequent interaction with industries lowers many of the barriers to traditional university-industry technology transfer (see Owen-Smith, 2012, chapter 9 this volume, for a discussion of some of these traditional barriers). Instead of working through a technology transfer office to market university research, academic researchers will likely have professional connections with the firms that will eventually commercialize the technologies (Chubin et al., 2010). The federal government's success in creating UIG collaborative research environments capable of developing new technologies provided a guide for local policymakers looking to use research centers to spur economic growth.

Phase 3: Fostering Collaborative Research Centers for Regional Economic Development

While the connection developed organically, researchers first noted the role universities played in the formation of regional industrial clusters in the 1980s and 1990s (e.g., Porter, 1990; Braunerhjelm & Feldman, 2006; Saxenian, 1994). In Phase 2, government policies were successful in helping build UIG research centers to advance research and technology development. In Phase 3, state and local governments became actively involved in supporting the economic contributions of UIGs.

The relationship between universities, industries, and local economic growth was formally articulated in innovation models such as the Triple Helix, developed by Etzkowitz and Leydesdorff (2000). The Triple Helix is a framework that describes how actors from multiple sectors of a local economy integrate to create a regional innovation infrastructure that will ultimately promote economic development. This focus on the regional or local innovation systems expanded upon existing theories, which were based on the concept of national innovation systems. A national innovation system explains how institutions such as firms, universities, and the federal government interact to create an innovation infrastructure to support economic growth and competitiveness at a national level (Nelson,

1993); however, much of the innovation within an economy occurs at the local level—and local innovation systems can differ significantly throughout a nation, particularly in large nations such as the United States.

The Triple Helix model was among the first to suggest that innovation infrastructures were critical at a local level, not just the national level. The Triple Helix is an interconnected network in which higher education institutions, state and local governments, and firms collaborate through a hybrid organization designed to optimize the interactions between parties. In the Triple Helix, each party takes on roles beyond those assigned in the traditional national innovation system model. In the national innovation system, universities perform basic research and train the innovation labor force. In a Triple Helix, colleges and universities have an additional mission of regional economic development, beyond their traditional roles of teaching and research. This focus on economic development is seen as an expansion of the university's traditional community engagement and service missions. Not only should universities be engaged in regional social and cultural development, they must acknowledge their ability to shape and grow the region's economy. Higher education institutions should collaborate with local industry to help them overcome technical challenges, provide access to university facilities, and work with them to provide appropriate training programs. Universities can also be actively engaged in supporting firms emerging from their laboratories through entrepreneurship training and support. These activities advance science and promote regional economic growth.

In a national innovation system, the primary roles of the federal/national government are to fund basic research through national laboratories and university-based principal investigators, fund the development of public goods, and support critical infrastructure such as the patent and legal systems. In the Triple Helix, regional governments take on an important role in the development of a local innovation infrastructure. This is done through funding, but moves beyond providing financial support for basic research. Local and state governments assume responsibility for ensuring the region has the research facilities required to support the growing cluster. Governments frequently achieve this mission through investment in UIG research centers. In addition, local and state governments must develop policies to support existing businesses and attract new ones. Examples of such policies include the provision of matching funds for private sector capital investments, tax exemptions, and the creation of regional development agencies (Boekholt & Thuriaux, 1999).

Within the Triple Helix, firms seek collaborative opportunities with university researchers and other local firms in order to take advantage of the unique innovation assets in the region. It is also important to note that Etzkowitz and Leydesdorff (2000) claim that a co-location of industrial, academic, and government entities is a necessary, but not sufficient, condition for the development of successful industrial clusters. That is, university and industry researchers working independently in a government-sponsored facility is not enough to create a Triple Helix. Efforts must be made to build networks and synchronize research activities between all actors to realize all of the benefits co-location offers.

Based on these theoretical models, policymakers in regional governments started to focus on investing in their regional economic growth through the development of UIG partnerships and research centers. Several states have made significant investments in regional innovation infrastructure to support longer-term economic growth. In 2001, New York announced a series of Centers of Excellence at universities across Upstate New York to build an innovation economy in areas that had lost significant manufacturing jobs. Texas introduced the Cluster Initiative in 2004 to create public-private partnerships focused on six high-tech industries in the state. Other states that have actively pursued university-industry research partnerships in the past decade include Oklahoma, California, South Carolina, Arizona, Michigan, and New Mexico (National Governors Association and Council on Competitiveness, 2007).

Several policy-oriented organizations have studied the effectiveness of UIG research collaborations in the creation of regional economic growth. The National Governors Association and the Council on Competitiveness (2007) published a report on cluster-based strategies for economic growth encouraging the development of human capital through locally based education centers and the development of collaborative innovation centers. The report highlighted several successful collaborations among industry, community colleges, comprehensive and liberal arts colleges, and research universities.

Another report by the State Science and Technology Institute (2006) encouraged the development of university-industry research centers designed to bridge the gap between academia and business. The report found that successful centers built on a region's existing industrial strengths, supported multidisciplinary work, and focused on collaboration. The National Research Council (NRC) has also focused on the issues of technology development for regional economic growth. In a 2002 study, the NRC concluded that successful research parks involve a large research university, a critical mass of human capital, funding, commitment of leadership, adequate physical infrastructure, and private sector commitment to commercialize the knowledge generated (Wessner, 2002). More recently they have focused on best practices. A 2011 report highlighted a handful of successful investments made by state governments with the intention of creating a high-tech cluster (Wessner, 2011).

In 2010, the federal government began to target its economic development strategy toward supporting local innovation systems, focusing on building research centers to support cluster development. The U.S. Economic Development Administration has made "Collaborative Regional Innovation" an investment priority. They seek to fund "initiatives that support the development and growth of innovation clusters based on existing regional competitive strengths" (www.eda.gov). One such initiative, the Jobs and Innovation Accelerator Challenge, provided $37 million in federal funding for twenty high-growth industrial clusters starting in 2011. These clusters will use the federal funding to leverage additional investments from local and state governments and industrial partners. In addition to being important for regional economic development, federal policymakers now view regional innovations systems as being critical to national competitiveness.

TYPES OF UNIVERSITY-INDUSTRY-GOVERNMENT RESEARCH CENTERS

University-industry-government research centers are designed to bring together the knowledge and resources of these three actors to facilitate cluster development and, as a result, support regional economic development. These centers provide facilities where researchers from universities and industrial partners can come together to advance science and technologies. Moreover, UIG research centers can generate economic growth through the commercialization of these technologies. Centers can take a wide variety of forms and have a range of technical foci. The scholarship on research centers has shown there is no one perfect or preferred formula for successful multisector collaboration and economic impact. Three of the most common forms of UIG research centers are collaborative research centers, research parks, and incubators. This section details each of these three formats, provides a brief case study as an example of the format, and reviews relevant literature. While there is some evidence to support claims that each of these variations of research centers are widely believed to serve as economic drivers, there does remain a dearth of scholarly literature on the subject.

Collaborative Research Centers

Collaborative Research Centers (CRCs) are research units consisting of researchers from multiple science and engineering disciplines, often spread across multiple higher education institutions, brought together to address a particular science or technology challenge. CRCs promote interactions between researchers with different backgrounds to enable and expedite the creation of knowledge and transfer of technology. University-based CRCs also engage researchers from industrial partners and government laboratories to support the center's research. They were first funded by the National Science Foundation and other federal agencies to address science and engineering challenges. CRCs often have secondary missions of providing advanced educational opportunities, often for graduate students, and promoting economic development (Bozeman & Boardman, 2004). It is for these reasons local and state governments have chosen to invest in CRCs. These investments often come in the form of state funding to build infrastructure and facilities at state universities to enable the performance of multisector, collaborative research in a region. The goal of the government is to attract intellectual capital, researchers, and innovative firms into the region to take advantage of the facilities offered by the CRC (Wessner, 2011).

One recent example of a highly successful university-based CRC is the University at Albany's College of Nanoscale Science and Engineering (CNSE) (part of the State University of New York). CNSE was created in 2001 as a New York State Center of Excellence in Nanoelectronics and Nanotechnology with $150 million in funding from IBM and the state of New York. The goal of the center was twofold: build a facility that will attract innovators in the emerging field of nanotechnology, and educate a nanotechnology-capable workforce that would attract nanoscale manufacturers to New York's Capital Region. The CNSE facility contains more than eighty thousand square feet of industrial grade cleanroom research space, making it the largest university-based nanotechnology research center in the world. In addition, the CNSE has set up a one-of-a-kind management structure to enable collaboration between corporate partners and the university. These collaborations were originally focused on overcoming the technical challenges facing semiconductor manufacturing. Over the past decade, CNSE has recruited 250 research partners including IBM, SEMATECH, Tokyo Electron, Applied Materials, Intel, Samsung, and Global Foundries from industry and universities such as Downstate Medical College, Columbia, Cornell, Yale, University of Texas, University of Central Florida, and Hudson Valley Community College. CNSE has attracted more than $10 billion in corporate investment into Upstate New York to date. CNSE offers undergraduate and graduate degrees in nanoscale science and engineering. The CNSE complex supports more than 2,500 jobs including industrial researchers, faculty, and students. Since the complex was established, companies including Vistec Lithography, Global Foundries, and M+W Group have relocated their manufacturing or management operations to New York's Capital Region. CNSE is now working to apply their success in the semiconductor industry to the emerging industries of alternative energy and nanobiotechnology (see Schultz, 2011 for a more extensive analysis of the development of CNSE).

The state government has played a number of important roles in the success of CNSE. Initially, it was a primary funder of CNSE's state of the art research complex, providing $50 million of the initial $150 million investment in 2001. It was the research capabilities of the complex that attracted many of the early industrial collaborators to relocate research operations on site. The New York state government also provided matching funds for private sector companies interested in making capital investments in the region's innovation infrastructure. The first investment made by IBM in 2001 was matched with $1 from the state government for every $2 from IBM. In CNSE's most recent announcement, private-sector collaborators (i.e., IBM, Samsung, and Intel) promised $4.4 billion of investment that will be matched with $400 million from New York, a ratio of 11:1. As the critical mass of innovators and the infrastructure within the facility grow, the government's role as funder has declined. New York has also offered incentives to nanotechnology-based companies to establish manufacturing operations in the communities around CNSE. These additional measures have further promoted the development of the nanotechnology-based industrial cluster in the region.

To date, little research has focused on the impacts of CRCs on regional economies; however, there has been considerable quantitative research focused on how these unique environments impact the research behaviors of affiliated parties. Indeed, many of the interactions facilitated by CRCs support higher education's ability to be an economic driver. Boardman and Coley (2008) found faculty affiliated with industry-aligned centers spent less time collaborating with academic colleagues and more time working with industrial partners. The frequency of these collaborations increased when the industry-affiliated CRC focused on multidisciplinary or programmatic research. Ponomariov and Boardman (2010) found that affiliation with a NSF Engineering Research Center increased a faculty member's number of publications, collaborators, collaborative institutions, industrial collaborators, and expanded the scope of their research. A survey of academic researchers showed that 48 percent of all CRC-affiliated researchers had industry interaction and about one-third of these interactions resulted in a co-authored paper with an industry researcher in the previous year (Boardman, 2009). The authors found that government involvement and industry presence at a CRC increases the level of researcher-industry interaction. Adams et al. (2001), in a study of industrial partners at CRCs, identified that membership in a CRC allowed firms to consult university faculty, promoted joint research, and provided access to an employee pool of graduates. Overall, the firms that participate in the centers and collaboration have higher levels of patenting and increased R&D lab expenditures. The body of research related to the impact of CRCs concludes that university-industry research centers make both faculty and industrial researchers more productive and collaborative. This suggests that research centers are successful at creating new technologies and expediting commercialization. These activities could be harnessed to promote economic development; though more research is needed in this area.

Research Parks

Research, or science, parks encourage and manage the flow of knowledge and technology between universities, companies, and markets. University Research Parks (URPs) are built with land, financial capital, and/or intellectual capital contributed by universities. Organizations or firms locate within the park to gain access to the faculty, students, and equipment that may have been otherwise unavailable. This access allows firms to expedite the development and commercialization of the technology. Universities benefit from the effective transfer of their knowledge and technologies developed by their faculty into commercially viable products (Link & Scott, 2006). In addition, local economies benefit through the creation of high-tech jobs in the region. Research parks began forming in the 1950s with the Stanford Research Park, Cornell Business and Technology Park and the Research Triangle Park of North Carolina. There was significant growth in the 1980s after the Bayh-Dole Act was passed because universities saw such parks as an effective tool for commercializing their research. Between 1951 and 1980, fourteen research parks were established. Between 1980 and 2007, eighty-five research parks were established in the United States (Link & Scott, 2006).

One of the most successful parks is Research Triangle Park (RTP) of North Carolina. The park was established in 1959 as a collaboration of state, industry, and academic leaders to boost the region's economy, which depended heavily on farming, furniture, and textiles. The park is located between Duke University, North Carolina State University, and the University of North Carolina and aims to generate economic activity by engaging the talent and technologies generated by the universities. RTP has strong ties with the local universities, but is run by the private sector. Universities provide the skilled workforce required for R&D and also share their expertise through subcontracting and faculty collaborations. The park is currently home to more than 170 companies. These include multinational firms, such as IBM, BASF, Bayer, Cisco, and DuPont, and startup companies. The park supports a wide range of industries, including biotechnology, alternative energy, nanotechnology, and information technology, that are buoyed by the expertise in the local universities. The park is also home to research facilities for several federal agencies. Over its fifty-year history, the tenants of RTP have been awarded 3,500 patents. As of 2006, it hosted more than 39,000 full time equivalent employees with an annual payroll of $2.7 billion (Weddle, Rooks, & Valdecanas, 2006).

The state of North Carolina provided relatively minimal infrastructural support for the formation of the RTP. Most of the facilities were constructed with private sector funding. Though, the state and local governments have continually supported and developed infrastructure for the region such as roadways and utility access. The state also provides incentives for companies to relocate their research efforts and operations into RTP. Tax credits are offered to companies interested in working at RTP. The state offers more extensive economic incentives targeted to specific high-growth industries such as digital media and biotechnology (The Research Triangle Park, 2011). The formation of RTP did not require significant physical capital investment by North Carolina, but the state took an active role in creating an inviting economic environment conducive to attracting high-growth high-tech companies.

Researchers have looked at the impact that URPs have on firms and economic development. Research parks generate jobs and economic output through their tenants. In addition, they have the potential to create spillover benefits into the region's economy through the production of R&D, creation of new companies, and attraction of additional firms in the supply chain (Link & Scott, 2007). Goldstein and Luger (1990) found evidence of URPs' positive impact on regional economies through surveys of URP directors. Löfsten and Lindelöf (2002) found that new firms affiliated with Swedish research parks have higher rates of job creation than their nonaffiliated peers. Siegel, Westhead, and Wright (2003) found that firms residing in URPs have greater research productivity as measured by patents and publications, which may lead to economic growth through commercialization. While there is qualitative evidence and case studies highlighting the impacts specific parks have on their host economies (e.g., Smilor et al., 2007), large-scale, quantitative evidence of the economic impact of URPs is scarce, likely due to the heterogeneous nature of URPs, which makes it difficult to conduct large-scale re-search on multiple parks.

Incubators

Incubators are a subset of research parks focused exclusively on entrepreneurial efforts to foster the creation and development of startup and spin-off companies. Regional economies invest in incu-bators to foster small business job creation, encourage growth in a local industry, and develop a region's entrepreneurial network. As of 2006, there were more than 1,100 incubators operating in the United States (Knopp, 2007). Almost all of these are nonprofits focusing on economic development. One-fifth of incubators are sponsored by universities. University incubators focus on the transfer of university research into the market through startup companies.

Like research parks, university-based incubators provide physi-cal infrastructure, access to faculty and students, and technical sup-port to encourage technology development. Incubators also offer programs targeted to startups such as management support and entrepreneurship training for emerging companies. Incubators will help new companies prepare business plans, offer legal assistance, and provide access to financing opportunities. The managers of in-cubators have networks of experienced entrepreneurs and financiers to offer the mentorship and financial support critical to the success of a new company. Some incubators even have seed funds that can be used to support member companies. More than half of research parks also have an incubator to support their earlier-stage tenants (Link & Scott, 2006).

One of the most established and successful university incuba-tors is Georgia Tech's Advanced Technology Development Center (ATDC). The ATDC was established in 1980 with funding from the state. Since its creation, the center has launched more than 130 companies, which have raised over a billion in funding. The incu-bator works closely with Georgia Tech's technology transfer office to help faculty, students, researchers, and entrepreneurs interested in commercializing Georgia Tech inventions. The incubator offers a wide range of services including informal networking opportunities among entrepreneurs, training, facilities at flexible rates, and grant writing assistance. In addition, ATDC manages a seed capital fund that matches companies' private sector investments. Georgia's state government initially supported the ATDC though the construction of its original facilities and still provides appropriations for the management of the incubator. These funds are leveraged to gain additional federal funding and industry service fees (Advanced Technology Development Center, 2012; Culp & Shapira, 1997).

Researchers have found limited evidence on the effectiveness of incubators. Mian (1996) surveyed graduates of six incubator programs and found that those firms that took advantage of the services offered by the incubator reported larger value added. In particular, firms reported that affiliation with the university incubator offered credibility to an emerging venture. Based on two studies of the ATDC, Rothaermel and Thursby (2005a; 2005b) concluded that ventures based on inventions from Georgia Tech faculty had higher chances of failure and longer time to graduation than those not from Georgia Tech faculty. The authors suggest this may be due to the fact that these ventures are often led by individuals who are juggling the two roles of entrepreneur and professor. However, as with URPs, incubators are extremely heterogeneous in nature. While there is some evidence of the successes of individual incubators, quantitative evidence of the success of incubators as a whole and their impact on local economies can be difficult to find.

CHANNELS FOR REGIONAL ECONOMIC IMPACT

UIG research centers have multiple channels through which they can create economic growth. First, they can be large employers of a highly skilled workforce. They require significant capital investment and generate economic activity in the region through their operations. Second, the research centers can become a hub of local high-tech knowledge. This knowledge spills over into the regional economy supporting growth for local firms, attracting new manufacturing, and spinning off new companies. Third, research centers can provide workforce development that will create a stock of uniquely qualified human capital. This section identifies the channels through which a research center can impact the local economy.

Employer and Purchaser

Many research centers attract economic activity onto sites through their day-to-day activities. In economic parlance, research centers act as economic units in that they engage in consumption, production, and the exchange of goods and services. Research centers create jobs that may not have otherwise existed in the region without the advanced research facilities. These centers employ faculty members, graduate students, and support staff. Those that host industrial research, support the employment of private sector scientists and engineers in the regional economy. These entities contribute significantly to a region's economic health. According to most recently available NSF data on workforce statistics, the average salary in the science and engineering workforce in 2006 was $60,000 (Hoffer et al., 2011). Over the same period the national average annual salary was approximately $36,500. In addition, employment in the science and engineering workforce is traditionally more stable. At the dawn of the recession in October 2008, the unemployment rate of scientists and engineers with a doctorate degree was 1.7 percent compared with the U.S. workforce average of 6.6 percent (Hoffer et al., 2011). This well-educated and well-paid work force brings stability and higher wages into the region, providing benefits that will spill over into the other sectors these employees support.

High-tech research centers also require significant capital investments to support the state of the art infrastructure. These investments are often made by industrial partners matched with university and government funds. CNSE and RTP, detailed in the previous sections, have both attracted billions of investment into their unique capital infrastructures. While not all of this money is spent in the local economy, a substantial portion does go to local contractors and suppliers. In the short term, these investments boost the region's construction and supplier industries. In the longer term, the investments provide returns though the continued attraction of users to the research facility—this is particularly meaningful when the users relocate from other regions, bringing new money into the local economy.

Knowledge Creation

There is strong evidence supporting the hypothesis that knowledge spills over from universities to entities in the regional economy and contributes to technology development (Anselin, Varga, & Acs, 1997; Audretsch & Feldman, 1996; Jaffe, Trajtenberg, & Henderson, 1993). These spillovers occur through channels such as direct personal contacts between researchers in a regional network of scientists and engineers and the hiring of graduates by local firms. This is one of the primary justifications for regional government investment in university-industry research centers. These centers create economic growth by serving as a critical component of a region's innovation infrastructure. State of the art research centers attract innovators interested in advancing the science and technology that will expand the stock of knowledge in the region. As the stock of knowledge expands, it draws interest from other firms and research institutions in the region who will perform additional complementary research. This will result in further growth in the regional knowledge stock. This knowledge stock creates economic impact through the expansion of a highly skilled labor force and the location of high-tech companies into the area interested in taking advantage of these spillovers. As a caveat, in assessing economic impact, it is important to try to distinguish those firms that locate in the region because of the research center versus those that do so for other reasons, such as geographic features, access to other resources the area has to offer, and personal choices of management. This separation is not always easy to accomplish, but failing to do so may artificially inflate the impact of the center.

Workforce Development

In addition to producing knowledge, colleges and universities have been tasked with training the labor force. University laboratories produce PhD students with expertise in cutting-edge research. The universities that house these research centers are also driving forces in the redefinition of curriculum at both the K–12 and university levels (Chubin et al., 2010). Researchers at CRCs are leaders in emerging fields of science and technology and are familiar with the research being performed in academia and industry. These experts are among the best qualified to identify the knowledge base and skill set that will be required for the continued development of the field and to formalize these requirements through the creation of formal educational curricula. For example, Stanford University and California Institute of Technology, at the center of Silicon Valley, led the development of new academic disciplines such as electrical engineering, computer science, and computer engineering (Saxenian, 1994). CNSE was among the first to offer degrees at the graduate and undergraduate level in nanotechnology-related fields (Schultz, 2011). Research centers often work with local community colleges to develop training programs for manufacturing jobs (Jacobs, 2012—chapter 7 this volume). In addition, the recent study of NSF Science and Technology Centers highlighted the multiple K–12 initiatives of centers designed to spread knowledge of emerging disciplines to students of all ages (Chubin et al., 2010).

Manufacturers developing new technologies will need employees at all levels familiar with these technologies. A robust education system at the K–12, community college, undergraduate, and graduate level will train a workforce that will meet potential employers' needs. This is a critical factor for firms making decisions about where to locate operations and manufacturing. A strong labor force training infrastructure is critical to attracting firms into the region and supporting employment and economic growth. In addition, local companies benefit from hiring local students with whom they had existing research ties. Research-oriented companies often collaborate with a faculty member's laboratory and will meet regularly with graduate students, which gives future employers the opportunity to assess a job candidate's skills over an extended period of time. Local companies also frequently offer internship opportunities to students. Students benefit from the professional experience and firms also view it as an opportunity to assess the skills of a potential new employee and begin training. Affiliation with a research center provides firms with access to a uniquely qualified employee pool. Hiring research scientists, technicians, operators, and production managers with whom the firm already has experience saves significant hiring and training costs.

The region benefits when students remain in the region upon graduation and accept a position at a local firm. In addition to building the labor force, the region benefits from the higher income tax revenues paid by these highly skilled, and likely higher-salaried employees.

MEASURES FOR THE UIG CENTER IMPACT

Stakeholders that contribute to the development of UIG research centers are often interested in knowing the return to their investment. Government funders are interested in knowing that their investments are creating a positive impact in the regional economy and benefit constituents. Industry partners want to be sure they are earning positive returns on their investments in collaborative research centers through benefits they would not have received through independent work. Universities are interested in advancing the productivity and learning of faculty and students. In addition, regular tracking of UIG center activities and impacts can be critical in informing future policy decisions. Regular evaluation of programs and outputs can provide insight to managers and stakeholders about the success of the center. It can highlight programs that should (or should not) be continued and others that may need to be modified and can lead to a more effective research center. Such evaluations also need to allow for an adequate amount of time for investments to yield results. Many research projects take several years of work before results are realized and evaluations need to account for such.

Despite the interest in and benefits that can be received from regular and standardized evaluation of research centers, standards for data collection and analysis do not yet exist. This is most likely due to the heterogeneous nature of research centers. There have been recent efforts led by organizations such as Association of University Technology Managers (AUTM) and the National Business Incubator Association to formalize the data collection related to the economic impact of university and incubator research. This section highlights best practices from the literature related to the data used, metrics created, and methods developed to evaluate the impact of UIG research centers.

Research Center Census

One way to assess the scale and scope of the research center is to directly survey research center tenants and researchers. A census of the research center can be collected on a quarterly or annual basis. At a bare minimum, a research center census can track the number of workers, both academic and industrial, as well as new capital investment made within the center. Additional data can be collected, such as payroll, position description (manager, researcher, technical, support staff, etc.), and annual operating expenses. Payroll and salary data can provide insights into the quality of the jobs created in the center. If salary data are unavailable from center tenants, the Bureau of Labor Statistics provides wage data categorized by occupation, industry, and geographic region that can be used to estimate the salaries and annual payroll within a center (Bureau of Labor Statistics, 1997). Tracking capital investments made in a given year on equipment and construction can provide further evidence of the amount of new economic activity occurring within a research center. Local government investment data are often a matter of public record and can be collected through sources such as government Web sites, press releases, and/or newspapers. Private sector tenants are frequently not required to publicly report investments, and the information will have to be collected through a census. Data on the number of visitors and list of suppliers can be helpful to quantifying impact on other parts of the regional economy. A list of suppliers and their locations can show the local businesses supported by center research activity and demonstrate how other businesses are benefiting. All of these data can provide some evidence on the scale of the research being performed in the center and the scope of its economic impact.

The data collected through a census can be used in conjunction with multiplier analysis to quantify the impact that research centers have in the regional economy. Multiplier analysis performed with tools such as IMPLAN or RIMS use data on the transfer of inputs and outputs between entities in an economy to track the role an institution plays in the regional economy. The reports are generated using employment and capital investment data to estimate the impact of the research center's annual economic activity on the region's economy. The advantage of this approach is that it is well recognized and commonly used to quantify the impacts of universities. Multiplier analysis performed on a regular basis can show how the role of a research center has changed over time. However, there are many concerns regarding the validity of these estimates. These include questions about the appropriateness and calculation of the inputs into the models and assumptions about geographic parameters. Therefore, the findings acquired through multiplier analysis must be used carefully. These and other concerns regarding estimating the economic impact of colleges and universities through multiplier analysis are detailed by McHenry, Sanderson, and Siegfried (2012—chapter 3 of this volume).

Measuring the impact of UIG research centers using multiplier analysis presents additional challenges not confronted when dealing with just university-related activities. First, these research centers are hybrid entities, which can make it challenging to determine what sector of the economy the center's activity should be classified under. They are not purely university entities nor are they just industrial complexes. They are research centers, but depending on the industries they support, the broad classification of Scientific R&D Services may not be adequate. Second, the capital investment and labor requirements for R&D vary greatly by industry. This lack of clarity makes it difficult to accurately classify the inputs into the multiplier model. One option is to use multiple permutations of inputs and industry classification to identify a range in which the center's impact may fall.

The end goal of these research centers is to develop a cluster of new high-tech industrial activity. A successful research center will create new infrastructure and attract new industry into the region. However, the multiplier analysis is often unable to take this into account. Detailed input-output data is collected every five years coinciding with the federal economic census of businesses conducted by the U.S. Census Bureau. This may not be a frequent enough interval to track the development of a new industry and corresponding suppliers in a region. While multiplier analysis is a commonly used approach to measuring the economic impact of universities, analysts may want to collect a wider range of data to track the growth and role of the research center in the economy over time.

Research and Development Funding

R&D funding is the most direct measure of investment in the region's knowledge stock. Some federal support for research center–affiliated principal investigators can be tracked through awards databases maintained by agencies such as the NSF and National Institutes of Health (NIH). On a more aggregate level, R&D expenditure data is tracked by the NSF and is available for state level analysis. In addition, NSF reports on R&D performance for universities by source of funding and academic field. Together these can provide a snapshot of the academic R&D performance within the region and the innovation infrastructure of the state. There are not currently any data publicly available on the performance of R&D by firms on a regional basis (Board, 2010).

Publication Output

Publications represent the output of earlier-stage, basic research. They are common outputs of university research projects and firms will use them to promote their technological advancements. Depending on the structure of the research center, annual reports of researchers can be used to collect information on publications directly affiliated with the center. Independent databases such as the Web of Science can be used to track peer-reviewed journal publications coming from a region. Search criteria such as topic area and author address or institution affiliation can be used to pinpoint papers directly related to the cluster. As a cluster develops, two trends should emerge. The first is a growth over time in the number of publications. As the cluster grows, more innovators and researchers will be attracted to the infrastructure in the region and will relocate research efforts. Secondly, there should be an increase in the number of institutions publishing in the region. While the hub of a cluster may be the university, the cluster does not form until other firms and institutions enter the region and contribute to the knowledge stock. As the cluster develops, other institutions in the region will begin to focus research activities on developing related technologies. This suggests that other regional universities and firms will also begin publishing in related areas.

Patents

Patents represent research applied to create a new technology. Inventors file for patents when their research has produced a new technology with commercial applications. Again, researcher reporting can be used to identify patents. The U.S. Patent and Trademark Office also has databases that track patent applications and awards (www.patft.uspto.gov). Searches can be performed using classifications or keywords and geographical areas to track the development of technologies in a region. As with publications, a growing cluster should exhibit a growth in the number of patents and assignees. Depending on the technologies being developed it may also be appropriate to track the number of copyrights and trademarks awarded.

Collaborative Research

In addition to growth of research outputs, researchers could also track the development of a network of researchers within a region using the bibliometric data. UIG research centers are established with the goal of forming a network of innovation in a region. If successful, centers should lead to greater collaborations between researchers at the university and industry. Collaborative publications are indicative

Figure 5.1. Sample Bibliometric Analysis of Research Outputs

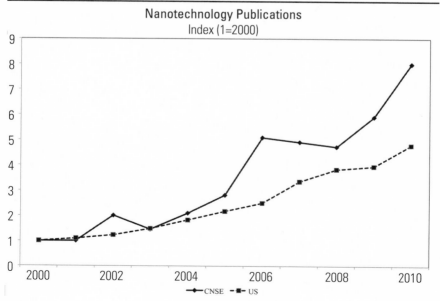

Figure 5.1. (*continued*)

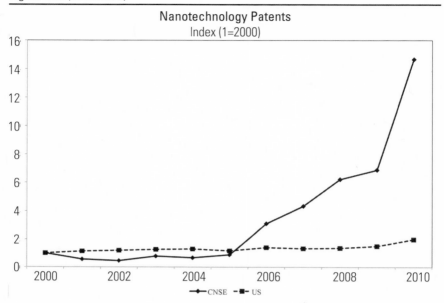

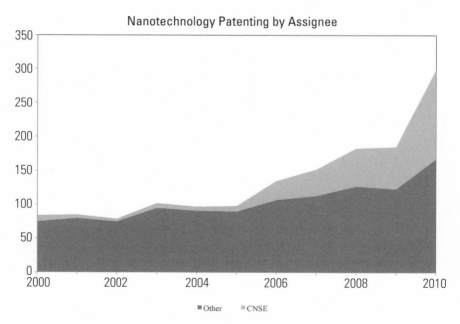

Figure 5.1. (*continued*)

Collaborations at Nanotechnology Research Centers					
Center	Collaboration (%)	Univ-Univ	Univ-Ind	Univ-Gov	Ind-Gov	Univ-Ind-Gov
CNSE	68%	74%	26%	12%	16%	0%
MIT	60%	90%	17%	8%	15%	2%
UTAustin	58%	76%	22%	16%	5%	2%
Georgia Tech	57%	84%	11%	11%	2%	2%
Rice University	56%	84%	14%	20%	0%	2%
Stanford University	55%	65%	38%	0%	4%	2%
CalTech	55%	84%	24%	15%	2%	4%
Cornell University	54%	81%	15%	9%	2%	0%
Harvard University	52%	90%	19%	12%	2%	2%
Northwestern	48%	79%	13%	19%	0%	0%

The above graphs and charts show how bibliometric data can be used to track research center activity overtime. Figure a) shows the growth of the College of Nanoscale Science and Engineering's (CNSE) publications compared with the trend of US nanotechnology publishing. CNSE's number of annual publications have grown 67% faster than the national average showing high levels of research growth. CNSE patent activities have grown over 7 times faster than the national average. Figure c) shows CNSE's share of nanotechnology patenting in the Capital Region growing indicating the growth of importance in the region's innovation infrastructure. Figure d. looks at the collaborative nature of CNSE's publications compared to other nanotechnology research centers. Authors at CNSE are more likely to collaborate than at other research centers suggesting that it may be more successful at building an innovation network.

of transfer of technology from university to industry. Faculty members work directly with their peers in industry on projects relevant to both parties. These collaborations remove much of the uncertainty and challenges associated with the technology transfer process. The university research will have a willing customer that has been engaged from the beginning of the project.

UIG CENTER IMPACT ON THE LABOR FORCE

The center can play a critical role in the development of the regional labor force through the graduates of its academic programs. The scale and scope of each center's involvement with academic programs is very heterogeneous. Many of the NSF-funded centers have an impact through the hosting of graduate and undergraduate researchers. Other centers support their own degree programs specific to the technology. Again, a data collection effort led by the center could provide valuable information. Graduates of the centers can be tracked on a regular basis. All alumni of the center could be required to fill out a survey upon graduation detailing employment plans, location, and what role their experience in the center played in their obtaining the position. The information collected can be used to estimate the impact of the center-related educational program had on each student, the regional economy, and the employer. Alumni employment rates and salaries can be compared with their peers graduating from the university but not affiliated with the center. Such comparison can provide insight into the value of the center affiliation to the graduate over a lifetime.

The Bureau of Labor Statistics (BLS) also collects information on occupations by region and industry. The Occupation Employment Statistics survey tracks more than eight hundred occupations and can be used to assess the science and engineering workforce developing in a metropolitan statistical area (Bureau of Labor Statistics, 1997). Analysts can identify jobs they would expect to see growing in a developing cluster and track them on an annual basis. For example, in a growing biotechnology cluster, analysts could track the number of jobs and wages of occupations such as natural science managers, medical scientists, biochemists and biophysicists, chemists, biological technicians, and so forth. Higher than average growth rates in related occupations would be expected of developing clusters.

IMPACT ON THE REGIONAL ECONOMY

One of the most direct ways centers create economic activity in a region is through the commercialization of their research through entrepreneurial activities. Centers and incubators often track the number of startup and spin-off companies that are established to develop center-created technology. A self-sustaining entrepreneurial system is critical for a cluster. New companies commercialize emerging technologies, generate growth, and create new jobs. In addition, entrepreneurs support the next generation of entrepreneurs. Entrepreneurial activities in the region could also be closely monitored. The number of startup and spin-off companies related to the center is the bare minimum data to be collected. Firms that graduate from (or leave) the research center can be tracked to assess their survival and growth rates. Growth is commonly measured by the amount of funding (government, venture capital, and equity) raised, revenue, shareholder wealth, and employment.

In addition, regional economic data can be collected on a regular basis from publicly available sources to track changes in the economic ecosystem over time. Regional employment can be tracked though the Bureau of Labor Statistics or the state Department of Labor. The BLS Quarterly Census of Employment and Wages collects regional data on the number of employees, employers, and wages at an aggregate and NAICS industry level. Industries related to a growing cluster can be identified and tracked over an extended period of time (Bureau of Labor Statistics, 1997). Output is the measure of all goods and services produced in an economy. Output data are available from the Bureau of Economic Analysis on aggregate and NAICS-industry levels for metropolitan statistical areas. These data should be compared with U.S. and state averages. In addition, regions with similar characteristics such as population size, geography, and industry composition may provide good comparisons. A developing cluster would expect higher than average growth in the relevant industries.

The use of these data should come with disclaimers. These datasets can be useful in assessing aggregate trends in regional growth, but their power to quantify the impact of a research center may be limited. As mentioned above, a number of factors contribute to the creation of a cluster and growth of a region's economy cannot be exclusively attributed to only one of these factors. In addition, these data may not fully track an emerging technology. Emerging technologies, such as nanotechnology, have a wide range of applications, making it difficult to accurately identify impacted industries. Not all firms will fall within the same sector and the wide-ranging impacts make it difficult to accurately assess the growth of the cluster. The final challenge associated with these data is that they are published with a lag. While these data sets may not be the most direct way to assess the impact of the research center, tracking them can help researchers identify developing clusters.

CONCLUSION

In recent years, governments have funded university-industry research centers with the joint goals of transferring university technologies into the marketplace and spurring technology-based economic development. Research centers allow university and industry researchers to work together to expedite technology development and commercialization. They are a pathway through which the spillovers can flow more freely into a regional economy. In addition, these centers are designed to serve as a hub of a high-tech cluster. They train and attract a uniquely qualified workforce into the region. This workforce will in turn attract established firms and entrepreneurs who wish to take advantage of this highly skilled labor.

This chapter has outlined the channels through which UIG research centers of all forms can impact the regional economy. It has also identified several metrics that can be used by managers, analysts, policymakers, and researchers to track the impact of the center and the development of a high-tech regional cluster over time. Tracking of these centers from their earliest stages is critical. It can provide important information on the impact the center is having, that is, the effectiveness of its policies, and it can inform and influence future directions.

REFERENCES

Adams, J., Chiang, E., & Starkey, K. (2001). Industry-university cooperative research centers. *Journal of Technology Transfer 26*, 73–86.

Advanced Technology Development Center. (2012). *About ADTC.* Available at http://atdc.org/about/about.

Anselin, L., Varga, A., & Acs, Z. (1997). Local geographic spillovers between university research and high technology innovations.

Journal of Urban Economics 42 (3), 422–448. doi:10.1006/juec.1997.2032.

Audretsch, D. B., & Feldman, M. P. (1996). R & D spillovers and the geography of innovation and production. *American Economic Review 86* (3), 630–640.

Boardman, C. 2009. Government centrality to university-industry interactions: University research centers and the industry involvement of academic researchers. *Research Policy 38*, 1505–1516.

Boekholt, P., & Thuriaux, B. (1999). Public policies to facilitate clusters: Background, rationale, and policy practices in internation perspective. In OECD (Ed.), *Boosting innovation: The cluster approach* (pp. 381–412). Paris: OECD Publishing.

Bozeman, B., & Boardman, P. C. (2004). The NSF Engineering Research Centers and the university-industry research revolution: A brief history featuring an interview with Erich Bloch. *The Journal of Technology Transfer 29* (3), 365–375.

Braunerhjelm, P., & Feldman, M. (Eds.). (2006). *Cluster genesis.* Oxford: Oxford University Press.

Bureau of Labor Statistics. (1997). *Handbook of methods.* Washington, DC. Available at http://www.bls.gov/opub/hom/.

Chubin, D. E., Derrick, E., Feller, I., & Phartiyal, P. (2010). *AAAS review of the NSF Science and Technology Centers Integrative Partnerships (STC) Program, 2000–2009.* Washington, DC: Advancement of Science.

Culp, R., & Shapira, P. (1997). Georgia's Advanced Technology Development Center: An assessment. In OECD (Ed.), *Technology incubators: Nurturing small firms.* OECD report, no. 60358, (pp. 63–74). Paris: Organization for Economic Cooperation and Development.

Etzkowitz, H., & Leydesdorff, L. (2000). The dynamics of innovation: From national systems and "Mode 2" to a Triple Helix of university-industry-government relations. *Research Policy, 29,* 109–123.

Feldman, M. P., Freyer, A. M., & Lanahan, L. (2012). On the measurement of university research contributions to economic growth and innovation. In J. E. Lane & D. B. Johnstone (Eds.), *Universities and colleges as economic drivers: Measuring Higher Education's role in economic development.* Albany: State University of New York Press.

Feller, I., Ailes, C. P., & Roessner, J. D. (2002). Impacts of research universities on technological innovation in industry: Evidence from engineering research centers. *Research Policy 31*, 457–474.

Goldstein, H., & Luger, M. (1990). Science/technology parks and regional development theory. *Economic Development Quarterly 4*, 64–78.

Gray, D. O., & Walters, G. W. (Eds.). (1998). Managing the Industry/University Cooperative Research Center: A guide for director and other stakeholders. Columbus, OH: Battelle Press.

Hoffer, T. B., Milesi, C., Selfa, L., Foley, D. J., Milan, L. M., & Proud, S. L. (2011). Unemployment among doctoral scientists and engineers remained below the national average in 2008. *Statistics*. National Science Foundation. Available at http://www.nsf.gov/statistics/infbrief/nsf11308/nsf11308.pdf.

Jacobs, J. (2012). The essential role of community colleges in rebuilding the nation's communities and economies. In J. E. Lane & D. B. Johnstone (Eds.), *Universities and colleges as economic drivers*. Albany: State University of New York Press.

Jaffe, A. B., Trajtenberg, M., & Henderson, R. (1993). Geographic localization of knowledge spillovers as evidenced by patent citations. *The Quarterly Journal of Economics 108* (3), 577–598.

Knopp, L. (2007). *2006 State of the Business Incubation Industry*. Athens, Ohio: NBIA Publications.

Link, A. N., & Scott, J. T. (2006). U.S. university research parks. *Journal of Productivity Analysis 25* (2), 43, 55.

Link, A.N., & Scott, J.T. (2007). The economics of university research parks. *European Review of Economic History, 23* (4), 661-674

Löfsten, H., & Lindelöf, P. (2002). Science parks and the growth of new technology-based firms—academic-industry links, innovation, and markets. *Research Policy 31*, 859–876.

McHenry, P., Sanderson, A. R., & Siegfried, J. J. (2012). Pitfalls of traditional measures of higher education's role in economic development. In J. E. Lane & D. B. Johnstone (Eds.), *Universities and colleges as economic drivers*. Albany: State University of New York Press.

Mian, S. A. (1996). Assessing value-added contributions of university technology business incubators to tenant firms. *Research Policy 25*, 325–335.

National Business Incubation Association. (2009). Business Incubation FAQ. Available at http://www.nbia.org/resource_library/faq/#1.

National Business Incubation Association. (2009). Business Incubation FAQ. Available at http://www.nbia.org/resource_library/faq/#1.

National Governors Association and Council on Competitiveness. (2007). Cluster-based strategies for growing state economies. Washington, DC: National Governors Association.

National Science Board. (2010). *Science and engineering indicators.* Arlington, VA: National Science Foundation.

Nelson, R. (Ed.). (1993). *National innovation systems: a comparative analysis.* Oxford: Oxford University Press.

Owen-Smith, J. (2012). Unanticipated consequences of university intellectual property policies. In J. E. Lane & D. B. Johnstone (Eds.), *Universities and colleges as economic drivers: Measuring Higher Education's role in economic development.* Albany: State University of New York Press.

Ponomariov B., & *Boardman,* P. (2010). Influencing scientists' behaviors through organizational design. *Research Policy 39,* 613–624.

Porter, M. (1990). *The competitive advantage of nations.* New York: The Free Press.

Porter, M. E. (1998). Clusters and the new economics of competition. *Harvard Business Review 76* (6), 77–90.

Porter, M. E. (2000). Location, competition, and economic development: Local clusters in a global economy. *Economic Development Quarterly 14* (1), 15–34. doi:10.1177/089124240001400105.

Research Triangle Park. (2011)

Rosenberg, N., & Nelson, R. (1994). American universities and technical advance in industry. *Research Policy 23* (3), 323–348.

Rothaermel, F. T., & Thursby, M. (2005a). Incubator firm failure or graduation? The role of University Linkages. *Research Policy 34* (7), 1076–1090. doi:10.1016/j.respol.2005.05.012.

Rothaermel, F., & Thursby, M. (2005b). University–incubator firm knowledge flows: Assessing their impact on incubator firm performance. *Research Policy 34* (3), 305–320. doi:10.1016/j.respol.2004.11.006.

Saxenian, A. (1994). Regional advantage: Culture and competition in Silicon Valley and Route 128. Cambridge: Harvard University Press.

Schultz, L. I. (2011). Nanotechnology's Triple Helix: A case study of the University at Albany's College of Nanoscale Science and Engineering. *Journal of Technology Transfer 36*, 546–564.

Siegel, D. S., Westhead, P., & Wright, M. (2003). Assessing the impact of university science parks on research productivity: Exploratory firm–level evidence from the United Kingdom. *International Journal of Industrial Organization 21* (9), 1357–1369.

Smilor, R., O'Donnell, N., Stein, G., and Welborn, R. (2007). The research university and the development of high-technology centers in the United States. *Economic Development Quarterly 21* (3), 203–222.

Weddle, R.L., Rooks, E., Valdecanas, T. (2006). *Research Triangle Park: Evolution and Renaissance*. Paper presented at 2006 International Association of Science Parks World Conference. Helskinki, Iceland.

Wessner, C. W. (2002). Government-industry partnerships for the development of new technologies. Washington, DC: The National Academies Press.

Wessner, C. W. (2011). *Growing innovation for American prosperity: Summary of a symposium*. Washington, DC: The National Academies Press.

6

THE CONVERGENCE OF POSTSECONDARY EDUCATION AND THE LABOR MARKET

ANTHONY P. CARNEVALE
AND STEPHEN J. ROSE

ABSTRACT

Over the past century, education became a primary means for achieving economic success in the United States. As more individuals pursued a postsecondary education, the country also benefited from enhanced economic competitiveness relative to other nations. However, America's comparative advantage of having a better-educated workforce has waned in the past two decades, slipping behind other nations such as Canada, Japan, Norway, and South Korea. This chapter analyzes how education influences a range of current public policy concerns from economic competitiveness to the rising income inequality. The authors also illustrate how the investment in a postsecondary education remains valuable, despite the rising cost of college. But they argue that as education's economic value increases, college and universities need to find a way to balance their intrinsic and extrinsic benefits.

INTRODUCTION

Since colonial times, Americans have relied on education to ward off false prophets, as well as to reconcile democratic citizenship with diversity and class differences. In the United States, education has also gradually become a reliable path to economic success, especially since the closing of the frontier at the end of the nineteenth century and continuing with the rush of industrialization and urbanization thereafter. The twentieth century ushered in the call for "high school for all," a goal that still frustrates us more than a century later. Yet, while high school degrees are still not universal, they were commonplace by the 1950s. And in the post–World War II era, a college degree became the preferred, if not the only, route to good professional and managerial jobs.

It is not news that in the post–World War II era postsecondary education became the preferred route to the best managerial and professional jobs. What is news is that since the 1980s postsecondary education and training has become recognized as the most reliable and most well-traveled pathway to middle-class earnings and status. As we elaborate below, the share of jobs that offer postsecondary wage advantages has increased from roughly one-third to two-thirds since the seventies.

The growing popularity of postsecondary education is driven by both economic and cultural factors. The popular acceptance of education as a legitimate arbiter of opportunity is deeply embedded in the United States' individualistic cultural and political biases. In theory, using education to mediate opportunity allows us to expand merit-based success without surrendering individual responsibility. After all, we each have to do our own homework to make the grades and ace the tests that get us into college and in line for good jobs. Using education this way also complements our other key preferences for a self-reliant citizenry, an open economy, and a limited government. Arguably, access to postsecondary education ought to give us each the earning power necessary to ward off public dependency and curb the expansion of the welfare state. Public support for education, especially access to college, thus provides the middle course in American politics.

The slogan "College for all" and the more humble country cousin "postsecondary education and training for all" certainly make good politics. While elected officials cannot promise to pay for college for all, they can promise to make college "affordable" for all who are qualified. This centrist consensus on postsecondary access and affordability is part of what remains of the common ground between the entrenched reds (Republicans) and the blues (Democrats). It has become the acceptable bipartisan political response to the risks and rewards in the global economy and the primary prescription for narrowing the family-income gap threatening the middle class. Education thus offers the middle course between the runaway free market always on offer from those located right of the political center and the directly redistributive "nanny state" alternative on offer from those on the left.

Promoting postsecondary access and success has other virtues: it unifies aspirations among a significant share of the populace. It creates common cause between the aspiring middle class and those who have already arrived but dread downward mobility for themselves and their children. Postsecondary opportunity also works as a public narrative, in part, because the public widely regards high school and vocational education as second-best. A great many people also believe high school students are not prepared to choose a career at such a young age and should not be steered toward one career or another.

Public opinion about college for all can be confusing. Several polls show two-thirds of respondents believe college is necessary for a solid career for their own children. At the same time, most respondents agree that not everyone needs a college education. We all tend to support alternatives to college for other people's children, but not for our own.

But, on balance, there's more economics in the growing agreement on college-going than there is in middle-class angst, cultural bias, and political posturing. The notion of *postsecondary education for all* resonates with our recent experience in the real economy. From the early assembly-line machines to the modern ubiquity of computers and the Internet, technology has revolutionized the workforce. America's relentless engine of technological development, fueled by increasingly fierce global competition, requires an ever-growing pool of workers savvy enough to integrate sophisticated new tools into their work routines. At the same time, our drive toward technical sophistication and automation has reduced the need for unskilled labor. Technological change has become the dynamic engine accelerating the value of and demand for postsecondary education and training.

The latest round of technology change began after the 1980–82 double-dip recessions ended the stagnant growth and high inflation of the seventies, setting the stage for a massive restructuring of our economy. The core mechanism at work increasing the demand for postsecondary education has been the computer. Computer technology automates repetitive tasks and increases the value of nonrepetitive functions in all jobs. Occupations with high levels of nonrepetitive tasks tend to require postsecondary education or training. As a result, the latest round of technology change does automate but is ultimately biased in favor of postsecondary skills or more precisely the complementarities between flexible computer technology and postsecondary skill.

EXPANDING EDUCATION TEMPORARILY INCREASED OUR COMPETITIVE EDGE

For many years, the United States was the undisputed world leader in education expansion; its rate of college completion was higher than any other country's. In the 1960s, when our lead in the share of the workforce with a college degree was still large compared to most other industrialized countries, we continued to expand access to college. Eventually, between 50 and 60 percent of each age cohort attended postsecondary institutions (approximately 35 percent earned a two- or four-year degree).

What looked like folly and waste to some turned out to be an economic boon, and other countries followed suit. As other countries expanded their educational systems, our comparative postsecondary advantage contracted. By 2008, the United States had dropped to second behind Norway in the share of its workforce with a four-year degree.[1] Figure 6.1, which includes short-term college degrees (our Associate's degree), places the United States third for prime-age adult educational attainment, behind Canada and Japan.[2]

The future is significantly bleaker for the United States among those aged twenty-five to thirty-four, the majority of recent college graduates. Here the United States ranks eighth in Bachelor's degree completion (Norway is again first) and tenth in all graduate degrees. Forty-two percent of that U.S. age group (25–34 year olds) have college degrees, far below the 55 percent of young adults in Canada, Japan, and South Korea (fig. 6.2).

A clear trend has emerged: We are losing ground to our competitors in postsecondary education attainment. President Obama and other leaders are rightly alarmed at our current position and have

Figure 6.1. Attainment of College Degrees for Prime-age Workers in OECD Countries, 2008[a]

Source: OECD, *Education at a Glance* (2010)
a. Prime-age workers are those between the ages of 25 and 64.

Figure 6.2. Attainment of College Degrees for Workers Aged 25 to 34 in OECD Countries, 2008

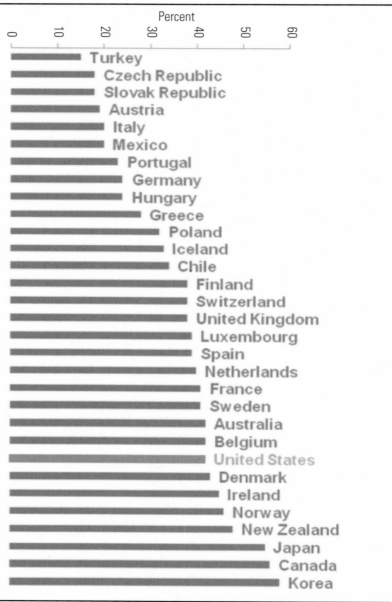

Source: OECD, *Education at a Glance* 2010: OECD Indicators

called on the nation to redouble its postsecondary education efforts and regain its comparative educational edge. The significance of these rankings goes beyond mere bragging rights: increasing our supply of skilled labor is central to our economic vitality. The expansion of American higher education while the nation was enjoying economic growth and global economic domination was not coincidental. Education was a primary driver of that growth and will need to continue that role in the future.

HIGH AND RISING WAGE PREMIUMS MEAN WE NEED MORE COLLEGE-EDUCATED WORKERS

Our increased focus on skilled labor in the United States is not an idle concern; the evidence clearly shows the United States needs more, not fewer, college graduates. Proof is apparent when applying the most fundamental concept of economics: supply and demand. In the labor market, workers supply their services for a price (or wage) and employers demand labor services (to fill jobs). The supply curve shows workers are willing to supply more labor at higher prices and less at lower prices. Conversely, the demand curve shows that employers are willing to hire more workers at lower prices and fewer at higher prices. The market clearing price or equilibrium wage rate is where the two curves intersect.[3]

Supply and demand are still the most important economic laws governing labor markets.[4] Ultimately, a company enforces these economic laws by hiring workers with the requisite skills to fill job openings and earn a healthy return on its investment. If qualified workers are in short supply relative to employer demand, the employer's rational response is to bid up wages, in this case, for college-educated workers. This increases the wage premium college-educated workers make relative to less-educated workers. Today employers are signaling that they want employees with a college degree or other forms of postsecondary training for the majority of jobs.[5] They want these employees so much that they are willing to pay workers with a Bachelor's degree 74 percent more on average than they pay workers with only a high school diploma.

This wage premium is not static, and all evidence suggests that employers are responding to the market, not just hiring degrees.

Figure 6.3. Wage Premium of Skilled versus Unskilled Labor, 1915–2005[a]

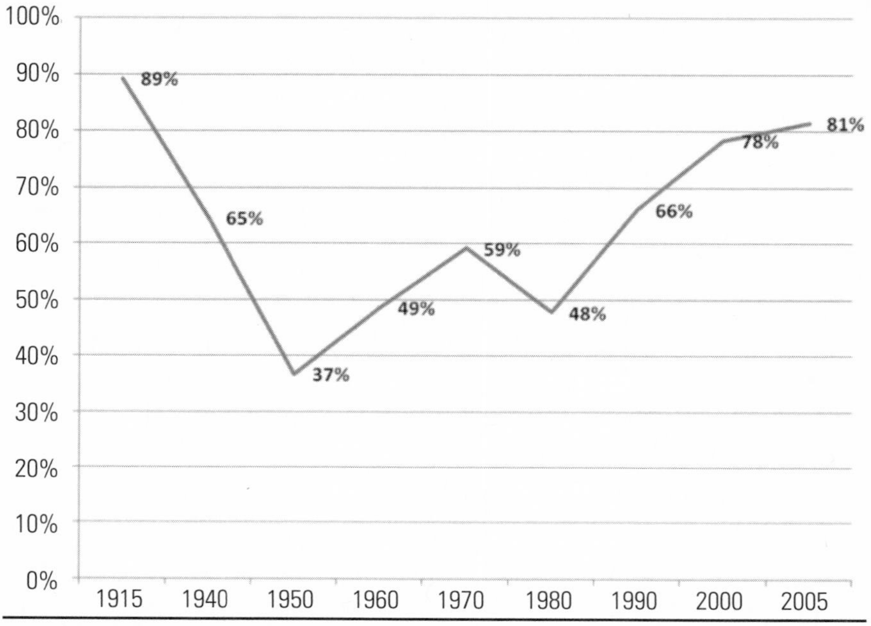

Source: Goldin and Katz (2008)
a. Skilled labor includes workers with a Bachelor's degree or better plus one half of those with some postsecondary education, including an Associate's degree. Unskilled labor includes workers who did not complete high school, those with a high school diploma and no postsecondary education, and the other half of those with some postsecondary education.

Historically, the wage premium has risen and fallen depending on the complex interaction between supply and demand.[6] As reported in Goldin and Katz (2008), the premium fluctuated throughout the twentieth century (Fig. 6.3).

In 1915, the few college graduates tended to be business leaders with earnings much higher than less-educated, rank-and-file workers. As the Great Depression dawned and jobs were hard to come by, the number of college-going young adults increased. That increase in supply combined with wage and price controls during World War II contributed to a dramatic decrease in the wage premium to just 37

Figure 6.4. Annual Change in Relative Demand for Workers with Postsecondary Education, 1915–2005

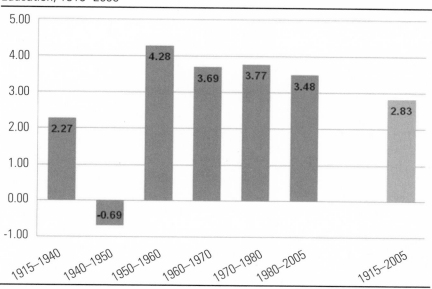

Source: Autor & Dorn (2009) and Goldin & Katz (2008)

percent by 1950. Thereafter the premium increased again, fueled by strong economic growth in the postwar years, hitting 59 percent by 1970. Over the next decade, the supply of college-educated workers spiked as waves of highly educated (by historical standards) baby boomers entered the workforce and, predictably, the wage premium dropped in tandem. From 1980 on, however, the supply of college-educated workers and the wage premium they received grew as the spread of information technology fueled the skyrocketing demand for skills throughout the economy.

Since we know the change in supply of educated workers during these years and the relative price of skilled versus unskilled labor, we can use the supply and demand model from Autor, Katz, and Kearney (2008) to compute the change in relative demand for skilled workers (Fig. 6.4). The demand for workers with postsecondary education grew at a rate of 2.8 percent per year during this entire ninety-year period. Relative demand was lower between 1915 and 1940 because of World War I and its economic aftermath and the Great Depression. From 1940 to 1950, the growth in demand was negative but attributable to strict wage controls instituted during World War II. From 1950 to 2005, the computed growth in relative demand was very high—more than 3 percent per year in each subperiod.These numbers demonstrate that increasing demand for skilled workers has a long, consistent history and is not based solely on the more recent history of rising computerization. However, computerization has accelerated these trends. In 1980, when mass adoption of personal computers began, 57 percent of the labor force had no postsecondary education. This figure dropped to 40 percent in 2005, but this up-grading of worker skills was offset by demand for college-educated labor rising by almost 3.5 percent per year. As a result, rising demand outstripped the modest increase in supply: workers with a Bachelor's degree who had earned 40 percent more than workers with a high school diploma in 1980 earned 74 percent more in 2005.

This rise in price, combined with the increasing supply, implies that demand for college-educated workers has been rising faster than the education system can provide them. Going forward to 2025, this trend will continue if we do not add significant numbers of college-educated workers to the economy. The share of college-educated workers is expected to increase very little while demand for skilled labor is expected to grow by 2 percent per year. The disparity between supply and demand through 2025 could increase the wage premium for a Bachelor's degree to an all-time high of 94 percent.

Finally, it is noteworthy that other industrialized countries have seen the same rise in relative demand. No one has done as compre-hensive a study of these countries as has been done for the United States, but we can compare the relative earnings on the basis of edu-cational attainment. Although the same forces are affecting the Unit-ed States' economic competitors, they were increasing their supply of college-educated people at a much faster rate. Consequently, the wage premium for a Bachelor's degree in the United States in 2005 was much higher than the average of all OECD countries (Fig. 6.5).[7] Only four small countries—namely, the Czech Republic, Hungary, Portugal, and the Slovak Republic—had wage premiums of more than 70 percent (or even 60 percent).

Figure 6.5. Wage premium for a Bachelor's degree or better, 2005

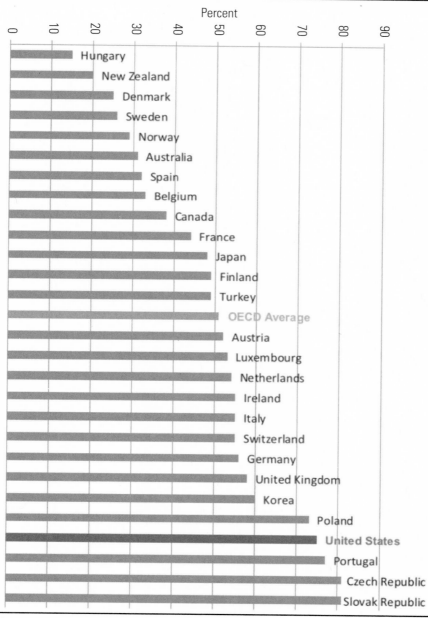

Percent

Source: OECD, *Education at a Glance 2010: OECD Indicators*

INCOME INEQUALITY IS DRIVEN LARGELY
BY ACCESS TO COLLEGE

One notable drawback to rapidly growing wages for more highly educated workers has been the concomitant rise in income inequality in the United States since 1980. Because earnings are the major component of household incomes, it is not surprising that the trends in income inequality follow the trends in earnings inequality. From the end of World War II to 1973, income inequality remained very stable. With the full implementation and expansion of Social Security, gains at the bottom of the income ladder were actually slightly greater than the gains in income at the middle.

Income inequality started to jump in 1982, after varying only slightly from 1967 to 1981 (Fig. 6.6).[8] This is largely in keeping with the trend in the wage premium for a Bachelor's degree. Earnings based on educational attainment changed during these same years: in 1979, those with a Bachelor's degree earned 40 percent more

Figure 6.6. Gini Coefficient for Household Incomes, 1967–2009[a]

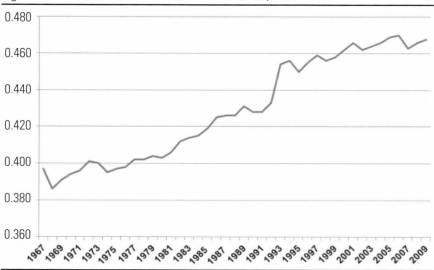

Source: US Census Bureau, Current Population Survey 2010.
a. The Gini coefficient measures the inequality of a distribution. A value of 0 expresses total equality, and a value of 1 expresses maximal inequality.

than those with a high school diploma and no postsecondary education ($44,792 versus $31,952 in inflation-adjusted 2005 dollars). By 1999, that wage premium had risen to 72 percent, with earnings of workers with a Bachelor's degree rising to $52,668 and earnings of workers with only a high school diploma falling to $30,586. By 2005, earnings had risen for both groups of workers ($54,502 and $31,242), but the wage premium had still increased modestly to 74 percent.

LIFETIME EARNINGS FROM COLLEGE ARE HIGH IN THE LONG TERM

College-educated workers earn more, but what is a degree really worth over a lifetime? A 2002 study from the Census Bureau estimated that in 1999 the average lifetime earnings for workers with a Bachelor's degree were $2.1 million ($2.7 million in 2009 dollars) or 75 percent more than earnings for workers with a high school diploma (Cheeseman Day & Newburger, 2002). Slightly more than a decade later, the wage premium for a college education has grown to 84 percent (Fig. 6.7).

Suppose people took the money they spent on college and invested it instead in AAA-rated, long-term government bonds. The investments would grow over a lifetime, but would the investment be more valuable than a college degree? The financial payoff from a college degree over forty working years is often measured differently because money in hand is more valuable than money in the future. To adjust for the difference, we calculate what economists and financiers call present value (PV) and examine a hypothetical cost-benefit analysis of attending college. Looking forward to the extra $1 million in wages earned over forty years, the PV reveals how much money is required at an assumed interest rate to yield the same amount in the future. Assuming an interest rate of 2.5 percent (the real interest rate of long-term government bonds in 2009), a conservative estimate of the PV for the lifetime average marginal return for a bachelor's degree over a high school diploma is about $300,000. To determine if a college degree is worth the expense, we must simply ensure that the discounted cost of the degree, which includes repayment of principal and interest, is less than $300,000 expressed in today's dollars.[9]

Figure 6.7. Estimated Median Lifetime Earnings by Education Level[a]

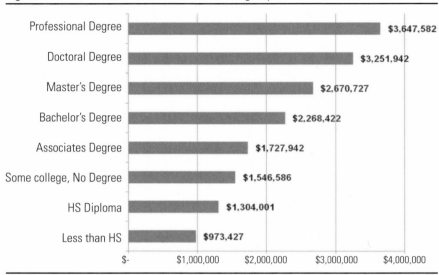

Source: Carnevale, Rose et al., 2011.
a. Median is used here because the average can be skewed by outliers or extreme values.

In addition, the economic costs of attending college should include the indirect cost of income forgone while students are in school plus the direct costs of tuition, books, and other necessities.[10] Two-thirds of students pay less than $15,000 per year for college, and more than three-quarters of students pay less than $24,000 per year in tuition and fees. Fewer than 5 percent of college students go to schools that cost more than $39,000 per year, according to the College Board, and almost 70 percent of these students do not pay the full sticker price (Baum & Ma, 2010).

For argument's sake, we have taken into consideration the larger of the estimates ($24,000 per year) for our calculations. We conclude that a four-year degree is estimated to cost about $80,000.[11] Costs for college are therefore well below the median expected net returns of $300,000. Furthermore, getting a Bachelor's degree is the path to graduate degrees and much higher earnings (37 percent of those with a Bachelor's get a graduate degree).

College is worth the cost not only in sheer economic terms, but also in terms of economic benefits such as career choice and employment stability. Workers with a college degree have had the lowest unemployment rates during the past three years, receiving the best possible shelter from the recession of 2007. They also have the best prospects for being hired in the recovery. They are the most trainable and adaptable workers in both good and bad economic times. Consequently, high school graduates and dropouts without postsecondary education or training are much more at risk of being left behind as the economy plods forward on the long march back to normalcy.[12]

A college education does not make one immune to economic recession. When it rains long enough and hard enough, everyone gets a little wet. In our current economy, where 59 percent of the population has at least some college education, even the most highly educated have lost jobs, and many college graduates have been scrambling for the reduced pool of jobs available. Unemployment rates at all education levels have climbed during the recession, and the unemployment rate of those with a Bachelor's degree or better reached a peak of 5 percent in November 2010 before declining again (Fig. 6.8).

Figure 6.8. Unemployment Rates by Level of Education, 1970–2010

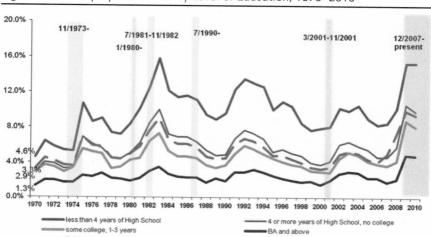

Source: U.S. Department of Labor, Bureau of Labor Statistics, Employment Situation, 2007–2010

a. Vertical gray lines indicate periods of recession.

Figure 6.8, which uses annual unemployment data from 1970 to the present, shows that workers with a Bachelor's degree were three times less likely to be unemployed than those with no high school diploma. In economic downturns, college degrees still make the best umbrellas, and college campuses not only provide the best rain shelters but also the launching pads for jobs and careers that will survive recession.[13]

The tangible benefits to postsecondary education, then, are clear. What's more, demand for postsecondary education has been increasing for decades, and the future promises more of the same.

THE DEMAND FOR POSTSECONDARY EDUCATION WILL CONTINUE TO INCREASE

Access to postsecondary education and training has become the essential goal for education reform in the K–12 system, and middle-class employability is now emerging as a key standard of educational adequacy in the postsecondary system. The statistics bear this out: since the early 1970s, the American economy has transformed from one that featured more jobs for high school dropouts than college graduates to one where the share of jobs for high school dropouts plunged from roughly one-third to one-tenth. In 1973, about 25 million jobs (28 percent) required applicants with at least some college education (Fig. 6.9).[14] By 2007, that number had nearly quadrupled to 91 million (59 percent) of all jobs in the U.S. economy.

The share of workers with an Associate's degree, postsecondary certificate, or some college has more than doubled from 12 percent to 27 percent of the workforce. The percentage of workers with a Bachelor's degree has more than doubled as well, from 9 percent in 1973 to 21 percent in 2007. The comparable percentage of workers with a Master's degree or better has increased at a slightly slower pace, from 7 percent to 11 percent over the same period.

The proportion of jobs with incumbents who have no postsecondary education and training has fallen commensurately. This declining share of opportunities for workers with some high school education or a high school diploma is now highly segregated by ten occupational clusters.[15] For example, by 2018 an estimated 61 million jobs (37 percent of all jobs) will be available for prime-age workers with a

Figure 6.9 Proportion of Jobs by Level of Required Education

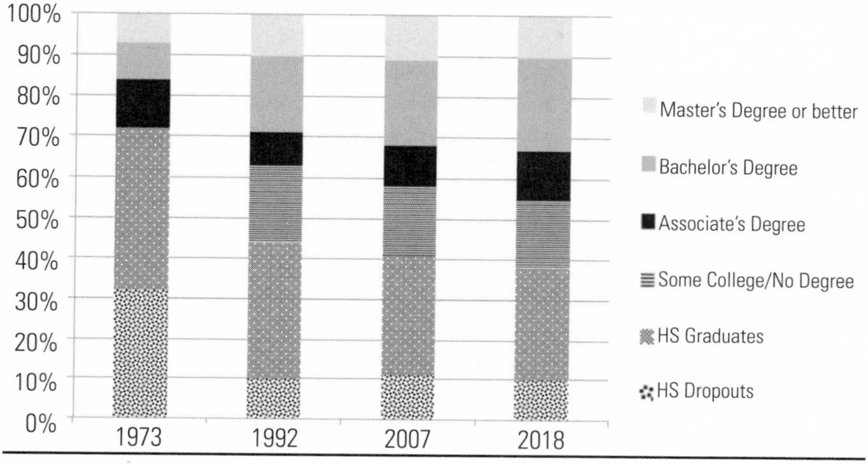

Source: Carnevale, Smith et al., 2010

high school diploma or less compared to 101 million jobs (36 percent of all jobs) for workers with at least some postsecondary education. Of those 61 million jobs, 87 percent will be found in only three occupational clusters: Blue Collar, Food and Personal Services, and Sales and Office Support. These particular clusters either have declining job opportunities or pay low wages. In addition, wage increases for people with a high school diploma or less are stagnant.

The proportion of workers who will need an Associate's degree, postsecondary certificate, or some college will increase from 27 percent in 2007 to 29 percent in 2018. The comparable share of workers who must have a Bachelor's degree will climb from 21 percent to 23 percent, while the number of jobs requiring a Master's degree or better may decline slightly, from 11 percent to 10 percent over the same period (Carnevale, Smith, & Strohl, 2010, pp. 13–14).

FROM AN ECONOMIC PERSPECTIVE, ALL JOBS AND ALL DEGREES ARE NOT EQUAL

Most data, including our own, understate the importance of postsecondary education and training because jobs data treat every job the same.[16] However, not all jobs are created equal. Workers with at least some postsecondary education have a better shot at full-time work and consistent work over a career. Low-wage service jobs account for about 20 percent of the workforce but only 14 percent of the hours worked in the economy (Autor & Dorn, 2009). Moreover, these jobs are commonly in low-wage service industries with large shares of part-time work or are jobs with very high turnover.

Some jobs that do not require postsecondary education provide opportunities for workers to settle into a career and earn a sustainable wage, particularly in manufacturing, professional and business services, and some technology positions.[17] The best opportunities for workers with a high school diploma or less are in male-dominated fields. For example, more than 80 percent of workers in blue-collar jobs that pay relatively good wages are male.

Many low-wage service jobs, however, are highly transitional; young people commonly take jobs in food services or other low-skill occupations as they work themselves through school or toward better, skilled jobs they can turn into a career. Roughly half the workers in low-skill, low-wage occupations move into higher wage categories within five years.

For an obvious example, many more doctors were once cashiers (before they finished their education) than cashiers who were once doctors, but the statistics treat the two jobs equally. For every new job for cashiers that will open up between 2008 and 2018, another thirteen will open up to replace people who leave cashier jobs. This is because of job turnover or "churn" as people in these jobs often leave the labor force or take a better-paying job. In contrast, for every new job for physicians, only 0.8 will open up to replace physicians who leave the occupation (Carnevale, Smith et al., 2010).

Just as jobs data treat all jobs alike, openings for low-skilled jobs are treated the same as those for long-term ones requiring higher education. This treatment exaggerates the significance of low-skilled jobs and, in turn, underestimates the demand for postsecondary education and training. Ultimately, about 11 percent of workers are stuck in low-wage, low-skill jobs in the bottom quartile of the wage distribution (Carnevale & Rose, 2001). In other words, as robust as the demand for higher education and training may seem in our forecasts, real demand may be even greater.

ALL COLLEGE COURSES, CERTIFICATES, AND DEGREES ARE NOT EQUAL

The traditional degree hierarchy from high school to PhD does not hold up when measured from an earnings perspective. Workers with higher degrees earn higher wages on average, but the overlap in earnings by degree level is significant (Fig. 6.10). Depending on industry and occupational choice, however, the link between better education and higher wages can sometimes be unclear. For instance, 28 percent of workers with an Associate's degree earn the same or more over the

Figure 6.10. Earnings Overlap among Workers with Different Levels of Education

	Less than high school	High school	Some college/ no degree	Associate's degree	Bachelor's degree	Master's degree	Doctoral degree
Professional degree	1.3%	2.4%	4.8%	4.9%	17.2%	24.2%	36.9%
Doctoral degree	2.3%	4.6%	8.6%	9.5%	26.7%	35.5%	—
Master's degree	4.6%	9.2%	15.9%	19.2%	39.9%	—	—
Bachelor's degree	7.3%	14.3%	23.1%	28.2%	—	—	—
Associate's degree	16.3%	29.8%	41.9%	—	—	—	—
Some college/ no degree	21.3%	36.6%	—	—	—	—	—
High school diploma	31.4%	—	—	—	—	—	—

How to read this chart: Beginning with the less than high school column and reading down, 1.3% of people with less than high school earn as much or more than the median earnings of someone with a Professional degree. Then 2.3% of people with less than high school earn as much or more than the median for someone with a Doctoral degree; 4.6% earn as much or more than the median for someone with a Master's degree, and so on.

course of their careers than their colleagues with a Bachelor's degree. About 23 percent of workers with some college but no degree earn the same amount or more than workers with a Bachelor's degree, and 40 percent of workers with a Bachelor's degree earn the same or more than their counterparts with a Master's degree (Carnevale, Rose, & Cheah, 2011).

Earnings can also vary more within a degree level than between degree levels. For example, while a Bachelor's degree garners an 84 percent wage premium over a high school diploma; the difference between the earnings for the top- and bottom-ranked Bachelor's degree is four times the wage difference between a high school diploma and a Bachelor's degree (Carnevale, Strohl, & Melton, 2011). Nonetheless, some awards and degrees are not worth the cost and debt burden, as the ongoing tensions between the federal government and for-profit schools demonstrate.

In addition, there is always a mismatch between a worker's skills and available jobs. Many people end up with the wrong degree in the wrong place at the wrong time. Others choose occupations that do not maximize earnings returns from their certificate or degree.

OCCUPATION MATTERS

The knowledge-based economy has not only shifted demand for postsecondary education, it has also fundamentally reshaped the way we think about careers. As we have moved from the industrial-based manufacturing economy, where a job was defined by the workplace, plant, and industry, work has become defined more by the tasks a worker performs. Today, the predominant unit of analysis for understanding the economy is occupation.

Although education matters enormously in determining earnings, an individual's earnings are not dependent solely on educational attainment. Occupation—the job someone works in—matters, too. Of course, occupation and educational attainment are closely linked, with some occupations requiring more education than others. Demand for workers with postsecondary education is tied tightly to occupations and the skills they require and more loosely to the industries in which those occupations reside.

Understanding the relationship between education and occupation is critical to understanding the forces driving demand for postsecondary education. Occupation is a simple, shorthand way of expressing all the tasks performed in a particular job and therefore the skills and level of formal education needed. While there is variation, occupations generally have similar requirements regardless of industry. Accountants, for example, perform comparable tasks whether they are working for a mining company or a hospital—the training required to do the work is virtually the same. As a result, the education requirements for occupations are relatively homogenous.

The educational requirement of an industry does not really pertain here. Industries are conglomerates of many different occupations and levels of educational demand. The day when people left high school, went to work in the local industry, and worked their way from the mail room to the corner office is no longer an option. Moreover, individuals who work in multiple occupations within a single industry (with the exception of the movement into management) over their lifetime are becoming rarer still.

The increasing complexity of work today requires more specific education and training focused on a particular occupation (labor-market specialization). More often now, education, training, and work are focused on the occupation, and careers reflect workers climbing an occupational hierarchy. Some occupations are tied tightly to particular industries (e.g., nurses in healthcare), but more and more occupations are dispersed broadly across industries

The best-paying jobs at the top of the education distribution overall are still doctors and nurses in the Healthcare Professional and Technical occupations, while managers and CEOs in Managerial and Professional Office jobs rank second for the size of their wage premiums. STEM jobs also pay well at every level, a trend consistent across time. Someone with an Associate's degree in a STEM occupation makes more than someone with a Master's degree working in Education.

Occupations that require the least amount of education still pay the lowest wages, however, even at the top of the education distribution. For example, college graduates earn only about $33,000 in Healthcare Support and $35,000 in Food and Personal Services. Although additional training accrues benefits in these occupational groupings, wage ceilings still make it impossible for these workers to climb comfortably into the middle class. The average wages of workers in Food and Personal Services has actually declined in real terms since the 1980s (Carnevale, Smith, & Strohl, 2010, p. 105).

Occupational choice also matters at the highest education levels. A Master's degree or better in Healthcare Professional, Managerial, and STEM occupations renders a vastly superior wage premium than a comparable degree in Food and Personal Services occupations. Ultimately, occupation-specific human capital ties people to their occupations and can lead to substantial wage premiums for specialized tasks.

Occupational choice highly correlates to earnings, regardless of educational attainment. High school dropouts in Managerial and Professional Office and STEM jobs, for instance, still earn twice as much as high school dropouts in Healthcare Support or Food and Personal Services jobs. Further, workers with a Bachelor's degree in Managerial and Professional Office or STEM occupations earned more on average than employees with a Master's degree or better in Blue Collar, Community Services and Arts, Education, Healthcare Support, and Food and Personal Services occupations.

MAJORS MATTER

Based on the wage results by occupational cluster, it necessarily follows that the earnings of individuals by undergraduate major also demonstrates that educational attainment is not the only factor driving earnings. While going to college is undoubtedly a wise decision, different majors have different economic value. Returns to different majors run a wide gamut primarily because different majors lead to different occupations. At the extreme, the highest earning major (Petroleum Engineering) earns 314 percent more at the median than the lowest-earning major (Counseling Psychology) (Fig. 6.11). The highest median earnings at the aggregate level are in Engineering majors ($75,000) and Computers and Mathematics majors ($70,000), while the lowest-earning majors are Psychology and Social Work ($42,000) and Education ($42,000) (Carnevale, Strohl, & Melton, 2011).

Figure 6.11. Median Earnings of Bachelor's Degree Holders by College Major

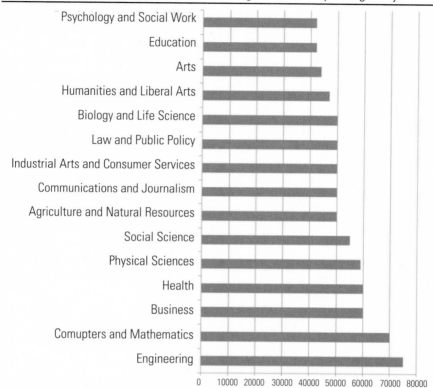

Source: Carnevale, Strohl, & Melton 2011, 36–37

COMMODIFICATION OR INTRINSIC VALUE?
HIGHER EDUCATION DOES NOT NEED TO CHOOSE

Some believe the increasing value of education may force a reckoning of narrow economic needs and broad educational goals, resulting in a commodification of education, where the social value of education is reduced to a mere product that can be bought, sold, or hired. Hence, the outcry from critics who lament that college students these days do not study enough Plato (Hacker & Dreifus, 2010). The critics are not entirely off the mark. Education has intrinsic as well as extrinsic value. The temptation to provide narrow vocational training rather than more general learning is strong in a market economy, especially in our current budgetary environment. In theory, the increasing power of economic markets in higher education can not only promote underinvestment in the value of self-knowledge and knowledge for its own sake but also reduce concern for the broader cultural and political value of knowledge in a democratic political system.

As the economic value of education increases, we need to remember that education, especially higher education, concerns more than dollars and cents. It should do more than provide new technology and new foot soldiers for the American economy. Even beyond these considerations, however, educators in secondary and postsecondary institutions have cultural and political missions to ensure that an educated citizenry can defend and promote our democratic ideals and freedom of thought.

We need to aspire to a dual bottom line in American higher education. A pragmatic balance can be struck between postsecondary education's growing economic role and its traditional cultural and political independence from economic forces. Ultimately, however, the inescapable reality is that ours is a society based on work. Those not equipped with the knowledge and skills necessary to get and keep good jobs are denied full social inclusion and tend to drop out of the mainstream culture, polity, and economy. In the worst cases, they are drawn into alternative cultures, political movements, and economic activities that threaten mainstream American life.

If secondary and postsecondary educators cannot fulfill their economic mission to help grow the economy and help youths and adults become successful workers, they will fail in their cultural and political missions to create good neighbors and good citizens. And increasing the economic relevance of education should, if done properly, extend the ability of educators to empower Americans to work in the world, rather than retreat from it.

NOTES

1. The Organisation for Economic Co-operation and Development (OECD) refers to a four-year degree as Type-A tertiary education.
2. Canada's and Japan's share of short-term degrees in the workforce are 24 percent and 19 percent respectively, compared with 10 percent for the United States.

3. We overstate the simplicity of labor supply and demand relationships here for the sake of clarity. In fact, the labor market is imperfect. Education and career decisions are heavily influenced by personal decisions. Further, politics often intrude on the labor market in the real world. State and federal governments, for example, set minimum wages, and workers can organize into unions to engage in collective bargaining. Government trade policies can affect the labor market, too, through imports produced by lower-paid workers from foreign countries. In addition, economists argue that employers sometimes pay higher wages than necessary to motivate their workers and help them identify with their companies, a concept called an efficiency wage.

4. See Autor, Katz, and Kearney (2008) and Hotchkiss and Shiferaw (2010) for quantitative proofs of this point.

5. Because of data limitations, we do not have complete historical data on workers with an Associate's degree, a postsecondary certificate, or some college/no degree. Although we analyze the wage premium for workers with a Bachelor's degree, it should be remembered that many other people obtain postsecondary education.

6. We would have liked to track the wage ratios for Associate's degree/high school diploma and Bachelor's degree /Associate's degree, but information for those receiving an Associate's degree (as distinct from some college/no degree) only became available in the Current Population Survey of 1992, after most of the increase in earnings inequality had occurred.

7. We use 2005 because it is the last year of data available in Goldin and Katz. Nonetheless, an average of the OECD data between 1998 and 2008 shows the same results.

8. Income information was first available in the U.S. Census Bureau's *Current Population Survey* in 1967.

9. For example, the PV of $1 million in forty years at slightly different interest rates will be $675,000 (1 percent), $453,000 (2 percent), or $307,000 (3 percent).

10. The direct costs per year for tuition and fees are $9,000; books, $1,500; and trips and extra costs, $1,500. Rent and food are not included; these costs are incurred whether one is attending college or working.

11. Salary foregone, which should be considered in the high school median earnings potential for four years, is excluded from the

immediate analysis because of the relatively high unemployment rates for recent young high school graduates irrespective of the state of the economy. We can, however, assume an average annual wage of $23,000 as income foregone for a college education.

12. Many critics have pointed out that the unemployment rate for recent college graduates is much higher than the rate for graduates as a whole. This is expected; college graduates typically have no labor-market experience. However, comparing the unemployment rate of recent college graduates, which was about 9 percent last year, with the overall unemployment rate of 9 percent presents a skewed picture of the benefits of college. It is more accurate to compare the unemployment rate for recent college graduates with that of recent high school graduates whose unemployment rate was about 35 percent last year, more than three times the rate for recent college graduates.

13. Recall that this very trend of increased college enrollment during hard economic times was observed during the Great Depression.

14. In this case the term *required* means employers paid applicants a significant premium for having a college degree.

15. The ten occupational clusters are Blue Collar, Community Services and Arts, Education, Food and Personal Services, Healthcare Professional and Technical, Healthcare Support, Managerial and Professional Office, Sales and Office Support, STEM (Science, Technology, Engineering, and Math), and the Social Sciences.

16. Our projections assume the United States was producing enough postsecondary graduates in the base year; therefore, we measure unmet demand going forward. Other evidence suggests we were not producing enough postsecondary graduates (Goldin & Katz, 2008; Carnevale & Rose, 2011).

17. A sustainable wage is one that exceeds the median, which can vary depending on the state where the job is located and the associated cost of living there. For the nation, the wage is about $35,000 per year.

REFERENCES

Autor, D. H., & Dorn, D. (2009). *The growth of low-skill service jobs in the United States and the polarization of the U.S. labor market.* Working Paper 15150 (July 2009), National Bureau of Economic Research. http://www.nber.org/papers/w15150.

Autor, D., Katz, L. F, & Kearney, M. S. (2008). Trends in U.S. wage inequality: Revising the revisionists. *The Review of Economics and Statistics 90* (2): 300–323.

Baum, S., & Ma, J. (2010). *Trends in college pricing 2010.* Trends in Higher Education Series. Washington, DC: The College Board. Available at http://trends.collegeboard.org/.

Carnevale, A. P. (1991). *America and the new economy: How new competitive standards are radically changing American workplaces.* Jossey-Bass Management Series. San Francisco: John Wiley and Sons.

Carnevale, A. P., & Rose, S. J. (2001). Low earners: Who are they? Do they have a way out? In R. Kazis & M. Miller (Eds.), *Low wage workers in the new economy* (pp. 45–67). Washington, DC: The Urban Institute Press.

Carnevale, A. P., & Rose, S. J. (2011). *The undereducated American.* Washington, DC: The Georgetown University Center on Education and the Workforce. Available at http://cew.georgetown.edu/undereducated.

Carnevale, A. P., Rose, S. J., & Cheah, B. (2011). *The college payoff: Education, occupations, lifetime earnings.* Washington, DC: The Georgetown University Center on Education and the Workforce. Available at http://cew.georgetown.edu/collegepayoff.

Carnevale, A. P., Smith, N., & Strohl, J. (2010). *Help wanted: Projections of jobs and education requirements through 2018.* Washington, DC: The Georgetown University Center on Education and the Workforce. Available at http://cew.georgetown.edu/JOBS2018/.

Carnevale, A. P., & Strohl, J. (2010). How increasing college access is increasing inequality, and what to do about it. In R. D. Kahlenberg (Ed.), *Rewarding the strivers: Helping low income students succeed in college.* New York: Century Foundation Press. Available at http://tcf.org/publications/2010/9/how-increasing-college-access-is-increasing-inequality-and-what-to-do-about-it.

Carnevale, A. P., Strohl, J., & Melton, M. (2011). *What's it worth? The economic value of college majors.* Washington, DC: The Georgetown University Center on Education and the Workforce. Available at http://cew.georgetown.edu/whatsitworth.

Cheeseman Day, J., & Newburger, E. C. (2002). *The big payoff: Educational attainment and synthetic estimates of work-life earning.* Current Population Reports. P-23 Series Special Papers (July): 23-210. Washington, DC: U.S. Census Bureau. Available at http://www.census.gov/prod/2002pubs/p23-210.pdf.

Cohen, J., & Balz, D. (2011). Poll: Whites without college degrees especially pessimistic about economy. *The Washington Post*, February 22. Available at http://www.washingtonpost.com/wpdyn/content/article/2011/02/22/AR2011022200005.html.

Eck, A. (1993). Job-related education and training: Their impact on earnings. *Monthly Labor Review Online 116* (10): 21–38. Available at http://www.bls.gov/mlr/1993/10/contents.htm.

Goldin, C., & Katz, L. F. (2008). *The race between education and technology.* Cambridge: Belknap Press of Harvard University Press.

Hacker, A., and Dreifus, C. (2010). *Higher education? How colleges are wasting our money and failing our kids—and what we can do about it.* New York: St Martin's Griffin.

Hotchkiss, J. L., & Shiferaw, M. (2010). *Decomposing the education-wage gap: Everything but the kitchen sink.* Working Paper 2010-12 (August 2010), Federal Reserve Bank of Atlanta. Available at http://www.frbatlanta.org/documents/pubs/wp/wp1012.pdf.

Krueger, A. B. (1993). How computers have changed the wage structure: Evidence from microdata, 1984–89. *The Quarterly Journal of Economics 108* (1): 33–60. doi:10.2307/2118494.

Organisation for Economic Co-operation and Development. (2010). *Education at a glance 2010: OECD indicators.* Paris, France: Directorate for Education, Organisation for Economic Co-operation and Development.

Rothstein, J. M. (2004). College performance predictions and the SAT. *Journal of Econometrics 121* (1–2): 297–317. doi:10.1016/j.jeconom.2003.10.003.

Thresher, B. A. (1989). *College admissions and the public interest.* New York: The College Board.

Turkheimer, E., Haley, A., Waldron, M., D'Onofrio, B., & Gottesman, I. I. (2003). Socioeconomic status modifies heritability of IQ in young children. *Psychological Science* 14 (November): 623–628. doi: 10.1046/j.0956-7976.2003.psci_1475.x.

7

THE ESSENTIAL ROLE OF COMMUNITY COLLEGES IN REBUILDING THE NATION'S COMMUNITIES AND ECONOMIES

JAMES JACOBS

ABSTRACT

As human resource issues become more important in the economic development process, the American community college is playing a greater role in the decisions made by companies and communities. Community colleges bring much strength to economic development issues. These institutions often are located in close proximity to major concentrations of private sector employment, have experience with technical training and meeting the needs of underprepared adults, and enjoy the flexibility to be able to offer programs and courses to suit the specific needs of their communities. Some of the roles community colleges have played in their communities include offering technical education to serve new technology industries and entrepreneurial training for displaced technical workers, developing local incubators for industry, and engaging in applied research projects with local businesses and industries. Community colleges are also beginning to develop relationships with local economic development agencies and four-year institutions in order to create and implement comprehensive economic revitalization strategies.

INTRODUCTION

In February 2009, Macomb Community College (MCC), in Michigan, held an unusual student "graduation" in a suburban Detroit office building. These students already had their Auto Body Design Associate's degrees from MCC, often acquired years before. There were twenty-five "graduates"—all males, many of whom had ten to fifteen years of experience as auto body designers working for original equipment manufacturers (OEMs) and their suppliers in the Detroit Metropolitan area. They were also unemployed, because their skills were no longer needed as a result of the downsizing of the domestic auto industry. However, with workforce development funding provided by the federal government and administered through a local workforce board, MCC and a local employment service firm, Talascend, provided these students with the opportunity to learn the lexicon and techniques of pipe design need in oil refineries. At the end of the program, the college helped connect these students to companies in Texas and New Mexico, who were in need of individual with pipe design skills. The end goal, however, was not for these individuals to leave the Detroit area. Rather, the strategy was to seek design work for projects that could be brought back into their communities, creating new markets and new opportunities for designers in the local market. This is one small example of how community colleges help create new jobs in their communities.

Macomb's small experimental program was not an atypical response by a community college. Following the great recession that began in 2008, lack of employment became a fundamental part of the "new normal" in many communities across the United States. High unemployment rates motivated community colleges to engage in activities to preserve jobs in their regions and extend economic development efforts within their communities. Their activities call attention to one of the often hidden assets that can be utilized in the struggle to stimulate economic development in many communities. Indeed, the community college can be an important asset for the development of economies across the United States. To understand this developing role for community colleges, it is worthwhile to start by examining the evolution of economic development strategies.

THE CHANGING NATURE OF ECONOMIC DEVELOPMENT STRATEGIES

What is meant by the term *economic development* is undergoing an important transition as economies move from being factor-driven to innovation-driven (Lane, 2012—chapter 1 in this volume). During the 1980s, the term referred to a process by which land preparation, access to suitable transportation such as railroad lines, and a number of other factors related to the physical assets of a site were marketed to a company for a relocation decision. These were combined with attractive tax incentives offered to prospective new investors in a community (Storper & Walker, 1984). If there was any discussion of training and education, it was restricted to the educational credentials of the technical and management staff of the company. In some instances, if firms had specific technical needs, they located in close proximity to a major research university, which resulted in the famous technology development clusters such as Route 128 in Boston, Research Triangle in North Carolina, and Silicon Valley, located near Stanford University (Schultz, 2012—chapter 5 in this volume).

As industries became more complex and knowledge-driven, this approach to economic development began to evolve, and the skills of workers at all levels of production and development needed to be enhanced. Much of the writing on this transition has focused on the need for more "knowledge" workers to help foster innovation. However, the implementation of innovation requires that production-oriented workers also enhance their own skill sets. This was particularly true as more computer-based tools and equipment entered the workplace. Initially, corporations viewed this equipment as money savers that would eliminate many jobs. However, corporate leaders soon learned that to realize the full productivity of their computerized workforce required a workforce with the skill set to run and repair the new computer-based equipment (Jacobs, 1994). This phenomenon is similar to that found in the broader economy, in that the benefits of new technologies cannot be realized unless the workers have the skills to be able to take advantage of those technologies. To take full advantage of potential productivity increases, companies began to emphasize human capital transformation. This meant not only the need to further the educational levels of all workers, but also the enhancement of specific skills of hourly workers.

However, companies could not simply send their workers to training seminars. Even when these skill sets can be "taught" through company-specific programs, the prospective workers must possess foundational learning skills to be capable of benefiting from this new training. That is, workers need to be able to learn, before they can acquire more skills and adapt those skills to their specific working environments. For example, when many Japanese and foreign firms set up shop in the United States in the 1990s, they recognized the need to adapt American workers to their foreign organizational culture. As part of the hiring process, they used elaborate assessment models to ensure that they selected a workforce that was able to accept continuous training at the workplace (Babson, 1995). This allowed the foreign firms to retrain the American workers to be able to adapt to the different organizational culture and technical expectations of the job. However, many companies do not have the capacity to implement training programs or hire an entirely new workforce. Instead, they rely on community and technical colleges to train students in certain skill sets and teach them to be critical thinkers.

Furthermore, the economic development considerations of community colleges focus not only on individuals, but also on retaining and growing local employment opportunities. For example, during the 1980s and 1990s, there began to be a buildup of support businesses and industries around large manufacturing centers. These firms became important for quickly providing the raw materials and parts that manufactures need to produce their outputs. Their effectiveness and efficiency were in part based on their close proximity to each other, allowing for goods and services to flow quickly and, when necessary, adjustments in the supply chain to be performed in a timely fashion. In good economic times, when manufacturing was booming, this was positive because all firms benefited. However, if one major manufacturer left the community or went out of business, it had a significant ripple effect upon all those firms that remained (Osterman, Kochan, Locke, & Piore, 2001).

These trends had enormous significance for the fashioning of economic development–related public policies. In the early 1990s, states began making funding available for customized training programs as a means to attract new investment. The promise of training workers in specific fields was meant to attract financial capital from outside the state. Most states rapidly adopted such practices in the 1990s as a response to the economic downturn experienced in the 1980s. The desire was to attract international investment, particularly from companies in Europe and Asia that were concerned about the availability of a workforce trained to handle their specific job expectations. In many states, programs were organized utilizing government training funds for the development of programs for incumbent workers in a specific industry or sector (Rosenfeld, 1992).

COMMUNITY COLLEGES AND WORKFORCE DEVELOPMENT

Emphasis on human capital as an essential vehicle for economic growth provided an enormous boost to the role of community colleges in economic development activities. The ultimate effect can be quite widespread given the vast network of community colleges spread across the nation and the number of students that attend them. As of 2011, there were more than 1,200 community colleges in the United States. They enrolled 40 percent of the 17.6 million college students in the United States. Moreover, more students start their undergraduate education at a community college than at any other type of postsecondary institution (U.S. Department of Education, 2011). While these institutions largely began as a means for preparing students to pursue a baccalaureate degree, their close ties with the local communities meant that one of the essential missions of community colleges became workforce development (Cohen & Brawer, 2008). Broadly speaking, the community college is the most accessible institution for educating the local workforce; and their popularity seems to grow as more occupations require more than a high school degree for entry-level work. Community colleges now prepare new workers within degree programs focused on business, allied health, and manufacturing occupational areas, as well as noncredit technical programs directed at incumbent workers or short-term programs for unemployed workers who need skill upgrades to help them find work. The American Association of Community Colleges (2011a, 2011b) maintains that community colleges provide some form of education to more than 60 percent of all healthcare providers, more than 70 percent of all first responders, and a majority of all elementary and secondary school teachers.

For many reasons, community colleges have emerged as drivers in the preparation of the nation's workforce. First, these institutions are located within a thirty minute drive of almost every major industrial concentration in the United States. They are easily accessible to both incumbent workers and those dislocated from their industry and are willing to customize both credit and noncredit programs to fit the needs of their communities.

Second, more than any other existing educational and training institution, community colleges maintain a comprehensive mixture of technical and academic faculty to deal with the diverse needs of industrial and business communities. Many community college faculty, both full-time and part-time, have work experience with a specific industry, and many faculty continue to engage with those industries as part of their teaching and research expectations. These experiences allow them to be familiar with the needs of the that industry and the specific learning requirements of current and future workers. This experience enables them to be able to integrate learning of basic foundation skills (e.g., mathematics, communication, and reading) within their technical training courses. In addition, many colleges maintain "advanced technology centers," with computer-based industrial equipment that can be used by adults to simulate real work experiences.

Third, whereas in the past community colleges focused their technical training efforts at entry-level jobs in various sectors of construction, healthcare, and manufacturing, there are increasing efforts to connect technical training with occupations that require four-year degrees. Designers are taught the skills at two-year programs to work in auto parts design, but encouraged to continue their studies in a design engineering program at a four-year institution. Programs devoted to electronics, mechanics, and informational technology are merging into "mechatronics" courses, which then transfer to engineering technology degrees in baccalaureate programs. Outside of manufacturing, many community colleges maintain teacher preparation programs, pre–social work courses, and business and information technology programs that are connected to four-year programs through articulation agreements that help students manage the transfer smoothly. In the past, students entered a community college vocational program as a terminal degree; however, the current trend is for an increasing number of students to anticipate transferring to one of the technical four-year programs—either right from the college or after a few years in the field (Jacobs, 2004; Lane, 2003).

As a result of this increasing demand for baccalaureate degrees, community colleges, in at least 17 states, maintain significant four-year programs on, or in close proximity to, their campuses (Lewin, 2009). Many have constructed "University Centers," which house four-year programs at their campuses. These centers are generally outposts of local four-year institutions that offer their courses at the community college. For example, Macomb Community College houses a branch of Michigan State University's Osteopathic Medical School. Beyond hosting a four-year institution, a few community colleges have even attempted to launch their own baccalaureate programs, often in specific applied technologies that are underserved by four-year institutions in the area (Lewin, 2009). The comprehensive community college has evolved into an organization that can handle short-term training, often in noncredit programs, while also providing a bridge or a direct conduit to baccalaureate degree programs.

ECONOMIC DEVELOPMENT ACTIVITIES OF COMMUNITY COLLEGES

There are four distinct areas where community colleges have developed significant engagement in economic development activities. First is preparing high-skilled technicians who will support the development of innovation that will likely drive future job growth in areas such as biotechnology, information technology, advance manufacturing, cybertechnology, and sustainable fuels. These are individuals who combine rigorous conceptual knowledge of science and mathematics with their practical applications in the specific industrial sectors. In 1992, Congress recognized that a problematic skills gap existed between the existing workforce and the skill needs of the emerging industries. In an attempt to redress this issue, it passed the Scientific and Advanced Technology Act (SATA), which allocated $35 million to the National Science Foundation for the development of advanced technology training programs at community colleges. For the past two decades, the Advanced Technology Education program established by SATA has provided more than $720 million to community and technical colleges in the United States to develop curriculum and programs that have played a role in anchoring specific technology sectors within the United States (Hull, 2011). These programs produce many of the technicians who provide the necessary local infrastructure for industry to grow and expand (Hull, 2011).

A second way in which community colleges serve as economic drivers is the creation of entrepreneurial programs aimed at displaced technical workers. These programs are designed to provide technical workers with the business skills to establish their own companies and/or better market their existing skill sets. In the past four years, the domestic auto industry has gone through a period of considerable downsizing. Individuals with technical skills in areas such as electronics and design were laid off from their jobs because of the shrinking of their companies. Many of these layoffs have come in the Detroit region, the historic home to America's auto industry. In response, community colleges in Michigan, Ohio, and Indiana have developed entrepreneurial skills programs for these individuals. The goal is for the retrained workforce to replace jobs lost through downsizing of major corporations by attracting or building small businesses. In fact, these programs have helped grow the number of jobs in places such as Lorain, Ohio, Kokomo, Indiana, and Detroit, Michigan, where companies have been formed to win jobs in other manufacturing industries (Macomb Community College, 2011).

A variant of this approach has been established in a creative national program initiated by the investment firm Goldman Sachs to establish economic growth in underserved communities. This program engages the local community college to deliver specific entrepreneurial training for indigenous small businesses with the intention of creating jobs in poor urban neighborhoods. Entitled "10,000 Small Businesses," the program has now been established at community colleges in urban communities such as New Orleans, Los Angles, Houston, Chicago, and New York. The initial results are extremely successful in growing jobs within communities with high unemployment and few institutions that offer job opportunities. The goal is to reach ten thousand small businesses and create jobs in communities that have attracted limited other investment (McGill Murphy, 2011).

Third, community colleges can play a role in the actual formation of companies through a business incubator approach. Many community colleges have formed specific structures that provide startup help and some form of technical assistance to new firms. While many four-year institutions have been actively engaged in the creation of incubators, some community colleges have begun to recognize they have a comparative advantage in terms of being able to support the creation of small businesses in specific fields where the community college has existing expertise. For example, LaGuardia Community College CUNY maintains a business incubator where fashion designers and artists can take initial steps to enter the New York City market with their creations. Mott Community College, in Flint, Michigan, along with several community partners, maintains a business incubator that offers support services to aspiring entrepreneurs in the region. In another approach, Lorain Community College (Elyria, Ohio), not only maintains a business incubator site, but also has created a local innovation fund which has become a source of capital for companies within the incubator. More than $4.9 million in the past four years has been awarded to seventy-one companies by the innovation fund, creating hundreds of new jobs in northeast Ohio.[1] The incubators allow local individuals interested in starting a company to take advantage of the technical and business expertise at the community college and receive the support they need to create the company.

Another variant of this approach is the use of the community college to aid current firms in refocusing their businesses from a shrinking industrial sector to another, more attractive, sector. The state of Michigan has initiated Procurement and Technical Centers (PTAC) at many Michigan community college campuses.[2] These PTACs are responsible for providing assistance to firms who wish to gain access to federal contracts in new areas beyond their current expertise. In many manufacturing communities this has meant that firms have shifted their product development and manufacturing away from the automobile industry and toward defense manufacturing. At Macomb Community College in the past year, the PTAC was responsible for the development of $18.5 million in contract awards in 2011, which created thirty new firms and more than 360 jobs in the area served by the center (Macomb Community College, 2011).

A fourth, and perhaps the most interesting form of economic development from the perspective of the community college mission, is the engagement of these institutions in specific applied research projects. As compared to many research-driven colleges and universities, community colleges tend to be more accessible to very small companies. Small firms often lack the knowledge of how to interact with the major research universities—and their issues are often very specific and their "research" questions could be considered mundane, not cutting-edge. Many community colleges have laboratory space and faculty that can engage in specific action-based research projects with companies, which can lead to small, but important, innovations that could lead to job creation. For example, Lorain Community College helped design a package for shipping small computer devices through the mail without damaging them. Macomb Community College has pursued a program with Siemens in the construction of electric vehicles to test their performance abilities. In North Carolina, local applied technology centers were located on community college campuses to develop research projects for the biotechnology industry. In fact, many community colleges maintain advanced technology centers for the express purpose of having companies bring specific problems for resolution through collaboration between the faculty of the college and the workers of the company (Rosenfeld, Jacobs & Liston, 2003).

CONCLUSION

The new roles being played by the community colleges in fostering economic development have yet to be documented fully, and their impact has not been measured in any systematic form. Many of these initiatives remain as new experiments, which have the potential to contribute to creating employment opportunities for the millions of Americans currently experiencing long-term unemployment as the result of the great recession. These efforts seem to evidence the emergence of yet another mission for community colleges. In addition to meeting the skill needs of manufacturers and training workers; these institutions are spurring the development of economic opportunities through the support and creation of new firms within their communities.

However, to take advantage of these new opportunities it becomes critical for community colleges institutions to be aligned with two other important economic development actors. First are the local economic development groups both public and private within communities. These organizations have rarely involved community colleges in the initial negotiations with companies or the development of strategies to entice specific companies or sectors into communities. This seems a problematic oversight as community colleges can play an important role in the development and growth of new and relocated firms. Indeed, in many Midwestern communities, the local community college has emerged as an important institutional anchor in local economic development efforts (Vey, Austin, & Bradley, 2010).

The second group that could partner with community colleges on economic development matters is four-year public colleges and universities. While community colleges have worked closely with their four-year counterparts on curriculum and course offerings, there has been little engagement on issues such as research and specific skills training of incumbent engineers and managers of many local companies. Much as community colleges have developed articulation agreements on curricular matters, it may be possible to create similar arrangements on research projects. Community colleges currently assist with applied research projects that support the productivity and growth of startup companies. In addition, this can include practical courses in accounting and basic management classes, which aid individuals in the writing of business plans and product development strategies. As firms become more sophisticated, their research and product development needs can expand beyond the capacities of the community college and could be of interest to students and researchers at a four-year institution. It could be useful if partnerships existed between two-year and four-year institutions to facilitate the support of increasingly complex and practical research projects. Yet, in practice such relationships are still uncommon.

More than three years later, the impact of the great recession upon the American economy is still being felt. Recovery efforts remain fragile, and there remains a need for increased economic development to create employment and economic activities. Revitalization of the economy will require experimentation with new strategies to promote economic development and job growth. Community colleges can and should be part of these new strategies. Collaboration among educational leaders, local economic development organizations, business and industry, and state officials will be required to realize the full benefits of community colleges as economic drivers.

NOTES

1. For more information about LaGuardia Community College's incubator see http://www.nydesigns.org/; Mott Community College's incubator see http://www.mcc.edu/; and Lorrain Community College and the Innovation fund see http://www.innovationfundneohio.com.
2. PTACS are now located nationwide and information is available from the U.S. Small Business Development Center (http://www.sba.gov/content/procurement-technical-assistance-centers-ptacs). More information about PTACs in Michigan is available at http://www.ptacsofmichigan.org/.

REFERENCES

American Association of Community Colleges. (2011a). A data-driven examination of the impact of associate and bachelor's degree programs on the nation's nursing workforce. Available at http://www.aacc.nche.edu/Publications/Briefs/Pages/pb03222011.aspx.

American Association of Community Colleges. (2011b). *First responders: Community colleges on the front line of security.* Available at http://www.aacc.nche.edu/Publications/Reports/Documents/firstresponders.pdf.

Babson, S. (Ed.). (1995). *Lean work: Empowerment and exploitation in the global auto industry.* Detroit: Wayne State University Press.

Cohen, A., & Brawer, F. *The American community college*, 5th edition. San Francisco: Jossey-Bass.

Community College Baccalaureate Association. (2011). Philosophy, purpose, and mission. Available at http://www.accbd.org/about/philosophy-purpose-mission/.

Hull, D. (2011). *Career pathways for stem technicians.* Washington, DC: National Science Foundation.

Jacobs, J. (1994). Skills and educational requirements. In G. Salvendy (Ed.), *Design of work and development of personnel in advanced manufacturing.* (pp. 159-186). New York: Wiley.

Jacobs, J. (2004). Integrating workforce development and institutional requirements. In W. J. Rothwell, P. E. Gerity, & E. A.

Gaertner (Eds.), *Linking training to performance.* (pp. 25-32). Washington, DC: AACC Press.

Lane, J. E. (2003). Studying community colleges and their students: Context and research issues. In M. C. Brown & J. E. Lane (Eds.), *Studying diverse students and institutions: Challenges and considerations* (pp. 51–68). (New Directions for Institutional Research, volume 118). San Francisco: Jossey-Bass.

Lane, J. E. (2012). Higher education and economic competitiveness. In J. E. Lane & D. B. Johnstone (Eds.), *Universities and colleges as economic drivers* (pp. 1–30). Albany: State University of New York Press.

Lewin, T. (2009). Community colleges challenge hierarchy with 4-year degrees. *New York Times*, May 3, p. A23.

Macomb Community College. (2011). *PTAC newsletter* (November).

McGill Murphy, R. (2011). Goldman Sachs's give to 10,000 small businesses. *Fortune Magazine.* January 18. Available at http://money.cnn.com/2011/01/17/smallbusiness/goldman_sachs_entrepreneurs.fortune/index.htm.

Osterman, P., Kochan, T. A., Locke, R., & Piore, M. J. (2001). *Working in America: A blueprint for the new labor market.* Cambridge: MIT Press.

Rosenfeld, S. A. (1992). *Competitive manufacturing: New strategies for regional development.* New Brunswick: Rutgers University Press.

Rosenfeld, S. A., Jacobs, J., & Liston, C. D. (2003). Targeting clusters, achieving excellence. *Community College Journal 73* (6), 34–40.

Schultz, L. I. (2012). University industry government collaboration for economic growth. In J. E. Lane & D. B. Johnstone (Eds.), *Universities and colleges as economic drivers* (pp. 129–162). Albany: State University of New York Press.

Storper, M., & Walker, R. (1984). Spatial division of labor: Labor and location of industries. In L. Sawers & W. Tabb (Eds.), *Sunbelt snowbelt: Urban development and regional planning.* New York: Oxford University Press.

United States Department of Education. (2011). *The condition of education 2011.* Washington, DC: Author.

Vey, J. S., Austin, J. C., Bradley, J. (2010). *The next economy: Economic recovery and transformation in the Great Lakes region.* Washington, DC: Brookings Institution.

8

THE INTERNATIONAL DIMENSIONS OF HIGHER EDUCATION'S CONTRIBUTIONS TO ECONOMIC DEVELOPMENT

JASON E. LANE AND TAYA L. OWENS

ABSTRACT

This chapter analyzes the role of higher education in international trade and investment. We first examine how colleges and universities address international measures in seventy institutional economic impact reports. These reports highlight three core areas of importance for institutions: educating international students, training a globally competitive workforce, and attracting international trade. We then review two of the more prominent international aspects of higher education: the movement of students and institutions across borders. With more students than ever traveling abroad, this chapter takes an in-depth look at current trends, national policies, and challenges regarding international student mobility. Finally, we examine a burgeoning realm of cross-border activity: multinational institutions and their role in foreign direct investment. Given the paucity of economic impact studies that directly address cross-border campuses and students, this chapter concludes by outlining a research agenda to inform a focused discussion of higher education's international economic engagements.

INTRODUCTION

Analyses of higher education's role in economic development tend to follow a domestic perspective. As discussed throughout this book, colleges and universities can be significant drivers of economic growth for the communities where they are located. These institutions improve the workforce, create jobs, foster innovation, and attract new business and industry. However, as globalization has fostered a worldwide market for goods and services, higher education is no longer a resource confined exclusively to the domestic domain. Both political and economic borders have become porous, allowing individuals and institutions to move more freely among nations and economies.

Increasingly, the local impact of higher education needs to be understood through the global context in which it exists. Higher education institutions attract students and resources from beyond immediate communities, and indeed beyond national borders. As beacons for international investment, some colleges and universities believe they can support the development or expansion of international trade within their local communities. Moreover, they attest to play a critical role in developing a workforce that is globally competitive; a workforce that is crucial for helping existing businesses expand internationally and attracting international businesses to set up shop nearby. This vision of international impact purports that economic activities grounded in local communities expand as ever-mobile graduates relocate internationally and as institutions invest their own financial and academic capital in foreign markets, contributing to other economies.

Despite the growing importance of higher education to international economics, there remain very few studies of these important economic contributions. There are two primary reasons for this omission. First, universities have only recently been thought of as having an important role in the international marketplace. Second, measures for determining the economic contributions of higher education at the international level are scattered throughout national and international surveys, as few agencies seek to compile this type of information. However, that such efforts are not (or cannot yet be) systemically analyzed does not signify that such activity does not occur or that it is marginal.

The purpose of this chapter is to examine the intersection of higher education institutions and the international aspects of economic development. In part one of this chapter, we explore the extent to which institutions in the United States consider the international dimensions of economic development in their own activities. We examine, through a content analysis, seventy economic impact reports produced by U.S. postsecondary institutions and systems in the last decade. Part two discusses policy and measurement issues concerning the economic impact of international student mobility, the largest component of the international trade of higher education. Part three focuses on the emergence of cross-border higher education as a form of foreign direct investment. The chapter concludes by setting forth a research agenda focusing on the growing role higher education plays in international trade and investment.

PART I: INSTITUTIONAL PERSPECTIVES— THINKING GLOBALLY

For at least three decades, colleges and universities have produced economic impact reports to demonstrate their local economic contributions; and, mostly for public institutions, demonstrate the return on investment of state appropriations to higher education (Leslie & Slaughter, 1992; Siegfried, Sanderson, & McHenry, 2007; McHenry, Sanderson, & Siegfried, 2012—chapter 3 in this volume). These reports serve as institutions' primary statements about the depth and breadth of their economic engagements. As such they serve as an exemplary means for understanding the dimensions with which institutional leaders prioritize, measure, and evaluate international economic activities, at least in terms of how they choose to communicate these ideas to external constituencies.

We reviewed seventy economic impact reports written by colleges and universities in the United States in the decade between 2001 to 2011. These reports include a broad cross-section of institutions from across the United States, including forty-eight public institutions, fourteen private nonprofit institutions, and eight state systems or regional consortia from thirty-six states across the country. The content analysis of the economic impact reports focused on determining to what extent institutions (1) prioritize global reach in these

Table 8.1. Top Three International Themes in Economic Statements

Theme	# of Institutions
International Students	22
Globally Competitive Workforce	15
Attracting International Trade	11

Source: Institutional economic impact reports

institutional reports through statements of recognition or intent; and, (2) measure or evaluate these activities through various indicators relative to institutional strategic visions. As is to be expected, the reports focused primarily on domestic measures, contributions, and contexts.

Our analysis revealed that forty-one of the seventy (58 percent) reports included some mention of the institution's global context.[1] Among those forty-one reports, three dominant themes emerged: (1) attracting international students; (2) educating a globally competitive workforce; and (3) helping attract international trade (see Table 8.1).

As illustrated in Table 8.1, only the theme of attracting international students appeared in more than half of the forty-one reports that acknowledged a global context. In fact, in many of the reports, no more than a few sentences were dedicated to global/international topics. Very few reports took as direct an approach as the University of Texas at Austin (2011), which declared in large bold font that the institution possessed "Global Reach, Local Impact." The report states:

> The University of Texas at Austin has about 20,000 international alumni. More than 5,700 students from more than 125 countries were enrolled for fall term 2009, the seventh-highest enrollment of international students in the nation. The estimated contribution to the Austin economy from international students enrolled at the university is about $132 million. (University of Texas at Austin, 2011, p. 6)

Institutions such as the University at Buffalo, University of Wisconsin, and the University of Virginia touted their role in raising international awareness of the region in which they are located and their critical role in attracting international investment in to the local economy. The University at Buffalo (UB) stated the issue this way:

> With the heavy international presence at its campuses, UB plays an important role in expanding the global awareness of Buffalo Niagara. For many overseas, the first time they hear of Buffalo is when they hear about UB. This association helps to cultivate an international image of Buffalo Niagara as a region that is plugged into the knowledge-based economy. Closer to home, UB's national profile assists efforts to re-brand the region from a snowy factory town to a center for innovation. (Foster et al., 2007, p. 23)

The University of Virginia went a bit farther in trying to rhetorically link state appropriations to increased out-of-state economic returns:

> The status of the University of Virginia as a nationally rec-ognized center of excellence in teaching and research lever-ages the state government's expenditures into a considerable inflow of economic value to the state. Investments in excel-lent teaching and research have increased the value of the University to knowledge customers from around the world. As the University's reputation has risen, the net flow of funds into the state has increased dramatically. (Knapp & Shobe, 2007, p. 10)

The University of Wisconsin makes a similar statement, linking their international prominence to the success of their economy and local businesses:

> The presence of a world class university in a state that is aver-age in population and economic resources creates a level of national and international recognition that helps the state in commerce and business development. (NorthStar Economics, 2011, p. 19)

Measuring reputational impact proves much more difficult than merely stating that there is a relationship between an institution's reputation and the economic prosperity of the local region. For many institutions, particularly those known widely overseas or who serve a large number of foreign students, benefits of ranking and reputation assume a spillover effect whereby knowledge of the institution leads to knowledge of the region, which may assist with facilitating international trade or foreign investment. In none of the reports was there a direct measure of reputational effect; although some did attempt to provide evidence of their international reputation. First, several institutions included some reference to their inclusion in international rankings. Second, institutions would list the number of international recognitions garnered by faculty. Third, one institution, the University at Buffalo, tracked the number of mentions the institution received in international media outlets (Foster et al., 2007). In all cases the measures were listed in a descriptive fashion, allowing readers to draw their own conclusion between the stated measure and the impact on the region's international reputation.

International Students

Higher education not only supports international trade in other areas, it also serves as a form of international trade in its own right. Like insurance and finance, higher education is considered a tradable service. Indeed, the national estimates of its economic impact have been substantial. For the United States, higher education consistently ranks among the top ten service exports. The economic contribution of tuition and living expenses of international students studying in the United States was estimated at around $20 billion in 2009 (NAFSA, 2011). Drilling down even farther, NAFSA (2011) also provides state by state economic impact statements For example, in Missouri and New York, international students in academic year 2010–11 were estimated to have contributed $383 million and $2.4 billion, respectively, to the state economy.[2] On the other side of the world, education services exports was valued in 2008 as Australia's leading service export and third largest overall export behind coal and iron ore, contributing $A15 billion to the economy (Australian Education International, 2009a, 2009b).[3] Yet, very few of the economic impact reports that we reviewed acknowledge the economic impact of higher education as a tradable service.

Across the reports, the most common approach to measuring the international aspects of their economic impact was to provide a count of the number of international students in attendance at an institution. The largest component of higher education's international trade comes in the form of students studying outside of their home nation. Twenty-two of the economic impact reports made specific mention of international students as part of their descriptive write up. While almost all of the reports differentiated between in-state and out-of-state students, it was only these twenty-two that specifically referenced foreign students. Very few reports provided a separate economic impact statement just for international students, such as Texas did in the statement listed in the beginning of this section. In most cases, the reports merely listed a number of international students attending the institution and grouped their economic contribution in with all out-of-state students. Because of the very large contribution of international students to international trade, we discuss this issue and its metrics in more depth in part II of this chapter.

Creating a Globally Competitive Workforce

Colleges and universities play a crucial role in developing the competitive advantages of economies. In our review of the reports, fifteen described the role of the university in fostering a "globally competitive workforce." The following statement from the University of Miami's report is representative of these types of statements, both implicating a global economy and noting the need for high-skilled labor to help the local region be competitive:

> [The university's] academic programs contribute to the economy and cater to marketplace demand by efficiently preparing students for knowledge-based careers in growing sectors of the global, regional, and local economies, such as health services, law, and business. These are fields in which Miami-Dade County, and Coral Gables specifically, enjoy a competitive advantage. (Washington Economics Group, 2008, p. 4)

Similarly, the University at Buffalo's (UB) report highlights the essential role that colleges and universities play in contributing to a globally competitive economy:

In the knowledge-based economy, human capital is the most critical resource. Companies require a skilled workforce to compete in national and global markets, while hospitals, schools and other institutions need skilled workers to provide high quality services. As Buffalo Niagara's largest and most comprehensive center of higher learning, UB furnishes the region with professionals ready to work in a wide variety of sectors. (Foster et al., 2007, p. 18)

The development of a high skilled workforce seems to be one of the more obvious contributions of a postsecondary institution to the comparative advantage of an economy. As such it was surprising that only 37 percent (15 out of 41) of the internationally focused reports mentioned their contribution to fostering a competitive advantage or economic competitiveness. More about higher education's contributions to workforce development can be found in Carnevale and Rose (2012—chapter 6 in this volume).

International Trade

As noted above, higher education institutions can also be useful in helping economies engage in international trade. Eleven of the economic impact reports included a statement about higher education's role in helping facilitate international trade or attracting international investment to the region. The University of Wisconsin made one of the most explicit statements in this regard:

The University [of Wisconsin's] extensive network of alumni creates contacts around the global economy. As the state seeks to increase exports and to attract direct foreign investment in the state, the University plays an active role in connecting with the global economy. (NorthStar Economics, 2011, p. 19)

The University of Virginia stated simply: "As the University's reputation has risen, the net flow of funds into the state has increased dramatically" (Knapp & Shobe, 2007, p. 10).

While these reports may not provide much evidence, extant scholarship does support a likely link between postsecondary institution and international economic flows. For example, research has demonstrated that the level and type of education within a nation influences a nation's ability to engage in export activities (Lall, 2000; Wood & Mayer, 1998, 2001). Offshoring of services, particularly in high-tech industries, is linked to the availability of tertiary graduates (Arora & Gambardella, 2004). Moreover, the ability to attract investment from other nations is tied to the skill development and education level of the local workforce (Zhang & Markusen, 1999; Akin & Vlad, 2011).[4] In considering the economic contributions of postsecondary institutions, one must account for their contributions to the economy's ability to be globally competitive.

Other Measures

There were several other measures used to demonstrate the flow of international resources into the local region, all mentioned in fewer than 15 percent of the 70 reports. Six institutions reported their domestic and foreign patents separately, although they did not disaggregate the amount of revenue earned from the different sources. Five institutions reported the amount of direct revenue to the institution produced from grants and contracts received from international sources. Furthermore, four of the reports suggested that institutions attracted high-skilled international migrants to the local region, either to work at the institution or in a company that was supported by the institution.

Finally, a small number of reports attempted to quantify the economic impact of the institutions in the larger global economy. This was accomplished in three ways. First, in a very interesting measure, one institution (University of Virginia) recorded the amount of money that its faculty and staff gave to "global" charities, although, as highlighted in chapter 3, it is difficult to attribute the economic effect to the institution as it is likely such giving would occur regardless for whom the staff members worked. In a second example, an institution counted the number of "global" companies that its graduates were responsible for creating. Hereto, attribution is also somewhat problematic in that it is not clear to what extent those graduates' ability to create companies can be linked directly to their experience with that institution.

One measure that can be clearly linked to institutions is in the form of investment in other countries. Three of the reports, all from private institutions (Brown University, Tulane University, and University of Notre Dame), specifically mentioned the international engagements of the institutions in foreign countries, citing that their work abroad has an economic impact overseas. None of the reports provided definitive measures in this regard, but these efforts are part of a growing phenomenon in which colleges and universities are expanding into multinational institutions and, thus, becoming economic drivers not just in their home country, but in foreign nations as well. This issue of the economic impact of overseas presence is discussed in part III below.

PART II: MEASURING STUDENT MOBILITY AS ECONOMIC IMPACT

Over the past decade, discussion about higher education and international trade has often revolved around the General Agreement on Trade in Services (GATS). This international agreement was established in order to regulate the trade of services among member nations while increasing the flow of services. Education was included as one of the service sectors to be regulated by the accord. These services are further categorized as one of four modes of supply: (1) cross-border supply: provision of a service where the service crosses the border; (2) consumption abroad: provision of the service involving the movement of the consumer to the country of the supplier; (3) commercial presence: the service provider establishes or has presence of commercial facilities in another country in order to render service, and; (4) presence of natural persons: persons traveling to another country in order to provide service.[5] During the 2000s, prominent scholars wrote about the potential impact of GATS on higher education (e.g., Knight, 2003; Van der Wende, 2005). Of utmost concern was the fact that GATS focused primarily on the process of trade, rather than the quality of the service. First and foremost, the notion of education as a traded service highlighted divergent national approaches to education, namely the role of higher education as a public good versus a private one, the right of the student to access this service free of charge rather than having to pay some or all of the cost, and the duty of the national government to educate their constituency according to their own beliefs and needs (Larsen & Vincent-Lancrin, 2002). Still other debates questioned the role of domestic quality assurance mechanisms as regulatory trade barriers, wondering whether nations would be required to reduce or eliminate such measures (Organization for Economic Cooperation and Development, 2003; Van Damme, 2002).

While GATS has crystallized recent attention on higher education's mobility, students have moved across international borders to pursue an educational experience for centuries (see Rashdall, 1895). Similarly, faculty have been part of an international market place, moving across borders in search of employment. More recent developments have included the use of the Internet and other distance education technologies, expanding service provision abroad. Moreover, some institutions have begun to invest in foreign outposts, physical presences that allow them to deliver their educational and research services directly within a foreign marketplace. Many of these activities have proliferated through the course of the GATS debates, despite the very limited education-related agreements reached via the GATS process. For example, the United States Department of Commerce estimates that from 2009 to 2010, education exports and imports have both increased healthily (see Table 8.2).

Between 2000–09, global international student mobility increased 77 percent from approximately 2.1 million to 3.6 million students attending some type of college outside of their home country (OECD, 2011). These students travel overseas in order to attend

Table 8.2. U.S. Private Education Services, by Category, in Millions of Dollars

Education	2008	2009	2010	2009–2010 % Change
Education - Exports	17,938	19,911	21,690	8.9%
Education - Imports	5,173	5,583	5,960	6.8%

Source: USDOC, International Transactions Accounts
Note: Data for 2010 are preliminary.

a wide variety of programs, institutional types, and degree or certificate programs, ranging from short-term language courses to extended graduate programs While the exponential increase of Chinese and Indian students has been the focus of commentary in the United States, foreign enrollments in Latin America and the Caribbean and Oceania have increased substantively as well. Even though less than 3 percent of the world's students choose to study abroad in Latin America, the 75,000 currently enrolled foreign students represent a 160 percent increase over the past decade. Similarly, international enrollment in Oceania, especially Australia, has increased by 180 percent from 120,000 to 335,000 students, almost 10 percent of the global share. Asian universities' and colleges' enrollments also have doubled, from just under 200,000 to 400,000 students.

But what of the economic impact of these students? Global statistics for educational trade, specifically student mobility, are incomplete, but several studies from Anglo nations have provided some evidence that suggests a considerable economic contribution to local communities. In the United States, NAFSA (2011) has estimated that in 2010–11 international students contributed about $28,000 per student to the local community through tuition and fees (see Table 8.3). This conservative estimate is limited to tuition and living expenses, without including any type of multiplier effect to track those student dollars into local economies. The Open Doors report (IIE, 2011) estimates that about 63 percent of the monies these students spend come from personal and family sources, and therefore are new to local economies. Similarly, a 2009 report commissioned by the Canadian Department of Foreign Affairs and International Trade estimated that international students contributed about $30,000 per student to local economies (Roslyn Kunin & Associates, 2009). This report further calculates that about 83,000 students worked during their stay, paying about $300 million to the Canadian government in various revenues. The Australian Council for Private Education and Training estimates that foreign students added a 30 percent value to local labor markets while their relatives coming to visit brought in an additional $365 million in tourism revenues (Access Economics, 2009). The Higher Education Policy Institute in the United Kingdom (where, in contrast to the United States, international students are allowed to be employed while in school) has calculated that international students spend their wages on essential accommodations,

Table 8.3. International Student Economic Impact in U.S. by Region, AY 2010–11

	Enrolled Students	Tuition & Living Expenses	US Based Support	Student Contribution	Economic Impact per Student
Northeast	181,847	$8,283,657,960	$2,452,502,388	$5,831,155,572	$32,066
South	207,433	$7,140,146,190	$1,982,668,855	$5,157,477,337	$24,863
Midwest	168,055	$6,340,402,776	$1,850,817,184	$4,489,585,595	$26,715
West	164,955	$6,148,147,022	$1,410,552,968	$4,737,594,055	$28,721
US Total	722,290	$27,912,353,948	$7,696,541,395	$20,215,812,559	$27,988

Source: NAFSA 2010–2011 Economic Impact Statements; Note: U.S. Total figures are a sum of data from the 50 states, plus DC, listed above.

food, and drink, while boosting revenues in nonessential categories as well (Vickers & Bekhradnia, 2007).

Several methodological issues are salient among these reports. First, the focus on measurement lies upon international students moving into any given community. However, characteristics attributed to the skills acquired by domestic students who study abroad could be included. Indicators would include postcompletion activities, such as a change in initial job placements, lifetime earnings, and international partners brought into the local community. The omission of these students in any attempt to determine economic impact underestimates the full value of a globalized student body (Lipsey, 2009). Other methodological issues are more systemic. No international organization consistently reports a full list of education as international trade indicators, leaving calculation methods and data sources to national statistics, which are often calculated in different ways, making comparison difficult if not meaningless. A further issue that hinders comparable measurement lies in the multiplier effect of dollars brought into communities. While NAFSA (2011) does not include any multiplier effect, the UK report multiplied dollars spent by 1.5 in order to more fully estimate the distribution of these revenues beyond educational expenses and immediate living accommodations. Still, the consensus among these reports indicates that international students contribute substantively to local economies, not only through the tuition and fees they pay to universities. As active participants in labor and consumer markets, they contribute revenues to governments and private business. Given these national advantages, several countries have established national or regional policies designed to promote international student recruitment.

In Europe, the Socrates and Erasmus programs have provided a framework for increasing student mobility, but perhaps the most famous national policy belongs to Australia. In the mid-1980s, the Australian national government announced intentions to actively expand educational exports (Verbik & Lasanowski, 2007). Since then, the government has aligned visa and immigration requirements in order to streamline educational opportunities with the skilled labor market. These legislative actions, alongside a reasonably priced, diversified education sector coupled with active student recruiters have culminated in a vibrant, global student body, one-fifth of which is comprised of foreign student enrollment (Access Economics, 2009).

A similar approach to policy has not occurred in the United States, mostly due to a decentralized state-based system rather than a coordinated national approach to higher education policy. However, members of Congress and several recent U.S. presidents have noted the relative decline in students choosing to study in the United States. Recognizing the importance of student internationalization in meeting modern political and economic challenges, national leaders have called for several policy measures, including visa and immigration reform (House Resolution 201, 107th Congress, 2001; Commission on the Abraham Lincoln Study Abroad Program, 2005). Although despite such calls, no federal legislation has yet established any legal framework similar to the Australian legislation. However, twenty-three state legislative assemblies have recognized the importance of internationalization in higher education through legislative proclamations and resolutions.[6] The state of Mississippi called upon state government to support and encourage international education, in part due to the

> evidence of the growing connection between Mississippi and the rest of the world [that] can be found in the Institute of International Education's Open Doors Report 2003,which indicates that Mississippi had 2,143 foreign students studying in the state for the 2002–2003 academic year, and these foreign students and their families contributed an estimated $44 million to the Mississippi economy in 2002–2003, in addition to shedding light on the existence of tremendous growth opportunities. (House Resolution 9, 2005)

Similar to these resolutions of intent, twenty-nine states have passed proclamations declaring a week in November as International Education Week, designed to attract foreign students to their higher education institutions through a variety of awareness campaigns. Along these lines, several states have developed a "Study" campaign (e.g., Study New York, Study Missouri, Study in Minnesota), intended to gather and disseminate information relevant to potential out-of-state students, mostly with a focus on international students. For example, the New York Department of Economic Development maintains the Study New York Web site (http://www.studynewyork.us/), complete with scholastic information on most accredited institutions, public and private, tourist attractions, and pertinent travel requirements or guidelines. As listed on the Web site, Study New York's raison d'être is to "position New York State as the destination of choice for students from around the world, thereby improving the visibility and global competitiveness of the State's institutions of higher learning, and expanding the State's services exports" (Study New York, 2011). The Study Maine Web site is maintained by the Maine International Trade Center (MITC), a public-private nonprofit funded by the state's department of economic and community development. MITC's mission is to expand Maine's economy through increased international trade in goods and services and related activities. Similar to New York's, this Web site promotes not only education, but also tourism and other state economic assets in order to attract potential students. Finally, another thread of state-based policy discussion focuses on the ever-present need to develop a globally competitive workforce by increasing the number of domestic students that study abroad. Given the well-touted claim that study abroad affects labor market participation, policymakers are seeking defined and reviewed indicators in order to empirically assess this assertion. The State Council of Higher Education for Virginia issued a white paper in 2009 calling for academics and professionals to compile data that can demonstrate the economic development benefits of current international education initiatives, both recruitment as well as study abroad, to state leaders.

In the United States, the proliferation of these internationally oriented state proclamations and white papers has coincided with a sustained reduction in state appropriations to public institutions. As full fee-paying students, most international students represent revenue streams to institutions as well as local economies. Consequently, policies and debates regarding the use of commission-based student recruiters have surfaced. Increasingly, more international students are employing third-party agents or recruiters during the college admissions process. In a recent study, Hagedorn and Zhang (2011) surveyed 257 Chinese students at four universities in the United States, both public and private. Of these students, 146 (56.8 percent) had used an agent at some point during the application process. The authors modeled students' demographic characteristics, family backgrounds, education experiences in China, and academic preparation for U.S. colleges and universities. According to their calculations, younger students whose parents had less education were more likely to use an agent to assist them in the college application process, indicating that recruiters are being employed to supplement a lack of knowledge on behalf of the consumer. Specifically, students used agents to assist in the college application process, visa application, and to provide information about higher education institutions in general. Even with Internet-based access to information, the widespread use of recruiters highlights students' need for clarity of information regarding college applications and admissions. In addition to students, some institutions have also begun to employ these recruiters, providing compensation to third-party agents for a variety of services rendered.

Opponents to such practices propose that irresponsible agents impact students and institutions negatively. The information asymmetry that can exist may allow recruiters to take advantage of students and institutions. Students can be steered toward poor academic choices while colleges and universities can be misrepresented. The State Department has argued that the use of commission-based agents is inequitable, can lead to biased and skewed advise for students, which in turn can lead to a poor choice of postsecondary institution, and thereby is unethical. The Department of State's Bureau of Educational and Cultural Affairs (ECA) Office of Academic Programs has banned advising and informational centers that receive financial support from ECA to engage professionally with recruitment agents of any type, commission-based or not (Education USA, n.d.). Despite the ECA policy, which technically governs a limited number of information centers, an increasing number of colleges and universities have proceeded to enlist the services of agents. Several professional organizations (e.g., National Association for College Admission Counseling; Association of Public and Land Grant Universities) have issued statements in support or against the use of these recruiters; currently a national committee has convened to examine the pros and cons.

In the 1990s, Australia struggled with ethical lapses in their system of recruiting, which inspired the country to enact the Australian Educational Services for Overseas Students Act (ESOS). Rather than ban commission-based recruiting by agents, the ESOS mandated a National Code of Practice for Registration Authorities and Providers of Education and Training to Overseas Students, which the Australian government enforces with severe penalties, including prison sentences. The code includes the following stipulation: "Registered providers take all reasonable measures to use education agents that have an appropriate knowledge and understanding of the Australian international education industry and do not use education agents who are dishonest or lack integrity." By contrast, the Council of Europe (2001) has placed responsibility for the agent squarely in the hands of the institution, "The awarding institution should be responsible for the agents it, or its partner institutions, appoint to act on its behalf. Institutions using agents should conclude written and legally binding agreements or contracts with these, clearly stipulating their roles, responsibilities, delegated powers of action as well as monitoring, arbitration and termination provisions. These agreements or contracts should further be established with a view to avoiding conflicts of interests as well as the rights of students with regard to their studies."[7]

While the policy debate surrounding recruitment echoes divergent sentiments voiced during the GATS debate of the early 2000s, what does appear evident is that despite a difference in student exchange policies, international student mobility has a calculable economic impact. Nations and states have recognized the importance of that impact through a series of laws, policies, proclamations, and marketing strategies. These policies are intended to not only attract students to a certain state, but also are designed with global economic competitiveness in mind; policymakers understand the value of internationally minded students to their local communities.

PART III: CROSS-BORDER HIGHER EDUCATION AND FOREIGN DIRECT INVESTMENT

The previous section focused on student mobility, or GATS mode 2: consumption abroad. In this section, we look at how some higher education institutions may contribute to the economic growth of foreign communities, specifically focusing on foreign direct investment (FDI) as one measure of this phenomenon, also known as GATS mode 3: commercial presence. The movement of students and scholars is not the only way in which higher education crosses borders. Since at least the 1950s, a small number of colleges and universities have established teaching outposts in foreign countries (Becker, 2009). One of the first such institutions, Johns Hopkins University, set up a campus in Italy to offer a graduate degree in international relations. The purpose of the program was to help facilitate multinational cooperation in a post–World War II era. However, it was also one of the earliest modern examples of an educational institution investing resources in an overseas market. In economic parlance, the investment of capital in a foreign market in return for at least some stake in the ownership of the foreign operation is referred to as FDI. This section briefly discusses the emergence of multinational universities, how their activities can contribute to foreign economies, and how conceptualizing this as FDI can allow for measurement of these contributions.

Higher education has become increasingly internationalized, with some colleges and universities evolving into multinational enterprises. Multinational colleges and universities (MNCUs) operate physical outposts in more than one nation and each of these outposts exerts its own impact on the economies in which it exists. These outposts can include outreach offices, teaching locations, and research sites. Indeed, universities have been operating international research sites and partnerships for decades. Many higher education institutions have established offices in foreign cities as a means of recruiting foreign students, keeping in contact with foreign-based alumni, and facilitating the development of international relationships such as joint research initiatives and double degree programs. These outposts have even been used to help attract international investment back to the economy where the home campus resides. In one interesting example, Troy University, a public institution in Alabama, shared an office in Germany with Alabama's economic development agency.

There is no accounting of the number of foreign outposts operated by colleges and universities, nor has there yet been developed a classification scheme for the myriad forms that an MNCU can take (Kinser & Lane, 2012). Even in terms of teaching engagements, MNCUs have developed different types of foreign outposts. Suffolk University once operated a junior college model in Senegal, where African students were supposed to take their first two years of classes before transferring to the main campus in Boston (Carmichael, 2011). The Indian university of Manipal operates a campus in Nepal which offers a Manipal curriculum taught by Manipal faculty, but because of national regulations, the degrees are awarded by Katmandu University (Kinser & Lane, 2012). Finally, several U.S.-based for-profit educational organizations (e.g., Laureate Education and Whitney International) have purchased foreign campuses, operating them as wholly owned subsidiaries of the for-profit company, but not changing the campuses' names or other aspects of their academic operation (Kinser, 2010). Each of these endeavors represents a form of FDI as capital is flowing into a foreign economy and the institution retains as least some ownership in the foreign educational operation.

One particular type of foreign outpost, international branch campuses, has received recent scholarly attention, and we use this subset of foreign outposts to illustrate how some higher education engagements serve as a form of FDI. The Cross-Border Education Research Team (2011) has identified nearly two hundred IBCs. They define an IBC as "an entity owned, at least in part, by a foreign education provider, operated in the name of the foreign education provider; engages in at least some face-to-face teaching; and provides access to an entire academic program that leads to a credential awarded by the foreign education provider" (Lane, 2011, p. 5). The home institution transfers financial and/or academic capital into a foreign market in order to provide an educational experience comparable to that offered on the home campus. Under this model, the organization is making a decision to internationalize its offerings by developing a multinational footprint. The foreign outpost receives organization-specific advantages such as curriculum design, instructional expertise, and international recognition derived from the home campus that allow it to compete directly with domestic educational institutions that might have advanced knowledge about local student expectations, educational pipeline flows, and regulatory/accreditation requirements. This sort of establishment allows for a higher degree of knowledge spillover than might otherwise be possible, as the benefits accrued by a higher education institution are now shared among two or more communities. By setting up shop in a foreign country, an institution is not only educating local students, it is also spreading knowledge through on-site faculty and research. This spillover effect can raise the skill level of human capital in the host country, help foster local innovation, and support local business development.

While there have been some meager attempts at tracking the FDI flows in education (e.g., International Trade Center), measurement, particularly in a comparative sense, has been difficult. Very few nations include education in their FDI metrics; moreover, nations have different definitions of FDI, primarily in terms of the ownership thresholds that must be met, and the reporting of reinvestment of retained earnings often lags significantly behind the time when they are realized (Razin & Sadka, 2007). Thus, inflows and outflows of FDI are not well matched on an annual basis. Globally, the amount of FDI has increased markedly in the last two decades, with a sevenfold increase occurring during the 1990s (Razin & Sadka, 2007). This rapid increase has been, in part, facilitated by governments adapting their regulations to be more receptive of FDI (United Nations Conference on Trade and Development, 2005). A similar trend has been seen in higher education, with nations creating more favorable policies, if not also providing incentives, to attract foreign education providers (McBurnie & Ziguras, 2007).

In studying the economic impact of cross-border higher education, there are two critical aspects of the FDI definition that must be considered. First, a transfer of capital must occur. Second, the institution transferring the capital must retain some ownership in the foreign endeavor. We'll discuss the second factor first. Whether the home campus of an institution is considered public, private nonprofit, or private for-profit, setting up an institution in a foreign environment requires the institution to meet the ownership requirements of the foreign country. In many cases, foreign governments require the creation of a locally registered organization.[8] At times, a university may create a wholly owned subsidiary that is legally a separate entity, but is entirely owned by the university. Some countries, such as Malaysia, have required that a local partner retain majority ownership in the local educational organization. For example, when Monash University (Australia) established a branch campus in Malaysia, it partnered with Sunway Corporation and both retained joint ownership of a new entity Monash University Sunway Campus Malaysia (MUSCM) (Lane, 2010a). In this arrangement, Sunway retained 74 percent ownership of MUSCM. Though they were a minority owner in the enterprise, Monash was investing financial and academic capital in the organization and that organization likely had an economic impact in its Malaysian community.

It is not unusual for IBCs to be established in partnership with a local entity, although the issue of ownership is not always as clear as that described in the case of MUSCM. For example, governments such as those in Abu Dhabi and Qatar have provided significant financial incentives to recruit foreign education providers, though the issue of ownership remains unclear (Lane, 2011). In most of these cases, the institutions ensure that they retain primary control over the academic enterprise, even though the physical infrastructure may not be owned by them. In a recent global survey of IBCs, the Cross-Border Education Research Team found that 28 percent of respondents wholly owned their overseas campus, while 18 percent rented their facilities (Lane & Kinser, 2011). The remaining 54 percent indicated that the campus facilities were owned by either a government, educational, or private partner.

While ownership is an important component of determining what constitutes FDI, it is the transfer of capital that usually forms the base of the metric—that is, FDI measures how much capital is being invested in the local economy by a foreign enterprise. There are both vertical and horizontal forms of FDI (Markusen, 1984). With vertical FDI, an organization invests in different levels of its supply chain. In this case, a college or university may invest in a foreign secondary school or a junior college such as Suffolk University did in Senegal as way to increase the flow of students into its home campus. However, most cross-border higher education activities would be classified as horizontal FDI, in that the institution replicates portions of its operation in one or more other countries. In deciding whether or not to engage in horizontal FDI, most organizations assess the cost of engaging in trade versus the fixed costs associated with starting a foreign unit (Markusen, 1984). It would make little sense for a higher education institution to establish an overseas campus to serve the same students that would otherwise travel to pursue their education at the home campus (unless the costs of the foreign campus were significantly subsidized by a foreign government or private partner).

With the creation of IBCs, the transfer of capital can be difficult to ascertain. In many cases and despite the ownership issues, IBCs are operated as extensions of the home campus and the "investment" of capital may be difficult to track. Faculty and administrators, particularly in the early years of startup, are shared between the campuses; so their salaries may not be associated with the IBC despite their relationship with it. Further, as already discussed, not all facilities are owned by the foreign education provider. Investments in the physical facilities may originate domestically, in the importing country, and would not be considered part of the FDI.

Beyond the issue of financial capital, the nature of higher education institutions is that academic capital is also transferred across borders. To our knowledge, no one has attempted to track academic capital as a form of FDI. In this case we define academic capital as the accumulated knowledge and instructional/research expertise of an educational organization. One of the specific advantages of higher education institutions is their academic capital. When considering whether to start a new university from scratch or have one started by a foreign education provider, an advantage of the latter is their organization's specific knowledge. They have the ability to transfer their expertise and knowledge to the new organization. In many cases this academic capital was generated after decades if not centuries of organizational evolution. As such, the economic impact of higher education institutions crossing borders can be different, and greater, than that of other multinational enterprises.

In some cases, governments can be quite directive in terms of the type of capital that an MNCU brings to their country. For those IBCs in Qatar's Education City, the government restricts the type of academic programs that can be offered. First, the government decided to import academic programs that were believed to support the economic pillars of the local economy. Second, institutions invited to set up shop in Education City could only import those programs approved by the government. For example, Texas A&M offers a petroleum engineering program, which supports the nation's petroleum industry, and Northwestern provides journalism degrees, which aligns with the nation's interest in becoming a regional media hub (Qatar is the home of al Jazeera) (Trani & Holsworth, 2010).

Conceptually understanding higher education as a form of FDI is much easier than actually measuring it. However, recognizing the increasingly important contribution that MNCUs play in driving the economic development of foreign nations is an important aspect of the connection between higher education and economic development and one that is largely missing from the existing discourse. Using this framing of FDI allows us to propose many important questions that need further examination. For example, what advantages might MNCUs have over domestic providers of higher education, and vice versa? How do IBCs contribute to the economic development of a locality and do these contributions differ from those of domestic institutions? If a government or private investor is looking to create a new college or university, what advantages or disadvantages exist for IBCs or domestic institutions? How do the spillover contributions of MNCUs compare to those of other types of multinational organizations?

Our purpose here is not to present specific measures of higher education–related FDI. Rather, we believe that this is an important component of the international dimension of economic development that is missing from economic development reports and the scholarly literature. Because metrics do not now exist to measure this phenomenon does not mean that it is not worthy of further study. Indeed, the economic contributions of higher education have been primarily framed from a local or national perspective, with the exception of the international flow of students. It may now be time for a broader understanding of how higher education functions as a form of international trade and foreign direct investment.

CONCLUSIONS

This chapter focuses on an important, though often overlooked, aspect of higher education's contribution to economic development. The increasing interconnectedness of markets, cultures, and countries fostered through globalization has propelled higher education into acting as a significant player in international trade and investment. However, while higher education's international engagements have become more expansive in the last decade; metrics to assess the full breadth of the economic impact of these engagements have yet to develop. In this chapter, we reviewed two of the more prominent international aspects of higher education, namely, the movement of students and institutions across borders.

In a review of seventy economic impact reports produced by colleges and universities in the United States over the past decade (2001–11), only 58 percent (n = 41) included any mention of global or international engagement. The three primary international themes identified in the analysis were (1) recruiting international students; (2) producing a globally competitive workforce; and (3) attracting international trade. However, while reports made mention of these issues, few provided concrete measures, opting instead for descriptive analysis and rhetorical linkages.

In order to illustrate the significant role that higher education now plays in international economics, we then analyzed existing documentation and data about higher education as a form of international trade and its activities with FDI. As discussed above, the movement of students across national borders to pursue their education is now one of the most prominent forms of international trade in nations such as Australia and the United States. Yet, only 31 percent (22/70) of the reports that we analyzed specifically included international students as a separate component of their analysis. Despite the minimal mention in institutional reports, groups as varied as the Organization for Economic Cooperation and Development (OECD), NAFSA—the association of international educators—and the U. S. government have all chronicled the economic contributions of international students.

Moreover, international engagements by colleges and universities do not just affect the economy in which the home campus operates, these engagements can also benefit foreign economies. Above, we looked at a very specific form of international engagement, international branch campuses, and argued that these institutions now operate as an important form of FDI, facilitating the movement of financial and academic capital across international borders. At present, evidence of such investments is mostly limited to qualitative data; however, the important role that higher education plays in developing economics (Lane, 2012—chapter 1 this volume) and the rapid expansion of foreign outposts of higher education institutions warrants the development of metrics to track and measure these investments in a more systematic manner.

In order to advance understanding and acknowledgment of the international dimensions of higher education's role in economic development, we propose that greater attention be given to developing a research agenda in this arena. First, a more systematic accounting for the international forms of economic impact fostered by a college or university in its local economy is needed. The analysis of economic impact reports provided above is only an initial step toward a more comprehensive understanding of these contributions. This analysis reveals what a few institutions are thinking in this regard, or at least what they are willing to discuss in a public domain. However, there may be other mechanisms not captured in such an analysis.

Second, additional information is needed about the nature and extent of the foreign outposts being developed by colleges and universities. Indeed, some colleges and universities are beginning to resemble multinational enterprises with offices, research sites, and teaching locations spread across multiple nations. While some scholars have begun to investigate the creation of international branch campuses, there are other types of outposts currently in existence that have not been acknowledged in the scholarly literature. Each of these outposts has an impact on the local economy, and research could focus on the channels and extent of such impact (e.g., workforce development, research productivity, knowledge spillover, etc.). Furthermore, comparison would be warranted between different types of foreign investments as well as between foreign and domestic education providers. However, without a more accurate description and accounting of such activities, it is difficult to engage in more advanced study about their economic impact in both the importing and exporting markets.

Third, an analysis of whether government economic policies incentivize or dis-incentivize the international activities of colleges and universities might reveal interesting patterns of economic growth and help inform policymakers regarding regulation and investment decisions. As mentioned above, some governments such as Abu Dhabi and Qatar are now providing financial incentives to attract foreign education providers. The African Development Bank is providing money so that Carnegie Mellon can set up a campus in Rwanda (Wilhem, 2011). Many U.S. states have set up marketing programs to help attract international students to their colleges and universities. Other governments have chosen to retain or create barriers to foreign investment in their higher education systems (McBurnie & Zyguris, 2007). However, there has yet to be any study of the economic impact of such policies.

Finally, there is a need for standardized indicators so that higher education institutions, governments, and businesses can establish a baseline of economic impact, determine growth (or shrinkage) over time, and employ informed data-based policy decisions at local, state, and national levels. At present, organizations such as NASFA and IIE provide some limited measurement of the impact of student activities abroad; however, colleges' and universities' international engagements extend far beyond the movement of students. As discussed above, some institutions, in their economic development reports, have also claimed to have raised international awareness of the local region, to have attracted international investment, and to have trained a globally competitive workforce. Yet the measures of such impacts are minimal at best and do not, at present, allow for comparative analysis. In some cases the metrics for studying international economics could be used or adopted; however, new measures will be needed to assess those contributions that are unique to higher education institutions.

NOTES

1. We searched each document for the following terms: global, international, foreign, world, trade, export, and import.
2. NAFSA (2011) did not use any multipliers in their calculation, so the reported numbers are likely lower than the actual contributions.
3. Birrell and Smith (2010) discuss some of the methodological concerns associated with AEIs calculations, suggesting that these numbers may be inflated. Readers interested in measuring the trade value of education are encouraged to review this article.
4. In these studies, the relationship was determined not to be direct. The countries with the highest and lowest levels of tertiary education received relatively little foreign direct investment. The nations with mid-level tertiary education development received the highest levels of foreign direct investment.
5. For more information on GATS modes of supply, see *Internationalisation and Trade in Higher Education* (OECD, 2004).
6. NAFSA has collected a comprehensive overview of federal and state-level initiatives, available for reference at http://www.nafsa. org/publicpolicy/.
7. *Code of Good Practice in the Provision of Transnational Education,* adopted by the Lisbon Recognition Convention Committee at its second meeting, Riga, 6 June 2001.
8. Places such as Dubai have created free zones that exempt foreign

corporations from such ownership requirements (Lane, 2010b); however, should an institution be established outside of the free zone they are obligated to abide by the federal law requiring all corporations in the United Arab Emirates to be at least partially owned by an Emirati.

REFERENCES

Access Economics. (2009). *The Australian education sector and the economic contribution of international students.* Prepared for Australian Council for Private Education and Training.

Akin, M. S., & Vlad, V. (2011). The relationship between education and foreign direct investment: Testing the inverse U shape. *European Journal of Economic and Political Studies 4* (1), 27–46.

Arora, A., & Gambardella, A. (2004). *The globalization of the software industry: Perspectives and opportunities for developed and developing countries.* National Bureau of Economic Research Working Paper 10538. Retrieved from http://www.nber.org/papers/w10538.

Association of Public and Land-Grant Universities (APLU). (2011). APLU expresses concern about possible ban of agents in international recruiting. Retrieved from http://www.aplu.org/page.aspx?pid=2098.

Australian Education International. (2009a). Research Snapshot, March.

Australian Education International. (2009b). Research Snapshot, June.

Becker, R.F. (2009) International Branch Campuses: Markets and Strategies. London: Observatory for Borderless Higher Education.

Becker, W. E., & Lewis, D. R. (Eds.) (1992). *The economics of American higher education.* Dordrecht: Kluwer Academic Publishers.

Birrell, B., & Smith, F. (2010). Export earnings from the overseas student industry: How much? *Australian Universities Review 52* (1), 4–12.

Blomstrom, M., and Kokko, A. (2001). FDI, human capital, and education in developing countries. Paper presented at FDI, Human Capital, and Education in Developing Countries Technical

Meeting in Paris, France. Organized by the OECD Development Center. December 2001.

Carmichael, M. (2011). Universities rethinking global expansion. *Boston Globe.* October 13. Available at http://www.bostonglobe.com/metro/2011/10/12/for-some-schools-including-suffolk-university-boston-boom-global-branch-campuses-goes-bust/KtTZj1Uz7G0NmzQUgZLs2O/story.html.

Commission on the Abraham Lincoln Study Abroad Program. (2005). *Global competence and national needs: One million Americans studying abroad.* Retrieved from http://www.nafsa.org/uploadedFiles/NAFSA_Home/Resource_Library_Assets/CCB/lincoln_commission_report%281%29.pdf?n=6097.

Council of Europe. (2001). Code of good practice in the provision of transnational education.

Education USA. (2011). Policy guidance for Education USA centers on commercial recruitment agents. Retrieved from http://chronicle.com/items/biz/pdf/policyoncommercialagents.pdf.

Foster, K. A., Entress, S. A., Lombardi, P. A., Stynes, B. A., & Teaman, R. M. (2007). *The difference a university makes: An impact analysis of the University at Buffalo.* Buffalo: Regional Institute, University at Buffalo.

Hagedorn, L. S., & Zhang, Y. (2011). The use of agents in recruiting Chinese undergraduates. *Journal of Studies in International Education 15* (2), 186–202.

House Concurrent Resolution 201, United States 107th Congress, 1 Sess. (2001).

House Resolution 9. Mississippi Legislature. Regular Sess. (2005).

Institute of International Education. (2011). International students by primary source of funding, 2009/10–2010/11. *Open Doors report on international educational exchange.* Retrieved from http://www.iie.org/opendoors.

Kinser, K. (2010). A global perspective on for-profit higher education. In W. G. Tierney, V. M. Lechuga, & G. Hentschke (Eds.), *Learning for earning in a globalized society: For-profit colleges and universities as schools and businesses* (pp. 145–170). Sterling, VA: Stylus Press.

Kinser, K., & Lane, J. E. (2012). Foreign outposts of colleges and universities. *International Higher Education 66,* 2–3.

Knapp, J. L., & Shobe, W. M. (2007). *The economic impact of the University of Virginia: How a major research university affects the local and state economies.* Charlottesville: University of Virginia.

Knight, J. (2003). *GATS, trade, and higher education: Perspective 2003—Where are we?* London: Observatory for Borderless Higher Education.

Lall, S. (2000). Foreign direct investment, technology development, and competitiveness: Issues and evidence. In L. Kim and R. Nelson (Eds.), *Technology, learning, and innovation* (pp. 13–68). Cambridge: Cambridge University Press.

Lane, J. E. (2010a). Joint ventures in cross-border higher education: International branch campuses in Malaysia. In D. W. Chapman & R. Sakamoto (Eds.), *Cross border collaborations in higher education: Partnerships beyond the classroom.* New York: Routledge.

Lane, J. E. (2010b). Higher education, free zones, and quality assurance in Dubai. Policy Paper. Dubai School of Government: Dubai.

Lane, J. E. (2011). Global expansion of international branch campuses: Managerial and leadership challenges. In J. E. Lane & K. Kinser (Eds.), *Multi-national colleges & universities: Leadership, administration, and governance of international branch campuses.* (New Directions for Higher Education). San Francisco: Jossey-Bass.

Lane, J. E., & Kinser, K. (2011). Reconsidering privatization in cross-border engagements: The sometimes public nature of private activity. *Higher Education Policy 24,* 255–273. Selected for the 2010 International Association of Universities—Palgrave Prize in Higher Education Policy Research.

Lane, J. E., & Kinser, K. (Eds.). (2011). *Multi-national colleges & universities: Leadership, administration, and governance of international branch campuses.* (New Directions for Higher Education). San Francisco: Jossey-Bass.

Larsen, K., & Vincent-Lancrin, S. (2002). International trade in educational services: Good or bad. *Higher Education Management and Policy 14* (3), 9–45.

Leslie, L. L., & Slaughter, S. A. (1992). Higher education and regional development. In W. E. Becker & D. R. Lewis (Eds.), *The *economics of American higher education*. Dordrecht: Kluwer Academic Publishers.

Lipsey, R. E. (2009). Measuring international trade in services. In M. Reinsdorf & M. J. Slaughter (Eds.), *International trade in services and intangibles in the era of globalization*. Chicago: University of Chicago Press.

Markusen, J. R. (1984). Multinationals, multi-plant economies, and the gains from trade. *Journal of International Economics 16* (3–4), 205–226.

McBurnie, G., & Zyguris, C. (2007). *Transnational education: Issues and trends in offshore higher education*. London: Routledge.

NAFSA. (2011). *The economic benefits of international education to the United States for the 2010–2011 academic year: A statistical analysis*. Washington, DC: Author.

National Association for College Admission Counseling (NACAC). (2011). Analysis of comments submitted to NACAC in response to preliminary board: Proposal on incentive compensation and international recruitment. Retrieved from: http://www.nacacnet.org/AboutNACAC/Policies/Pages/IntlIncentiveComp.aspx.

NorthStar Economics. (2011). *The University of Wisconsin-Madison's $12.4 billion impact on the Wisconsin Economy*. March.

Obst, D., Kuder, M., & Banks, D. (2011). Joint and double degree programs in the global context: Report on an international survey. New York: Institute for International Education.

Organization for Economic Cooperation and Development (OECD). (2003). *Enhancing consumer protection in cross-border higher education: Key issues related to quality assurance. Accreditation and recognition of qualifications*. Report. Trondlheim, Norway: OECD/CERI.

OECD. (2011). *Education at a glance 2011: OECD indicators*. Paris: Organization for Economic Cooperation and Development.

Rashdall, H. (1895). *The universities of Europe in the Middle Ages*. London: Henry Frowde.

Razin, A., & Sadka, E. (2007). *Foreign direct investment: Analysis of aggregate flows*. Princeton: Princeton University Press.

Roslyn Kunin & Associates, Inc. (2009). *Economic impact of international education in Canada final report*. Presented to Foreign Affairs and International Trade Canada. Vancouver, BC: RKA, Inc.

Siegfried, J. J., Sanderson, A. R., & McHenry, P. (2007). The economic impact of colleges and universities. *Economics of Education Review 26* (5), 546–558.

State Council of Higher Education for Virginia. (2009). *Higher education, globalization, and economic development in Virginia.* Richmond, VA: Author.

Study Maine Web site. (2011). studymaine.net.

Study New York Web site. (2011). studynewyork.us.

Study New York. (2011). About study New York. Available at http://www.studynewyork.us/?q=about.

Trani, E. P., and Holsworth, R. D. (2010). *The indispensable university: Higher education, economic development, and the knowledge economy.* Lanham, MD: Rowman & Littlefield.

United Nations Conference on Trade and Development. (2005). World investment report. Accessed from http://www.unctad.org/Templates/WebFlyer.asp?intItemID=3489&lang=1.

United State International Trade Commission. (2011). *The year in trade 2010: Operations of the trade agreements program.* Washington, DC: Author.

University of Texas at Austin. (2011). *An investment that pays off for Texas.* Austin: Author.

Van Damme, D. (2002, May). Trends and models in international quality assurance and accreditation in higher education in relation to trade in education services. Paper presented at the Economic Cooperation and Development/U.S. Forum on Trade in Educational Services.

Van den Berg, H. (2001). *Economic growth and development.* New York: McGraw-Hill.

Van der Wende, M. C. (2005). Globalisation and access to higher education. *Journal of Studies in International Education 7* (3), 193–206.

Verbik, L., & Lasanowski, V. (2007). *International student mobility: Patterns and trends.* London: Observatory on Borderless Higher Education.

Vickers, P., & B. Bekhradnia, (2007). *The economic costs and benefits of international students.* London: Higher Education Policy Institute.

Washington Economics Group. (2008). *University of Miami: Driving community progress.* Available at http://www.edu-impact.com/author/washington-economics-group.

Wilhem, I. (2011). Carnegie Mellon U. to open campus in Rwanda, a milestone for Africa. *The Chronicle of Higher Education.* September 14. Retrieved from http://chronicle.com/article/Carnegie-Mellon-U-to-Open/128991/.

Wood, A., & Mayer, J. (1998). Africa's export structure in a comparative perspective, Study No. 4. In *African development in a comparative perspective.* Geneva: UNCTAD.

Wood, A., & Mayer, J. (2001). Africa's export structure in a comparative perspective. *Cambridge Journal of Economics 25* (3), 69–394.

Zhang, K. H., & Markusen, J. R. (1999). Vertical multinational and host country characteristics. *Journal of Development Economics 59* (2), 233–52.

9

UNANTICIPATED CONSEQUENCES OF UNIVERSITY INTELLECTUAL PROPERTY POLICIES

JASON OWEN-SMITH

ABSTRACT

While national legislation such as the 1981 Bayh-Dole Act created common pressures for American universities to commercialize the outcomes of faculty and student research, the act also created new tensions on campus. Those tensions hinged on the university's new role as owner and therefore arbiter of the use of faculty inventions and on the mandate to share royalties from such inventions between faculty and their institutions. Different campus-level approaches to managing these tensions in policy and in practice resulted in widely varying processes and outcomes for technology transfer. This chapter draws on interviews with licensing professionals and faculty inventors as well as close readings of intellectual property policies on two campuses to explicate the ways in which common institutional tensions can result in unanticipated organizational consequences associated with academic efforts at technology transfer.

INTRODUCTION

The last three decades have witnessed an impressive transformation in the societal meaning and roles played by academic science and engineering. This shift is most apparent in dramatic increases in the depth and variety of academic engagement with the world of commerce. From patenting and marketing of intellectual property (IP) to active venture capital investment and intimate involvement in the dense contractual networks that represent the center of gravity of the knowledge economy, American research universities are playing more active, complex, and prominent commercial roles than ever before.

The university research mission has shifted from dominance by a largely academic focus that is (at least rhetorically) distinct from concerns involving commercial application and use (Dasgupta & David, 1994; Merton, 1957), to one in which the "knowledge-plus" (Geiger, 1993) emphasis that has been a quiet component of academic life for decades is made explicit in the conduct, evaluation, and dissemination of academic research and development (R&D). This chapter situates that transformation within a broader framework, theorizing it as an instance of institutional change that sparks varied processes of organizational transformation.

The ways in which particular campuses respond to increasing commercial pressures can yield surprising outcomes for academic research. Unanticipated consequences occur because now commonplace contradictions and ambiguities are resolved in distinct fashions through often highly local negotiations and conflicts among campus actors. In this way, supra-organizational pressures toward similar policies and practices result in disparate organizational arrangements with lasting implications for both the positive and the negative outcomes of academic research commercialization. In other words, the case of university research commercialization offers an opportunity to examine the ways in which common institutional pressures generate heterogeneity in policies and practices at the organizational level.

After introducing my data-sources and highlighting the methodological choices that bound this analysis, I present a brief overview of the institutional shifts associated with widespread academic engagements with commerce. Legal changes that vested ownership of faculty inventions in the university, the rise of a professional group dedicated to managing and marketing university technologies, and contradictions resulting from the pursuit of private rights to public knowledge exert similar pressures on all research universities. The relative positions those universities hold in existing academic status orders and their local efforts to appropriately resolve the challenges of commercial engagement jointly drive a long-standing organizational form toward greater heterogeneity in practices and outcomes.

In this chapter, I attend to key contradictions surrounding the ownership and control of faculty inventions and the appropriation of revenues they generate. Two relevant professional groups, faculty scientists and engineers and university technology licensing officers, come into contact and often conflict around these issues. Both of these groups share important commonalities in their responses to commercial engagements. Those points of similarity often hold across campuses. Nevertheless, particular faculty-staff interactions around patenting and licensing help to cement important campus-level differences in approaches to technology transfer. I first examine faculty researchers' decisions about whether to disclose inventions to their local technology transfer office. Next I consider licensing professionals' decision about whether to pursue patents on new invention disclosures. Finally, I discuss interactions around patenting and licensing on two campuses characterized by very different commercialization policies and outcomes.

Faculty and technology licensing officers come into contact most closely and frequently in the process of discovering, protecting, marketing, and licensing intellectual property. At each stage of this process, members of both groups must make decisions that constrain their own future choices and those of relevant members of the other group. For example, a core uncertainty for technology licensing officers centers on the "pipeline" of new, potentially patentable, innovations. On most campuses, however, technology licensing officers lack both the time and the expertise necessary to actively seek out new inventions in diverse faculty labs and research groups. Thus, the success of licensing professionals depends, in large part, on the willingness of faculty to disclose potential inventions. Once such disclosures are made, however, the decision of whether to pursue IP protection (most often in the form of a patent) and of how to market and where to license such IP lies in the hands of technology licensing officers. The disposition and commercial success of faculty inventions, then, depends upon the skill, experience, and decisions of licensing professionals.

Professors and licensing officers often have distinct interests. This is particularly the case when faculty have the potential to benefit significantly from commercial activity (as is the case when professors seek to base new firms upon their university-owned inventions). Decision points related to faculty choices about disclosure, licensing officers' assessments of patentability, and their joint determinations of how to commercialize findings offer insight into the relational sources of organizational transformations and thus illuminate some of the ways in which broad institutional changes can generate increased heterogeneity in organizational practices and outcomes.

FIELDWORK IN ORGANIZATIONAL TRANSITION

Defining a field research project on organizational transformation requires an investigator to ask what, conceptually, is changing and where, empirically, that transformation can be observed. My answer to the former question is a core mission of the postwar American university and with it a societal and policy conception of the meaning and utility of "academic" science. That claim has two important theoretical characteristics: first, the notion of a shifting mission for a class of organizations suggests that outcomes and processes of enactment may vary depending on the particular organizations where they take place. Organizational missions and policies are interpreted, enforced, and "performed" on the ground. At the same time, largely stable and widely shared conceptions of academic R&D (and of the "academy" more generally) suggest that varying processes of change may share common features across organizations. In more abstract terms, this case highlights a real tension between supra-organizational pressures toward convergence and situational pulls toward heterogeneity. My initial effort to unravel that tension requires a tight empirical focus on what is changing, but also attention to how that change occurs in particular locations and to who is driving the transformation.

The character and outcomes of U.S. universities' increasing engagements with commerce are shaped by three common factors: (1) the well-worn institutional distinction between an academic research system dominated by peer-reviewed publications and grants and concerned primarily with status-based rewards (Dasgupta & David, 1994; Dasgupta & David, 1987; Merton, 1968) and a more commercial system focused on excludable intellectual property rights and pecuniary rewards (Etzkowitz, Webster, & Healey, 1995; Merton, 1988; Rip, 1986); (2) the careers of faculty members, which increasingly span multiple universities and the academic/commercial divide (Murray, 2004; Powell & Sandholz, 2011) ; and (3) the infrastructure of policies, offices, and individuals arrayed on university campuses to administer technology transfer under shared rules imposed by the 1980 Bayh-Dole Act (Nelson, 2004; Kenney & Patton, 2009).[1]

Examining these points of stability requires that attention to the fundamental change at issue (shifting relationships between academic and pecuniary R&D on campus) be filtered through the dual lenses of research administration and faculty perceptions. Despite broad similarities, however, individual universities vary widely in their practices and policies regarding intellectual property and commercial outcomes.

More than 2,700 patents were issued to the United States' eighty-nine most research-intensive universities in 2000.[2] The four most prolific patentors[3] were granted more than 28 percent of those patents and the top ten accounted for nearly 45 percent. Results are similarly stark in terms of commonly used metrics of commercial returns to academic research. The top ten revenue earners garner more than 65 percent of the more than $1 billion intellectual property licensing returned to universities. The ten most successful institutions on several other measures (licenses that include equity in start-up firms, number of new start-ups, licenses executed, and licenses generating income) account for between 35 and 50 percent of all the commercial action (Association of University Technology Managers [AUTM], 2000). By 2010, the most recent year in which data are available, the ten highest revenue-earning U.S. universities accounted for 57 percent of the more than $1.79 billion in gross revenue generated by campus licensing efforts. Similar levels of concentration persisted on other measures as well.

While certain types of changes associated with research commercialization will be apparent across campuses, the actual processes of transformation that specific universities follow may vary dramatically with organizational arrangements and (in particular) with campus position in the stable stratification system that characterizes academic R&D. In order to examine both the broad institutional changes and the effects of their particular enactments on campus, I opt for a comparative research design that focuses specifically on similarities at the level of collectivities while emphasizing variation in the organizationally situated relationships among them.

COMPARATIVE CASES AND DATA

The fundamental data underlying this research are drawn from transcripts of semi-structured interviews with eighty-nine scientists, engineers, technology licensing officers, and research administrators on two different campuses.[4] These interviews were conducted in 1999 and 2000. In addition to interviews, observations in a variety of settings (e.g., laboratories and research groups, technology licensing offices, regents' meetings) and archival data from both public (e.g., United States Patent and Trademark Office, National Science Foundation Science Indicators Data) and university (e.g., licensing and sponsored project records) sources were used to supplement information gathered in interviews.

The proposition that common institutional catalysts of change result in different organizational trajectories and outcomes suggests a somewhat novel research design. I selected campuses to maximize variation in organizational arrangements and outcomes. Big State University (BSU) and Elite Private University (EPU) are very different organizations.[5] The former is a land-grant campus widely recognized as one of a set of up and coming state universities in the public science hierarchy. With significant strengths in optics, materials science, nanotechnology, and translational biomedicine, BSU faculty conduct considerable research that is potentially commercializable. EPU, in contrast, emerged as an elite science and engineering university in the postwar era and has maintained its broad preeminence across physical and life science disciplines. While there are clear differences in the breadth and depth of their academic reputations, both campuses rank among the top recipients of sponsored project funds.[6] In terms of academic reputation and capacity, then, these two campuses represent widely varying but not wildly inappropriate comparison cases.

More important for my focus on commercialization are these campuses' fundamental disparities on common measures of technology transfer infrastructure and output. Where EPU was an early entrant into the technology transfer game (founding a formal technology licensing office more than a decade prior to the passage of the Bayh-Dole Act), BSU is a relative newcomer whose office was among the last founded in the late 1980s. Differences in experience are matched by differential levels of university support. At the turn of the twenty-first century EPU's office boasted more than twenty-five full-time equivalent personnel while fewer than ten people were wholly dedicated to commercialization efforts at BSU. Given persistent findings that university patenting and licensing efforts manifest increasing returns to scale (Siegel, Waldman, & Link, 2003), it is not surprising that these capacity differences are reflected in huge outcome disparities.

By the end of the 1990s, EPU licensing officers received three times more invention disclosures than their counterparts at BSU. Similarly, BSU filed nearly ten times fewer new patent applications and executed only one-quarter of the licensing deals. As one might expect, these "input" differentials are matched by widely varying returns. EPU was issued nearly five times more patents than BSU and translated that property into yearly licensing revenues in the tens of millions of dollars. BSU's income stream is a full order of magnitude smaller (AUTM, 1998; AUTM, 1999; AUTM, 2000). In 2010, these differences became even more dramatic. That year, EPU was issued more than thirteen times the number of patents that BSU received. In terms of revenue streams, 2010 saw BSU's efforts yield just 1.1 percent of the returns that flowed to EPU. Experience, infrastructure, magnitude, and even luck matter in explanations of cross-campus outcome differences. My contention, however, is that that the first three of those factors are endogenous outcomes of an ongoing process that has brought technology licensing officers and research faculty into close contact around issues of disclosure, patentability, and approaches to commercialization.

Put another way, the thirty-year history of academic technology transfer efforts since the 1981 Bayh-Dole Act has resulted in marked and persistent concentration in both activities and returns on just a few campuses. The members of this small number of research universities represent the pinnacle of scientific productivity in American academia, but there are also dramatic differences in status among them, with a handful of high-profile private institutions and an even more circumscribed group of very visible public campuses perched atop the contemporary scientific status hierarchy. The most commercially

productive and profitable campuses do not map uniformly onto either existing scientific status or raw levels of experience with technology transfer (Owen-Smith, 2003). Instead, part of the reason for
persistent differences in commercial performance as well as for the
relative stability of those outcomes over time has to do with the character of particular local efforts to solve the common organizational
dilemmas raised by technology transfer. The process by which these
challenges were recognized (or not) and resolved (or not) on specific
campuses may also yield insight into the complicated and sometimes
negative effects increased commercial engagement is having on the
practice of academic research.

FROM REPUTATION RACES TO OWNERSHIP RIGHTS

Importing commercial standards to academic research is potentially
corrosive precisely because it represents a shift in the core rules of
the academic game. The outlines of this change are best conveyed
in terms of the divergent implications of patents and publications as
mechanisms for the dissemination of novel research findings. Both
patents and publications are explicit mechanisms for publicizing new
information, but they differ dramatically on several dimensions.

Consider Arie Rip's (1986) evocative analogy linking publications to funnels and patents to fences as an entry point into a discussion of academic and proprietary approaches to scientific findings.
Both publications and patents are markers of accomplishment and
means to disseminate information. Publications, however, are funnels
precisely because their success depends on the breadth of future use.
Articles represent an author's formal release of control over the uses
to which a finding is put.[7] "Ownership," then, is a matter of priority and recognition (Merton, 1968, 1988). Returns to publication
accrue in reputation and both priority and rewards are intimately
linked to others' uses of an author's findings. In short, articles have
(and to be successful can have) no presumption of exclusivity. In contrast, patents are fences in the sense that they demarcate a "plot" of
knowledge legally owned by its inventor. Property ownership con-
veys a bundle of rights. For this argument however, excludability (the
right to prevent others' use of your property) and appropriability (the
right to capture economic returns from the use of your property) are

central and their various implications have generated much of the hue and cry that has accompanied academic commercialization.

The distinctions I draw between patents and publications are particularly important for universities and faculty because the Bayh-Dole Act imposes standard rules on the patenting of federally funded innovations. Most tellingly, Bayh-Dole requires that ownership of intellectual property be vested in the university and not in the individual faculty inventor. This provision has a number of important implications. First, it necessitates that universities (which had traditionally been ill equipped to manage intellectual property) develop administrative units and policies to facilitate the identification, prosecution, marketing, and management of IP developed on campus.[8] Second, vesting ownership rights in the organization fundamentally alters the relationship between faculty and their institutions, shifting the locus of control of a scientist's research output from the individual to the institution. Questions about how to use intellectual property and how to divide revenues from its use have the potential to set researchers and their institutions at loggerheads.[9] If this tension is really central to both the broad institutional transformations shaping the academy and the varying organizational outcomes that accompany it, then university policies and procedures should focus explicitly (though perhaps with different valences) on the dual issues of ownership/control, and distribution of returns.

Ownership and Profit in Policy

Differences in policies governing IP ownership and royalty distribution are important. Focusing attention upon those variations draws attention to the divergent formal approaches universities have developed as they strive to address tensions arising from commercial engagements. Thus, an analysis of policies on the two campuses must elucidate the shared origins of the divergent rules while demonstrating that their particularities could result in disparate commercial outcomes. While they may tell only part of the story, I argue that organizational policies are rules that represent the outcomes of situated processes of organizational learning.

Policies are not exogenous inputs into a stream of organizational activity; instead, they represent the crystallization (perhaps also the

Table 9.1. Intellectual Property Policies, EPU and BSU, 2000

Policy Focus	EPU Language	BSU Language
IP Ownership	Title to all potentially patentable inventions conceived or first reduced to practice in whole or in part by members of the faculty or staff (including student employees) of the University in the course of their University responsibilities or with more than incidental use of University resources, belongs to the University. . . . The inventor, or inventors acting collectively when there are more than one, is free to place inventions in the public domain if that would be in the best interest of technology transfer and if doing so is not in violation of the terms of any agreements that supported or governed the work. The University will not assert intellectual property rights when inventors have placed their inventions in the public domain.	If intellectual property is developed by an employee within his or her area of expertise or responsibility, then the intellectual property is owned by the University. The determination of ownership of intellectual property is not dependent upon the person's physical location. *For example, if a chemist is working on a new chemical structure and a related idea comes to him while showering at home, the intellectual property is owned by the University. But a chemist working in a home workshop, creating a new wooden toy, is the owner of that intellectual property, although such intellectual property should be disclosed to the University Designated individual.* In general, decisions concerning intellectual property ownership are based on common sense. That is, if it is reasonable and logical to assume the employee's discovery was made without any influence of the University or its resources, then ownership is the employee's.

Table 9.1. (continued)

Policy Focus	EPU Language	BSU Language
Royalty Split	Pursuant to EPU's present policy on royalty sharing, net cash royalties [15% of gross removed for TLO budget and costs] are divided 1/3 to the Inventor, 1/3 to the Inventor's department, and 1/3 to the Inventor's school. The Invention Disclosure Form requests that the inventor indicate the department that supported development of the invention. Unless TLO is notified otherwise, the indicated department and its school will receive the department and school's share of royalties.	All income repays any University Expenses incurred in creating the income. The royalty schedule listed below is net of 'first income' (1) Net income up to $10K—100% to inventor (2) Net income $11K-$50K—50% Inventor, 30% Inventor Discretionary account, 20 % University Intellectual Property account. (3) Net income $51K-$500K—40% Inventor, 25% Inventor Discretionary account, 20% University IP account, 5% Inventor's Department, 5% Vice President's fund for the Promotion of Research. (4) Net Income $501K-$1M—35% Inventor, 20% Inventor Discretionary account, 30% University IP account, 10% Inventor's Department, 5% VP's Fund (5) Net Income > $1M—25% Inventor, 20% Inventor Discretionary, 40% University IP account, 10% Inventor Department, 5% VP's fund.

idealization) of past activities (March, Schulz, & Chou, 2000; Zhou, 1993). As organizational rules, policies encode past experiences. They are articulated and enacted by specific sets of actors. Hence, the effects of capacity, experience, and magnitude upon commercial outcomes at EPU and BSU will be mediated by the relationships instantiated in technology transfer and faculty work and most especially at their intersection. Thus, I emphasize that rules and procedures have both ostensive and performative characteristics (Feldman & Pentland, 2003).

The two core tensions that Bayh-Dole ensured would be shared across campuses center on ownership and profit from intellectual property. Table 9.1 highlights policies relevant to university ownership of faculty-developed IP and to the distribution of royalty income on licensed IP as of the year 2000 when the bulk of my fieldwork took place.

At both EPU and BSU, patented faculty inventions are owned by the university as a condition of the employment contract. The proximate cause on both campuses is the Bayh-Dole Act. At BSU the state constitution—which mandates that property developed by state employees in the course of their duties be owned by the state—adds another impetus to establishing ownership over faculty-developed IP. Despite the similar concerns that are manifest in these policy snippets, they also manifest two key differences that revolve around establishing ownership and control over the eventual distribution of inventions (excludability).

Note that EPU takes ownership of innovations developed during the course of a faculty member's responsibilities qua faculty member or with "more than incidental use" of university resources. The latter section is routinely cited by faculty to explain how they came to own patents separate from the university. On EPU's campus the level of resource usage that surpasses the incidental is negotiable, as is the breadth of "university responsibilities." In contrast, BSU's policy does not mention resource usage and expands university responsibilities to encompass any innovation within an employee's "area of expertise or responsibility." The phrasing here is much more constraining than that found in the EPU policy, as it suggests that any invention in any way related to a faculty member's academic responsibilities belongs to the university regardless of whether BSU resources were used.

Indeed, the BSU policy goes on to make this idea explicit in a hypothetical discussion (highlighted in italics) of ownership in the case of an invention developed by a chemist in the shower. Even in the extreme case of a chemist who invents a "new wooden toy" (certainly an invention that is far removed from her professional competencies as a chemist and associated duties in the university) BSU's policy states that rights to the toy are the inventor's, but that the innovation should be disclosed to a university official. Where the EPU ownership policy holds out some hope of flexibility on the question of ownership, thus implying a degree of discretion for faculty inventors, BSU's policy strictly demarcates university-owned property to encompass any invention made in the area of competency for which a faculty member is employed. In the language of the policy, any chemical invention made by a chemist is unequivocally the property of BSU.

The second notable feature of these ownership policies has to do with control over the eventual disposition of an innovation. As was the case above, the EPU policy implies greater discretion for faculty inventors at the potential expense of university control. Note that while BSU's policy makes no mention of placing it in the public domain (presumably through publication), EPU explicitly allows faculty to decide to do just that on the condition that such an action does not violate the terms of any existing agreements and that it be "in the best interests" of transferring the technology. Under such conditions, EPU "will not assert intellectual property rights." In other words, EPU's policy limits university ownership to those instances where faculty inventors opt to pursue intellectual property. This passage reprises the theme of faculty discretion that is largely absent from the language of BSU's more restrictive policy. While interviews and observations suggest that neither office spends any time "policing" the scientific literature for instances of faculty innovations wrongly released to the public, EPU's explicit recognition that inventions can be transferred through publication signals (at least rhetorically) the primacy of the traditional academic research mission over and above more commercially oriented outcomes.

Both policies demonstrate concern with the transfer of ownership rights from faculty researchers to the university itself, but the discretion accorded to faculty and the breadth of expectations for ownership by the university vary dramatically across campuses. Similar variations are evident in policies governing royalty sharing.

The second row of Table 9.1 highlights differences in those policies. Contrast EPU's fairly simple policy—a three-way split between the inventor, the inventor's department, and the inventor's school net of 15 percent removed to cover operating costs and overhead—with the complicated "sliding scale" used by BSU. Several BSU inventors bemoaned the complications of their institution's policy. One senior life scientist noted that the inventor's share dropped precipitously "just as things got interesting," while another noted, with tongue firmly in cheek, that "the thing is so complex that if we ever got any royalties they'd all be spent on an accountant to figure out the split."

Both comments highlight important differences across the policies. Note that the inventor's share of royalties remains constant at EPU whether royalties amount to $300 or $300 million. The inverse relationship between the magnitude of the royalty stream and the inventor's share in those monies at BSU is explicitly designed to reward "base hits" rather than "home runs" in the licensing game. Also notice who shares the royalties. At EPU, funds go to the inventor, her department, and her school (e.g., school of arts and sciences). In each case the returns to an invention remain plausibly within the reach of an inventor. The source of a yearly influx of funds into department chairs' and deans' discretionary accounts is likely to be noticed when successful inventors make requests of administrators. Contrast this with BSU's policy where an increasingly large share of royalties goes into a general intellectual property account administered by the university's vice president for research.

EPU inventors ascribe some importance to the proximity of their royalty funds. A senior physical scientist who has held university-level administrative posts highlights the importance of this difference for faculty.

What is really unusual and absolutely motivating [about the royalty policy] was that 1/3 went to the inventor, 1/3 to the department, but the remaining 1/3 did not go to the university general fund, it went to the school instead. [That was] absolutely critical [because] there was then and there is today a mistrust by faculty members of monies that go directly into the general fund. If it goes to the general fund of a university it might as well go to the federal government. The reasoning is, I'll never see it, it will never benefit me.

The benefits associated with royalty income play an important role in the rhetoric of incentives technology licensing officers (and to a certain extent university administrators) mobilize to convince sometimes skeptical faculty to disclose their inventions. To the extent that concerns about being able to "reach" the royalty income associated with one's inventions are common among faculty, policies that return funds to units in close organizational proximity to inventors may help to generate greater rates of faculty disclosure. Similar outcomes might result from another feature of the policies. Note that BSU mandates a division of the inventor's share of royalties across personal and academic ("inventor's discretionary account") uses, whereas EPU's more flexible policy makes no such separation, leaving the distribution of funds up to the faculty inventor.

Beyond their relationship to faculty decisions about disclosure, such policies also have distributional consequences for the allocation of "unrestricted" funds across campuses. At universities where a portion of royalty income is distributed from a university-level fund, there is at least some possibility that units on campus that have little to no engagement with commercial activity (for instance, most humanities and social science disciplines) might benefit from the university's licensing activity. Under a system that keeps royalty funds close to inventors, in contrast, those units (e.g., engineering, genetics, pharmacology) that patent most extensively will reap the benefits of their commercial engagement, raising the possibility that significant royalty funds could exacerbate already existing funding differentials across fields within universities.

Finally, note the subtle, but important, difference in the policies' treatment of overhead costs. EPU sets a limit (15 percent of gross) on overhead, while BSU simply notes that such costs will be defrayed before royalties are split. BSU inventors whose patents have generated income often report that BSU's overhead costs are difficult to predict and can swell to encompass the lion's share of revenues. One senior life scientist, who has invented several lucrative technologies, sums up this concern: "As it is, it's not even worth our while. After they whack that off the top we get a little dribble five years down the road. To hell with it."

Variations in institutional responses to the key contradictions inherent in mixing proprietary and academic approaches to science and engineering imply very different organizational contexts for those activities. BSU's policies indicate a strong conception of ownership, imply lesser discretion for faculty inventors, and describe a royalty split that reduces rewards for spectacular success, while removing an increasing portion of monetary returns from the inventor's reach. The acting director of BSU's technology licensing office highlighted both the income-focused incentive structure of the policy and the inflexibility of ownership requirements in an interview:

> The main incentive to disclose is the one I mentioned. We share income with faculty. That is the upside. The downside is that it is required. Faculty are state employees. Their inventions are state property. As state employees they are required to disclose. So that is the carrot and the stick.

The potential for conflict between faculty inventors and licensing professionals is close to the surface in this director's comments. BSU's formal policies also bear the stamp of conflicts over who should control faculty inventions and as a result help to cement distrust between faculty inventors and licensing professionals into a somewhat adversarial technology transfer process.

The rigidities in this policy are explicable in terms of both the constraints placed upon a public university by its state constitution and a desire to spread any returns from commercial success as broadly as possible across a university that routinely faces budgetary pressure from an overwhelmingly conservative state legislature. In sum, strong efforts to control faculty inventions and to turn their proceeds to support the campus as a whole have the effect of increasing conflicts and thus decreasing commercial involvement at BSU.

In contrast, EPU policies include a more flexible conception of ownership, a greater range of discretion for faculty inventors in terms of both royalty use and the decision to place a new invention in the public domain, and a royalty policy that limits overhead expenses while keeping income within the organizational "reach" of an inventor. Here the model more clearly subordinates decisions about intellectual property to an academic logic and in doing so helps to frame technology licensing professionals as servants of the university's academic mission rather than as watchdogs for its commercial interests. A nod to faculty discretion and royalty-sharing policies that keep profits within the reach of inventors help to decrease conflicts between licensing professionals and inventors and thus to increase rates of commercial involvement on campus. Those increases, however, may come at the cost of growing disparities among faculty as well as across units, disciplines, and fields that are more or less far removed from the immediate needs of the market.

EPU's policies, then, help to establish an organizational environment conducive to faculty members' simultaneous pursuit of public and private science precisely by hewing more closely to a traditional "academic" approach that places a great deal of discretion in the hands of faculty and that decentralizes efforts to "invest" commercial returns in scientific pursuits. The overall impact of those policies favors faculty autonomy and situates returns at the level of the school rather than the university. One senior life scientist at EPU frames these issues clearly in a comparison of the policies at his university and at a peer institution of BSU, which had recently attempted to recruit him: "EPU trusts its faculty, they have a pretty good track record with trust and they really give you freedom. Across campuses there are examples where they run it this way and examples where they run it more like Leningrad State." He goes on to note that the lack of discretion afforded by "Leningrad State" played a large role in his decision not to accept an appointment there.

As these comments suggest, policies in and of themselves cannot enact change within an organization. Formal rules do, however, set the stage upon which specific organizational transformations play out. Differences in responses to the same set of tensions across campuses are suggestive. Divergent policies can catalyze very different dynamics in relationships between faculty and licensing officers and thus, result in wide-ranging trajectories.

FACULTY RESPONSES AND THE DECISION TO DISCLOSE

For an academic scientist, the decision to pursue a patent via an invention disclosure to a university technology licensing office is complicated. Faculty frame such decisions at three levels of analysis, speaking in terms of (1) broad conceptions of the effects commercial endeavors have on the university and academic science; (2) the general environment their campus offers for entrepreneurial science; and (3) perceptions of their local technology licensing office, its staff, and policies. Faculty accounts of the decision (not) to disclose are accordingly complex and often ambiguous. Professors offer explanations for their decisions that range from broad concerns about commercialization's effects on the academy, to simple ignorance about IP, and specific complaints about the policies and procedures surrounding technology transfer on their campus (see Jensen, Thursby, & Thursby, 2003).

What is immediately striking about such accounts is that there is little cross-campus variation on the first dimension highlighted above. Almost without exception both EPU and BSU faculty share a range of perceptions about the relationship between commercial and academic science on campus and those perceptions color their thinking about the benefits and detriments of patenting.

Faculty Responses to Commercialization and Incentives to Patent

Two distinct, though related, sets of issues permeate faculty discussions of patenting. The first has to do with general concerns regarding the increasing commercialization of academic research (particularly in the life sciences). The second manifests greater interest in the particular uses to which intellectual property can be put and the professional and personal benefits of patenting. While these discourses are apparent on both the EPU and BSU campuses, their valences shift with the discipline of the researcher being interviewed. Faculty decisions to disclose are driven by their general conceptions of the "fit" between academic and proprietary science and by their perceptions of the potential outcomes and benefits of patenting, but with respect to both sets of issues their comments suggest that meanings, implications, and uses of intellectual property vary dramatically across physical and life science fields.

As universities become more deeply engaged with a wide range of commercial activities, faculty face more complex professional and intellectual environments. The shifts at work in the academy are most apparent in the life sciences (Powell & Owen-Smith, 1998) on more research-intensive campuses, and at the top of the academic status hierarchy (Blumenthal et al., 1986; Owen-Smith, 2003). Thus, I begin with a brief analysis of life science faculty responses to commercialization, highlight differences in physical scientists' perceptions and then link broader conceptions to the uses to which these two broad groups of faculty typically put intellectual property.

The professional world of life science research has fundamentally transformed over the last quarter century. New scientific discoveries enabled closer linkages between cutting-edge science and industrial development and helped spark the rise of an industry (biotechnology) that has maintained its historically close roots to the university and to academic research (Powell, Koput, & Smith-Doerr, 1996). At the same time, expanded possibilities to patent living organisms (catalyzed by the 1981 *Diamond v. Chakrabarty* Supreme Court decision) increased acceptance of academic patenting, a rising tide of venture capital funding (Gompers & Lerner, 1999) and influxes of both federal and industrial support for biomedical research have shifted the center of gravity of the American research university from its post–World War II focus on physical science and engineering research (often conducted with defense applications in mind) to biomedical and particularly genetically based research that is often conducted in close collaboration with industry and with human therapeutic applications in mind (Kennedy, 2003; Slaughter & Rhoades, 1996). A mix of new funding opportunities, novel scientific techniques, shifting institutional mandates for universities and their researchers, and changing life science career trajectories have brought basic and commercial research into much closer proximity and placed life science fields and research at the leading edge of university transformations (Powell & Owen-Smith, 1998).

Against this broad backdrop of change, the complications in life science faculty accounts of their responses to commercialization are best understood in terms of two fundamental assumptions. Faculty perceptions of changes to the academy and thus their decisions about whether and how to pursue intellectual property are colored by their beliefs about the degree to which academic and commercial mandates for research overlap and the extent to which such overlaps are corrosive to distinctive features of the university and its science.[10]

The most "traditional" of commercially active life scientists pursue invention disclosures and market opportunities in a fashion designed to separate those endeavors from their academic pursuits and reputations. In this view, science and commerce are not necessarily at odds, but the latter is less challenging and rewarding than the former and is best pursued after academic reputations have been cemented. These scientists largely see the relationship between academe and commerce as a one-way street. Academic success can sometimes be "cashed in" for pecuniary returns, but those returns are understood to have little bearing on academic achievement. For such scientists, control over inventions is less problematic than profiting from commerce, and as a result they are less likely to fight with licensing professionals than they are to pursue commercial efforts on their "own time" through consulting arrangements and scientific advisory board memberships.

Two, more novel, approaches diverge from this view by emphasizing inextricable linkages between proprietary and academic research. These researchers cite the groundbreaking science conducted in firms and the market value of university discoveries as evidence for the growing convergence between public and private uses of scientific knowledge. Perceiving that connection, however, raises significant issues surrounding control of inventions. One group of faculty takes this overlap to be corrosive for the university and responds, paradoxically, by turning to aggressive pursuit of intellectual property in order to protect their freedom to conduct academic research. These "reluctant entrepreneurs" are highly likely to spar with licensing professionals for the simple reason that they believe the disposition of their patents bears directly upon their ability to conduct the academic research upon which their careers and reputations rest, so that, while profits may be personally important to such researchers, they are subordinated to concerns with control.

Another selection of life scientists, though, turn the close connections between proprietary and academic uses of science to their advantage by aggressively pursuing both types of activities at once. These "new school" faculty members are deeply concerned both with control over their inventions (particularly to the extent that they hope to found companies to commercialize their academic discoveries) and with the distribution of profits (to the extent that they perceive returns to commerce as a source of support for cutting-edge academic research). Where engaged traditionalists maintain an active separation between market and academic activities and incentives and reluctant entrepreneurs turn to patents to protect their academic laboratories, new school life scientists trade on their research in two overlapping worlds. When new school researchers are active on campus both conflicts and commercial returns may increase.

While the life sciences (and their faculty) stand at the center of academic entrepreneurship, they are by no means the only active researchers (or even patentors) on campus. Physical scientists and engineers manifest similar positions as their life science colleagues, but the distribution of faculty across those positions varies in part because of the long history (particularly in physics, chemistry, and engineering) of defense- and industry-oriented research.

According to physical scientist informants, the historical position of applied academic research has been that of the engaged traditionalist whose commercial endeavors are either kept separate from academic pursuits or are simply considered a necessary component of those pursuits. In both instances the focus in physical scientists' accounts is not specifically on potential dangers to the academy but instead upon developing policies and procedures to guide researchers' attempts to manage the conflicts of interest and commitment that can easily emerge from commercial engagement. While many physical scientists fall into the engaged traditionalist category, another group has affinities with the new school life scientists.

These researchers' general focus on managing the individual conflicts brought about by commercial activity, however, help explain why physical scientists and engineers in this position are less likely than biomedical scientists to actively commercialize (through, for instance, a start-up company) their intellectual property while maintaining university affiliations. Where new school life scientists often wear multiple hats, it is more common for physical scientists to take leaves of absence or depart the academy altogether in order to direct the commercial endeavors of the firms that develop their inventions. These characteristic differences in focus suggest that the distribution of conflicts and the trajectories of change on individual campuses will also be shaped by variations in faculty engagement across disciplines.

As one senior physical scientist and university-level administrator at EPU colorfully noted, physical scientists and engineers began developing standards for the management of commercially valuable research in the immediate postwar period, and those standards are more often observed in the breach by "newly" entrepreneurial life scientists.

You can't legislate reality and you can't even legislate good manners or appropriate behavior. So, when new opportunities arise in new areas university faculty sometimes behave in ways that are not appropriate. They might involve themselves in an outside arrangement more than they should, or they might immerse themselves in outside activities, in research and consulting, that get them out of line with their commitments to teaching and research at EPU. The way our former provost[11] used to say it was the engineers have been doing this for fifty years and they know how to walk the street without looking like prostitutes. By that he meant that his newest, youngest colleagues were interacting with companies and doing stupid things that made them look pretty ugly as they were out on the street selling their wares.

While a greater range of variation is apparent in life science faculty's responses to commercialization, the spirit of this comment suggests that when new arenas and opportunities open, faculty respond in novel ways. Over time, however, standards develop that enable the maintenance of faculty engagement with commerce while maintaining the distinctive character of academic research work. The process by which such standards emerge (and are eventually drawn into question by future alterations to the environment) is one of change at the level of both professional communities and organizational arrangements. The fruits of just such a change are being harvested in today's entrepreneurial academy.

On this view, faculty accounts of the benefits and dangers of commercialization are shared across campuses but vary by broad field of study. That bifurcation (between more recently commercializing biomedical fields and research areas that have been more closely connected to application throughout the postwar period), I have suggested, is one of history, experience, and the development of legitimate and taken-for-granted means to balance potential conflicts of interest and commitment. The major effect of these differences is to limit the on-campus appearance of aggressive new school physical science faculty while opening a broader space for activities that follow the pattern of the engaged traditionalist. Physical scientists with new school tastes, my informants suggest, are likely to take leaves or depart the academy altogether for a period of time to pursue industrial interests.

The challenge, according to the administrators of physical science units, is to ensure that such researchers are able to (and desirous of) returning to the university after a commercial interlude. Indeed, as numerous scientists informed me, this path of leaving and returning was the exact pattern followed by the current provost at EPU.

A long history of commercial linkages in federal science and engineering fields may increase those researchers' belief in both the distinctiveness and the resilience of academic norms and institutions. Nevertheless, another important distinction bifurcates physical and life scientists' approaches to intellectual property on campus. The technologies and industries most commonly associated with physical and life science commercialization shift scientist's thoughts about incentives to patent.[12]

Faculty accounts of their decisions about invention disclosure are driven by their perceptions not only of the relationship between commerce and science, but also by their sense of the possible outcomes and potential benefits of pursuing patent protection. In accounts of why they have chosen to pursue patents through their universities, life and physical science faculty highlight the same general classes of benefits, but their conceptions of two of the most commonly mentioned consequences of IP—protection and leverage—suggest widely disparate understandings and uses to which patents can be put. While they vary across research area, these assessments are remarkably stable across campuses, suggesting that inter-campus differences in invention disclosures are less a result of varied perceptions of the benefits and meanings of IP, than of the ways local processes and environments for commercialization attend to complex motivations to disclose.

Here again, supra-organizational characteristics of faculty attitudes are filtered through local arrangements, policies, and processes. Similar institutional starting points result in divergent organizational outcomes because different organizations have the capacity to resolve similar ambiguities and contradictions in a variety of ways. Organizational performances in the face of supra-organizational alterations, then, orient trajectories of change that (if they become the norm for imitation) will eventually stabilize both organizational and institutional outcomes.

One such point of departure has to do with faculty's perceptions of inventors regarding the meanings and implications of intellectual property and another with the potential benefits (personal and professional) of patenting. Both are discrepant across broad research fields but the source of that variation appears to be more historical and institutional in the former case and more closely tied to technology and industry structure in the latter.

Scientists' accounts of their decisions to disclose innovations to their local technology licensing offices often invoke the concepts of leverage and protection, but the same terms hide different meanings. The director of EPU's technology licensing office captures these subtle distinctions very succinctly: "Physical scientists patent for freedom of action, life scientists patent for strategic advantage." More elaborately, life science inventions (and in particular innovations aimed at the development of therapeutic and diagnostic products) have a larger potential to open new markets where the returns to patent ownership are less likely to be constrained by existing products and overlapping intellectual properties. The possibility of being first to market with a new drug or diagnostic tool, however, is balanced against the arduous and expensive regulatory process. Thus, patents in biomedical fields can be taken to offer protection from competition in the form of licenses that transfer exclusive rights to practice and invention, and in turn the possibility of complete appropriability (though for a limited time) offers leverage in the form of incentives to shepherd a new innovation through the sometimes treacherous FDA approval process.

In contrast, physical scientists and engineers most often describe innovations, such as new techniques for magnetic resonance imaging or data storage, that often enter crowded markets where overlapping property rights to complementary technologies make it highly unlikely that a single piece of IP will return large revenues absent widespread nonexclusive licensing. In such an environment, intellectual property offers protection to faculty in terms of ensuring freedom of action to pursue their own research[13] in a world crowded with IP while conveying leverage that can be used (through cross-licensing, for instance) to ensure access to other proprietary technologies or to open relationships with other organizations upon whose technologies one's research depends.

While subtle, the distinction is potentially an important one, as it bears upon strategies for commercializing university technologies, and thus has implications for campus policies and the emphases of licensing officers. At the extreme, an "either/or" focus on physical and life science technologies can result in mutually contradictory regimes for IP use on campus. The standards and approaches associated with more established engineering approaches to commercial engagement may even help explain the chagrin with which commentators and informants view more distinctively biomedical approaches to IP and technology transfer.

If life scientists often seek strategic advantage (through exclusivity that enables certain varieties of protection and leverage) for the novel entities that can underpin market-opening therapeutics, diagnostic tools, and medical devices, then these faculty will largely view patents as tangible objects to be bought and sold. Rather than using intellectual property to open multiple nonexclusive arrangements with numerous partners (as in the physical scientists' notion of protection and leverage in IP rights), these scientists will be concerned with finding the best partner to develop and market a drug or device.

This more strongly strategic and proprietary conception of the protection and leverage benefits to IP protection may underpin increasing concerns with potential conflicts of interest and commitment among life scientists engaged in commercial biomedical research (see Krimsky, 2003). Perhaps more importantly for this argument, this more strategic view of IP protection suggests greater potential for university-level ownership and control of intellectual property to generate conflicts between institutions, administrators, and faculty (Mirowski, 2011). Under a freedom of action regime that emphasizes multiple, nonexclusive licenses to open a field of play (and not inconsequentially, relationships with established players), decisions about individual licenses may be perceived as less consequential.

Needless to say, then, the campus-level effects of a widespread turn to proprietary science will have to do with (1) the distribution of life and physical science entrepreneurs on campus (and within those groups, of the multiple approaches to commercialization and IP documented above); and (2) with the development of local policies, procedures, and institutional environments that can accommodate multiple, complex, and potentially contradictory sets of approaches to IP. On most campuses, enacting the latter is the province of the technology licensing officer and is most apparent in their decisions about when (and how) to pursue intellectual property protection for inventions disclosed by faculty.

LICENSING PROFESSIONALS AND THE DECISION TO FILE

The explosion of patenting and licensing on U.S. university campuses in the last three decades was catalyzed by federal policy changes that formally located ownership rights to intellectual property based on federally funded research in the organizational performer of that research rather than in the agency that funded it. As I noted above, this move had important implications for the university, as it altered the character of the relationship between an institution and its faculty and necessitated the development of some organizational means to identify, prosecute, manage, and market IP developed by faculty researchers.

Universities could (and routinely did) hold title to IP developed on their campuses prior to the passage of the Bayh-Dole Act. Policy changes in the 1980s, then, did more to accelerate a trend toward academic patenting and technology transfer than to create one (Mowery et al., 2001). Bayh-Dole and other changes associated with it, succeeded primarily in making technology transfer a standard and expected component of the university research mission in the United States (Owen-Smith, 2003). In doing so, the act created a burgeoning market among universities for employees whose job was to evaluate and administer intellectual property, widespread diffusion of internal technology licensing infrastructures in U.S. universities, and thus development of a new type of campus research administrator.

A professional and practical locus of the changes occurring in U.S. universities is the technology licensing office. Such formal arrangements for technology transfer are increasingly common on U.S. campuses. In a 2000 survey of American universities, all but ten of the 142 institutions responding reported a date of founding for a technology licensing program. Only six of the ten that did not report a date of founding dedicate less than one FTE staff person to technology licensing duties (AUTM, 2000). These offices, and their occupants, are essential players in the elaboration and enactment of the policies and practices that represent organizational responses to broader institutional changes, and they are staffed by a new professional group complete with its own international association.

Founded in 1973 as the Society of University Patent Administrators (SUPA), the Association of University Technology Managers (AUTM) witnessed dramatic growth in membership and influence

in the period following the passage of Bayh-Dole. In 1976, soon after its founding, the association had only fifty individual members,
but those numbers swelled to more than three thousand by the early
years of the twenty-first century (AUTM, 2003). The swelling ranks
of AUTM were matched by a dramatic acceleration in foundings of
university technology transfer programs. Nearly 77 percent (109) of
the 142 universities surveyed by AUTM in 2000 founded technology
transfer programs after 1980 and fully 30 percent (43) founded such
programs in the 1990s (AUTM, 2000).

Along with dramatic increases in membership and university
penetration, the 1990s saw AUTM begin to develop metrics for technology transfer through their yearly "licensing survey," to extend
efforts at outreach and lobbying, and to develop professional training opportunities for members ranging from multi-unit courses and
didactic seminars at meetings to formalized resources such as a new
technology transfer practice manual and a "toolkit" aimed at the
directors of technology licensing offices. While these efforts have not
gone uncontested—for instance, several universities have expressed
concern with the AUTM survey's focus on income as a primary metric for success—AUTM and its members seem to be clearly engaged
in a project of professionalization.

In keeping with this effort, informants active in AUTM's administration report that a current focus of debate surrounds the development of standard credentials and certifications for technology
licensing professionals. The development of university technology
managers as a recognizable and distinct professional group and their
increasing involvement in university technology transfer efforts represents another supra-organizational transition associated with increasing commercialization in the wake of Bayh-Dole.

On individual campuses, technology licensing officers are responsible for day to day decision making and management of intellectual
property. Where the decision to disclose an invention offers a win-
dow onto faculty perceptions of commercialization, the decision to
file patents on such disclosures provides insight into the unique positions professionalizing technology managers occupy in the ecology of
the entrepreneurial university.

Technology licensing officers occupy a sometimes uncomfort-
able middle ground between industrial clients, faculty inventors, and
the university administrators who oversee their work. In this sense

licensing professionals on campus share much in common with other service occupations in that they are (at least) "dual agents" (Jensen, Thursby, & Thursby, 2003), whose objectives and activities are simultaneously shaped by faculty on whom they depend for invention disclosures and expert information and by the central administration on their campuses on whose behalf they administer the ownership rights that accompany title to intellectual properties.[14]

Across BSU and EPU campuses, licensing professionals' accounts of the considerations that go into a decision to file share several common features: (1) the importance of faculty input into the decision, (2) search for signals of potential value and industrial interest in licensing, and (3) concern with the accessibility of findings and similarly with avoiding actions that might allow the university to be cast as acting in pursuit of narrowly commercial interests.

The comments of an experienced EPU licensing associate highlight the importance of the multiple "parameters" that structure a decision to file. His description emphasizes the complications inherent in evaluating the potential of an early stage, often ill-defined, innovation. Common methods for overcoming such difficulties deepen licensing professionals' connections to multiple (sometimes competing) constituencies while blurring the very boundaries—between the inventor and the invention, between marketing and evaluation, and between the university and commerce—that licensing offices are charged to help maintain (Guston, 1999).

> You have to be able to get a quick understanding of the technology, but you can never understand it at the level of PhD. You may be pretty good in one area but there is no way to understand enough of it, the novelty, what it will take to put it into a commercial product and the hurdles that will have to be overcome to make it a commercial success. There is not a crystal ball to look at, so we have to consider some very rough parameters. For instance we look at the inventor and even if you are not sure you put more weight on somebody who has been successful before. You also look at where the market is and the technical barriers to implementing the technology. The other aspect of what we do is listen to industry. We definitely value the information that we get from companies.

The complicated picture presented here focuses our attention on the central role the faculty inventor plays as a source of information about their technology and a parameter in decision making. The central importance of this "inventor factor" is common in licensing professionals' accounts of decision making on both campuses, but the valence of that attention varies dramatically and in a fashion that seems wholly congruous with the different policy orientations described earlier.

While both EPU and BSU licensing professionals are tasked with evaluating and marketing university innovations and (in the process) with managing the increasingly porous boundary between the university and the market, the different offices have adopted very different approaches to those duties. Nowhere are the differences more clear than in the relationships between licensing officers and faculty inventors.

Efforts at "inventor management" play a large role in licensing professionals' accounts of the technology transfer process, but as was the case with physical and life scientists, conceptions of protection and leverage benefits to IP, the shared term masks interesting variations. In this case, the variation stems from an indissoluble mix of differences in campus resources for technology transfer and in licensing professionals' conceptions of their particular roles vis-à-vis faculty inventors and inventions. Both approaches represent local accommodations to the pressures that formal ownership rights place on the relationship between faculty and their institutions and are easily apparent in different approaches to staffing a technology transfer office.

On EPU's campus, licensing efforts are framed largely as a service provided to faculty at their discretion while BSU's office focus more on "policing" the boundaries of the university to ensure that faculty do not take inventions that are legally university property "off the reservation." Where EPU's focus is on marketing faculty innovations in concert with their inventors, BSU emphasizes a more restrictive and legal approach to protecting and licensing IP. Where the former stresses the formation and maintenance of relationships via intellectual property (and does so with the help of slack resources available due to prior licensing successes) the latter is concerned (in large part because it lacks a track record of success or an established revenue stream) with establishing ownership over properties that may return blockbuster income streams to the institution.

Such blockbuster returns are most likely to emerge from life science research that generates fundamental research tools or that offer broad protection for a therapeutically valuable compound. These types of intellectual property are precisely those of the greatest concern to reluctant entrepreneurs and new school life scientists respectively (Powell & Owen-Smith, 2001). At BSU, then, restrictive policies and a history of adversarial relationships between faculty and licensing professionals are exacerbated by organizational and environmental pressures to generate revenue; pressures that bring technology managers into close contact with precisely the faculty groups whose interests in disclosing and lack of established disciplinary methods for handling commercial engagements make conflict most likely.

These different approaches and relationships are also reflected in the staff of technology transfer offices. Every (non–support staff) member of BSU's small technology licensing office is trained to the PhD level in a science and engineering field or is an attorney specializing in intellectual property. In contrast, only one member of EPU's (2.5 times larger) licensing office held a doctoral degree at the time of my fieldwork. There were no attorneys, and the bulk of licensing associates were trained to the bachelor's degree level in a science or engineering field. Several associates also held (or were pursuing) graduate degrees in business administration or marketing.

Staffing and focus differences also resonate with perceptions of the inventor's proper role as a participant and parameter in decision making. Consider two very different accounts of the inventor factor in decisions to file. The first, offered by BSU's outgoing director, emphasized the need to separate inventors from their inventions and determine the marketability of the researcher as well as the technology while purging estimations of potential value of the irrational exuberance of faculty.

> Inventors are very important to our decisions as long as you remove their overenthusiasm. There is something called the inventor factor, and that is something we have to consider. Can you work with this guy? Can you dress him up and take him out? Is he going to shoot down every deal as soon as he meets someone in the business, or is he going to keep secrets from us so that we will the technology back to him. Sometimes we get disclosures and say there's no information here.

> There's no data. You know damn well that the inventor is excited about something, but you haven't got a clue what. We just can't evaluate it. What happens in that case is that we release the invention to the faculty member.

Compare this account, in which the inventor factor is largely a negative outcome of (only partially muted) conflicts surrounding the ownership of technologies, to the account offered by a very experienced EPU licensing officer whose decades of experience have concentrated on physical science technologies.

> When I'm doing an analysis of whether I'm going to accept something, I look at who the inventor is. I look at how enthusiastic they are, because they play a critical role in the process. I've learned from experience that the passion of the inventor can tell me a lot. You may think that an invention is worthless, but if the inventor is totally committed to it and believes in it strongly, then that counts a lot for me.

Where the inventor factor is framed predominantly as a hindrance (or in the worst case as a disingenuous performance) in the BSU account, EPU's licensing officer highlights the central importance inventor appraisals of a technology's worth play in decision making. What should be clear here is that the central relationship driving cross-campus differences in accounts of patenting is that between faculty inventors and technology licensing officers. The tensions and complications that play out in accounts of faculty's decision to disclose and licensing professionals' decisions to file are common to both campuses and are embedded in changing policy regimes, faculty's shifting perceptions of their professional environments, and the rise of a new class of university administrators who must manage the boundary between the academy and industry while skirting potential rifts that formal ownership rights open between faculty and their institutions.

CONCLUSION AND DISCUSSION

Accounts of key decisions underlying patenting efforts on two disparate campuses manifest very similar features that result from shared supra-organizational characteristics of a transformation at work in one of the core missions of the academy. These shared catalysts, though, spark change trajectories on individual campuses that result in widely disparate campus environments for commercialization and similarly divergent outcomes. The theoretical challenge posed here is to link the contours of supra-organizational institutional changes that are common to variously organized universities with different patterns as well as magnitudes of change. How do common institutional starting points result in divergent processes of situated change? In what sense does a change in the "academy" manifest and depend upon typical patterns of change at work in individual universities? These questions require a novel approach that emphasizes two features of large scale but differentiated transformations: (1) their nested character (e.g., tensions introduced to an entire class of organizations are enacted and resolved in very different situated processes and thus develop multiple instantiations and legitimate meanings); and (2) their relational character (e.g., processes of situated organizational change are relational and political in that shared tensions generate characteristic patterns of conflict and resolution among key collectivities in organizations).

The argument presented in this essay situates these dual features of institutional/organizational change in an analysis of the processes by which supra-organizational pressures associated with academic research commercialization are enacted in divergent processes of organizational change on particular campuses. I selected widely divergent campuses as research sites precisely to enable a dual figure-ground focus on very different organizational trajectories and outcomes that emerged through the resolution of tensions introduced by changes common to both institutions (e.g., shifting ownership rights, the rise of a new professional group, and shifting faculty conceptions of their professional environment). On this view of emergence, relationships among core organizational constituencies offer insights into the specific trajectories taken by different organizations.

Accounts of patenting on both campuses manifest notable similarities. They describe a process less like a race between well-defined starting and ending points than like a rugby scrum[15] where a diverse mass of players come together to push an ill-defined object toward a general goal. These accounts describe faculty decisions to disclose, and licensing professionals' decisions to file as key points of contact that provide articulation points for particular change processes. The motor of that change is relational and situated (at least metaphorically) in technology licensing offices where a newly professionalizing group of technology managers and a variegated set of faculty inventors come together to co-constitute patentable technologies and in the process an entrepreneurial environment on their particular campus.

NOTES

The research reported has been supported by the National Science Foundation (# 0097970, # 0545634) and the Sloan Foundation (Industrial Studies Program). I am indebted to the faculty, staff, and students on two campuses who shared their time and knowledge with me.
 1. Bayh-Dole enables universities to patent the outcomes of federally funded research provided that title to those inventions is held by the institution and that the patented innovation be commercialized (e.g., transferred to the market).
 2. The institutions represent about 2 percent of all postsecondary institution in the United States. While hard counts of academic patents are difficult to establish, the U.S. Patent Office estimates that 2008 saw some 2,891 utility patents issued to U.S.-based universities and colleges (United States Patent and Trademark Office, 2010). A 2000 survey of technology transfer activity at 141 U.S. universities conducted by the Association of University Technology Managers reports that 3,222 patents were awarded to those institutions in that year. Patenting activity on university campuses is thus highly concentrated at a very small number of research intensive institutions.
 3. The University of California system, MIT, Stanford, and Caltech. Data extracted via assignee searches from the U.S. Patent and Trademark Office's online database.
 4. The bulk of these interviews are with faculty members, but in some instances graduate students and post-docs located in commercially active research groups were also interviewed.
 5. In keeping with the need to maintain informant confidentiality, names and characteristics of the individual informants and the institutions they are affiliated with are pseudonyms.

6. EPU's nearly $500 million/year sponsored research budget clearly outweighs the approximately $350 million BSU receives yearly. In relative terms, however, both campuses fall near the top of the grants distribution for research intensive institutions, and within one standard deviation of each other.

7. Publication (or any form of public disclosure) bars the possibility of patent protection and, in the case of articles, even the particular expression of a finding (e.g., the copyright) is signed over to the publishing journal by a faculty inventor.

8. Throughout this chapter, I focus attention on universities with internal offices of technology transfer. Such arrangements are by no means the only possibility, though they are model arrangements on research-intensive U.S. campuses. Other models include reliance on an independent patent management firm (Mowery et al., 2001) and the creation of a separate nonprofit entity associated with the university.

9. I do not wish to imply that simply allowing professors to own (and thus control) the outputs of their research would reduce challenges associated with commercialization. Instead, I contend that the processes by which commercialization works changes upon the organization and practices of the academy will be structured by such distinctions. Thus, we might expect the effects of academic commercialization to manifest distinctively in systems that do not remove control of IP from faculty inventors.

10. For a more detailed discussion of life science faculty's responses to increased commercialization see Owen-Smith and Powell (2001).

11. A well-known life scientist.

12. In what follows, I pay little attention to the incentive offered by royalty sharing at universities. It is undoubtedly the case that the potential for monetary rewards is an important component of faculty entrepreneurship, however, the fact that very few inventions ever return significant income, that only a portion of that income accrues to the faculty members themselves, and that many faculty are aware of their chances of becoming rich directly from a piece of IP means that income streams are less salient than other perceived benefits. See Owen-Smith and Powell (2001b) for a more detailed analysis of life and physical science faculty's decisions to disclose.

13. In this short space, I cannot draw out all the interesting points at which physical and life scientists' conceptions of the benefits of IP meet, but note the similarity between the conception of freedom of action used here, and the reluctant entrepreneur's focus on using intellectual property to ensure autonomous use of research tools and materials in biology.

14. At both BSU and EPU, technology licensing offices are administrative units under the umbrella of the central research administration.

15. I borrow this metaphor from Rosenbloom and Spencer (1996).

REFERENCES

Association of University Technology Managers (AUTM). (1998). *Licensing survey, FY 1998: Full report.* Northbrook, IL: Association of University Techology Managers.

Association of University Technology Managers (AUTM). (1999). *Licensing survey, FY 1999: Full report.* Northbrook, IL: Association of University Techology Managers.

Association of University Technology Managers (AUTM). (2000). *Licensing survey, FY 2000: Full report.* Northbrook, IL: Association of University Techology Managers.

Association of University Technology Managers (AUTM). (2003). *Licensing survey, FY 2003: Full report.* Northbrook, IL: Association of University Technology Managers.

Blumenthal, D., Gluck, M., Louis, K. S., Soto, M. A., and Wise, D. (1986). University-industry research relationships in biotechnology: Implications for the university. *Science, 232,* 1361–1366.

Dasgupta, P., & David, P. (1987). Information disclosure and the economics of science and technology. In G. R. Feiwel (Ed.), *Arrow and the ascent of modern economic theory* (pp. 659–689). New York: New York University Press.

Dasgupta, P., & David, P. A. (1994). Toward a new economics of science. *Research Policy 23,* 487–521.

Etzkowitz, H., Webster, A., & Healey, P. (1995). Science as intellectual property. In S. Jasanoff, G. E. Markle, J. C. Petersen, & T. Pinch (Eds.), *Handbook of science and technology studies.* Thousand Oaks, CA, and London: Sage.

Feldman, M. S., & Pentland, B. T. (2003). Reconceptualizing organizational routines as a source of flexibility and change. *Administrative Science Quarterly 48*, 94–118.

Geiger, R. L. (1993). Research and relevant knowledge: American research universities since World War II. New York: Oxford University Press.

Gompers, P. A., & Lerner, J. (1999). *The venture capital cycle.* Cambridge: MIT Press.

Guston, David H. (1999). Stabilizing the boundary between US politics and science: The role of the Office of Technology Transfer as a boundary organization. *Social Studies of Science 29*, 87–111.

Jensen, R. A., Thursby, J. G., & Thursby, M. C. (2003). *The disclosure and licensing of university inventions.* NBER Working Papers 9734. Cambridge, MA: National Bureau of Economic Research.

Kennedy, D. (2003). Industry and academia in transition. *Science 302*, 1293–1293.

Kenney, M., & Patton, D. (2000). Reconsidering the Bayh-Dole Act and the current university ownership model. *Research Policy 38* (9), 1407–1422.

Krimsky, S. (2003). *Science in the private interest: Has the lure of profits corrupted biomedical research?* Lanham, MD: Rowman & Littlefield.

March, J. G., Schulz, M., & Chou, H. (2000). *The dynamics of rules: Change in written organizational codes.* Stanford: Stanford University Press.

Merton, R. K. (1957). Priorities in scientific discovery: A chapter in the sociology of science. *American Sociological Review 22*, 635–659.

Merton, R. K. (1968). The Matthew Effect in science. *Science 159*, 56–63.

Merton, R. K. (1988). The Matthew Effect in science II: Cumulative advantage and the symbolism of intellectual property. *Isis 79*, 606–623.

Mirowski, P. (2011). *Science mart: Privatizing American science.* Cambridge: Harvard University Press.

Mowery, D. C., Nelson, R. R., Sampat, B. N., & Ziedonis, A. A.(2001). The growth of patenting and licensing by US universities:

An assessment of the effects of the Bayh-Dole Act of 1980. *Research Policy 30*, 99–119.

Murray, F. (2004). The role of academic inventors in entrepreneurial firms: Sharing the laboratory life. *Research Policy 33* (4), 643–659.

Nelson, R. R. (2004). The market economy and the scientific commons. *Research Policy 33* (3), 455–471.

Owen-Smith, J. (2003). From separate systems to a hybrid order: Accumulative advantage across public and private science at Research One universities. *Research Policy 32*, 1081–1104.

Owen-Smith, J., & W. W. Powell. (2001). Careers and contradictions: Faculty responses to the transformation of knowledge and its uses in the life sciences. *Research in the Sociology of Work 10*, 109–140.

Owen-Smith, Jason & Walter W. Powell (2001b). To Patent or Not: Faculty Decisions and Institutional Success in Academic Patenting. *Journal of Technology Transfer* 26(1): 99-114.

Powell, W. W., Koput, K. W., & Smith-Doerr, L. (1996). Interorganizational collaboration and the locus of innovation: Networks of learning in biotechnology. *Administrative Science Quarterly 41*, 116–145.

Powell, W. W., & Owen-Smith, J. (1998). Universities and the market for intellectual property in the life sciences. *Journal of Policy Analysis and Management 17*, 253–277.

Powell, W. W., & Sandholz, K. (2011). Chance, necessité, et naiveté: Ingredients to create a new organizational form. In J. Padgett & W. W. Powell (Eds.), *The emergence of organizations and markets*. Princeton: Princeton University Press.

Rip, A. (1986). Mobilizing resources through texts. In M. Callon (Ed.), *Mapping the dynamics of science and technology: Sociology of science in the real world*. Basingstoke, Hampshire: Macmillan.

Rosenbloom, R.S. & Spencer, W.J. (1996) The Transformation of Industrial Research. *Issues in Science and Technology*. 12(3), 68-74.

Siegel, D. S., Waldman, D., & Link, A. (2003). Assessing the impact of organizational practices on the relative productivity of university technology transfer offices: An exploratory study. *Research Policy 32*, 27–48.

Slaughter, S., & Rhoades, G. (1996). The emergence of a competitiveness research and development policy coalition and the commercialization of academic science and technology. *Science, Technology, and Human Values 21*, 303–339.

United States Patent and Tradmark Office. (2010). U.S. colleges and universities – utility patent grants 1969-2008. Available at http://www.uspto.gov/web/offices/ac/ido/oeip/taf/univ/doc/doc_info_2008.htm.

Zhou, X. G. (1993). The dynamics of organizational rules. *American Journal of Sociology 98*, 1134–1166.

10

THE IMPACT OF THE 2008 GREAT RECESSION ON COLLEGE AND UNIVERSITY CONTRIBUTIONS TO STATE AND REGIONAL ECONOMIC GROWTH

D. BRUCE JOHNSTONE

ABSTRACT

At the time of the September 2011 SUNY conference on *Universities as Economic Drivers,* the United States and most of its colleges and universities were recovering from, or accommodating to, the collapse of state budgets, endowments, and family incomes. These economic changes stemmed from the Great Recession of 2008–10, which by the start of 2012 still left most states with serious budget shortfalls. Ironically, public colleges and universities, which are generally assumed to be one of the keys to restoring the nation's economic competitiveness in the increasingly competitive global economy, were themselves suffering from worsening austerity due to, in part, significant cuts in state appropriations. This chapter examines the linkages between their heightened financial austerity and their ability to contribute to the state and regional economic recovery, concluding that states must elevate the budget priorities of higher education, but also that public colleges and universities can enhance their contributions to economic restoration in spite of the worsening austerity.

INTRODUCTION

The Great Recession of 2008 began with a crash in the United States market for mortgage securities and derivatives, and then spread quickly to the entire financial sector and to the rest of the U.S. and most of the industrialized world economies. By early 2012, the U.S. economy was recovering very slowly, with unemployment still just over 8.5 percent. In late 2011, however, the central concern of the advanced industrial economies was moving from America, where the worldwide economic downturn began, to Europe, and especially to Southern Europe (Greece, Italy, Portugal, and Spain), where a combination of slow economic growth, high deficits, and exploding (and unfunded) future pension and health care obligations threaten the Euro Zone itself—and are threatening America's economic recovery as well.

As of the end of 2011, the usual monetary and fiscal tools for supporting economic recovery, such as lower interest rates and enhanced governmental spending, appear to have been insufficient to the task as well as mired in a political stalemate. The American Recovery and Reinvestment Act (ARRA) of 2009, which included more than $30 billion in part to address college affordability and access and $7.6 billion for scientific research, helped to stave off some of the recession's effects on America's colleges and universities; in particular, the effects stemming from the collapse of state treasuries and the loss of income of so many U.S. households with students in college. However, the ARRA money has since dried up, and many economists believe that the stimulus was insufficient to restore the United States economy anyway, quite aside from its ability or inability to shield American higher education from the effects of the 2008 recession.

The U.S. president and most Democrats, joined by most academic economists, continue (as of early 2012) to call for more federal fiscal stimulus, which in turn calls for either higher federal deficits in the short run or increased taxation or both. The Republican Party, animated by its right wing, but also encouraged by a widespread malaise with government generally, calls for more cuts in federal and state spending, lower taxes (especially on individuals and corporations), and priority attention not to the current high levels of unemployment or relief to hard-pressed state and local public sectors, but to the size of government itself and to the high and increasing levels of government debt. The Republicans, who, as of 2012, controlled the House of Representatives and many statehouses, saw the priority need to cut government spending, cut taxes, and attempt to bring down what they believe to be the increasingly unsustainable entitlements for pensions and health care.

Public higher education, like all state revenue-dependent sectors and services, is vulnerable to collapsing state revenues, which, unlike federally funded services, are unable to be relieved by deficit financing. But public and private colleges and universities alike are also vulnerable to the anticipated cuts in federal financial assistance (especially federal Pell Grants and the federal subsidized student loan program), as well as to cuts in federal research support. This chapter examines the impact on public colleges and universities of the economic downturn that began with the 2008 recession and the effect that the ensuing austerity of public higher education may have on college and university contributions to state and regional economic recovery and growth.

Most of this analysis will be speculative, as the combination of economic austerity and uncertainty are both ongoing and too recent to allow data driven analysis. Nonetheless, the juxtaposition of the widespread belief that colleges and universities are key to economic growth and recovery—the very theme of this volume—alongside the fact that a worsening higher educational austerity brought on the very economic downturn that many believe needs a vibrant sector of higher education to correct makes this topic relevant. I will attempt in this chapter to examine:

- the depth of the current (public) higher education austerity and the likelihood of imminent recovery—as opposed to a long-range or even a permanent financial downturn that will have both a profound and a lasting effect on the ability of colleges and universities to carry out their traditional functions of, for example, teaching, vocational and professional preparation, applied and basic research, and community and regional service; and
- the possible special impact of such higher education austerity on the contributions that colleges and universities can make to their regional economies.

HIGHER EDUCATIONAL AUSTERITY FOLLOWING
THE 2008 GREAT RECESSION

Financial austerity in higher education has been around for decades—perhaps forever—quite apart from the impact of any slowdown, recession, or turbulence in the general economy. This austerity is a function not simply of higher education's high costs, which are indeed very high, whether measured in dollars per student or in dollars per anything else that those of us in universities do. Far more significantly, this austerity is a function of an annually increasing trajectory of costs, and therefore of annually increasing revenue needs, that will in most years outpace the prevailing rates of inflation, and that will almost certainly exceed the likely trajectory of available revenues, especially from the state governments—many of which have been disinvesting in their public universities for years and all of which have been shifting more of the burden of support on to parents, students, and donors.

To add a personal note to this assertion, in 2001 I co-edited a book titled *In Defense of American Higher Education*, in which I contributed a chapter examining those supposed "out of control" costs that were then, as now, coming under such criticism. As a part of this defense, in a footnote, I recounted my personal experiences with austerity over the fifteen years as a State University of New York college president (1979–1988) and then as SUNY system chancellor (1988–1994), stating:

> In almost every one of those fifteen years and frequently more than once in a single fiscal year, I and my administrative team have had to cut faculty, staff, and operating expenses (on more than one occasion extending to the removal of tenured faculty), totaling approximately 20 percent of the full-time faculty and staff of the State-operated system. (Johnstone, 2001, p. 174)

In fact, the downturn in state finances and in the financial fortunes especially of public colleges and universities since 2008 has been far more profound than this, and gives every indication of being lasting. Nationally, in the crippling 2008–09 recession and the subsequent prolonged downturn and persisting unemployment, the only factor that saved universities in many states from even deeper cuts was the so-called federal stimulus money mentioned above, much of which went into higher education. For example, in 2009, fifteen states used $2.3 billion from the ARRA to support their higher education institutions (SHEEO, 2011). Without the stimulus money, state support for higher education would have dropped from 2008 to 2010 by 6.8 percent. Even with the stimulus, total state support for higher education decreased in Vermont in 2010 by 16.4 percent, in Virginia by 10.4 percent, in New Mexico by 10.2 percent, in Iowa by 9.5 percent, in Ohio by 7.9 percent, in Michigan by 7.1 percent, and in California by 6.8 percent (Stripling, 2010).

According to the Delta Project on Postsecondary Education Costs, from 2008 to 2009, net tuition revenue per student at public research universities increased by $361, while per-student appropriations declined by $751 (Delta Cost Project, 2010a, p. 3). Tuition increases made up for less than half, on average, of what institutions lost in state funds. Moreover, the gap between the spending by top private colleges and universities and the top public institutions, already widening for at least a decade, has been accelerating since the recession (Delta Cost Project, 2010, p. 16).

Focusing on New York, the site of the September 2011 conference on *Universities as Economic Drivers,* the following information helps brings greater clarity to these financial dilemmas:

- New York State spending on higher education—public and private, institutional and student support—fell from 2009 to 2011 by 3.6 percent (Grapevine, 2011a).
- New York's total spending on higher education was twenty-third (from the top) in per capita, and sixteenth in funding per $1000 of personal income (Grapevine, 2011b)

This is actually a little better than the State University of New York had experienced in the early 1990s—which sends a mixed message regarding the prospect for future improvements in state funding for public higher education in New York. State tax support for public higher education is somewhat low largely because of the small proportion (relative to the proportions in other states) of students being educated in public colleges and universities. At the same time, this funding is not so low as to signal a literal financial collapse of New York State's public colleges and universities.

Most important (or discouraging to those in New York's systems of higher education), New York is still a very high tax state, and the prospects for substantial state tax increases are dim—and the odds of SUNY and CUNY significantly benefiting from additional tax money are dimmer still, particularly in terms of increased annual appropriation. One small glimmer of increased funding comes from a special state-funded competition designed to spur growth in the economic development of SUNY's research centers, and Governor Andrew Cuomo announced in January 2012 his desire to create a similar program for the system's comprehensive universities. In an era of austerity, such targeted funding mechanisms may become more common.

AN UNCERTAIN FINANCIAL FUTURE

Whether the Democrats or the Republicans prevail in the 2012 elections, or whether an effective compromise is reached in 2012 or 2013 on the competing priorities of addressing unemployment and rising poverty, or addressing the nation's long-range deficit, a continuing and almost certainly rising austerity seems to be the future of higher education, public and private alike, even with the eventual economic recovery that is almost inevitable (if far more prolonged than any would wish for).

The principal question for public colleges and universities and their presidents, chancellors, and governing boards facing this long-run paucity of state tax revenues, then, is whether this is a period of austerity they can continue to ride out by further expenditure reductions and tuition increases, or whether at least some institutions need to radically alter their underlying higher education production functions and produce their learning at significantly—and sustainably—lower per-student costs. In other words, rather than continuing on the track of reducing expenditures through faculty and staff attrition; replacing needed full-time faculty lines with lower cost, part-time adjunct lecturers; deferring maintenance; and increasing non-tax revenue through increasing tuition and fees and ramping-up private philanthropic giving, public colleges and universities might need to turn to measures such as:

- increased teaching loads of research university faculty who are not producing significant research at the highest level;
- fuller use by students and faculty alike of the teaching day, week, and year (e.g., more undergraduate late afternoon classes, and year-round calendars);
- greater use of self-paced learning, credit by examination, and credit for e-learning;
- measures to significantly lower course and program redundancy;
- measures to increase three-year bachelor's degree completion, in part by more effective incorporation of college-level learning in high school; and
- measures to lower significantly failure and noncompletion rates, in part through better alignment of the academic preparedness of incoming students with the academic standards of the institution and program.

Whether most colleges and universities, public and private alike, will be able to ride out the continuing (as of early 2012) American economic downturn and return to a familiar way of doing the business of higher education—that is, with two fourteen or fifteen-week semesters, full-time student course loads of four or five courses taught mainly in lecture theatres and classrooms, and taught mainly by professors who can at least aspire to long-term employment with significant control over their curricula, standards, and instructional methods—or have to change in very fundamental and unsettling ways is uncertain at best. So the long-run effect of this austerity on most colleges and universities (like the long-run financial futures of the American economy, the public sector generally, and the lower and lower-middle socioeconomic classes) seems in early 2012 to be in some doubt. But whatever the long-term future, it appears safe to say that many or even most colleges and universities will continue trimming expenses and shedding lower priority programs as well as aggressively seeking more non-tax revenues, especially from tuition and fees. The question posed in this chapter, then, is how such measures will affect the contributions that colleges and universities make toward their state and regional economies—the question to which I now turn.

THE EFFECT OF THE 2008–2012 ECONOMIC DOWNTURN ON THE IMPACT OF COLLEGES AND UNIVERSITIES ON THEIR STATE AND REGIONAL ECONOMIES

There has not been sufficient time to gather evidence on the impact of the recent (and in some ways, in 2012, still current) economic downturn on public college and university contributions to their state and regional economies, but it is possible to make at least some informed conjectures about the effects that severe and prolonged public college and university austerity might have on state and regional economies. We can begin with examining three significant—and quite different— ways in which colleges and universities contribute to the economic growth and vitality of their states and regions in the best of economic times—and then speculate on the likely impact of a continuous austerity. These three ways are:

1. contributing directly to the development of new, innovative, knowledge-driven, export-oriented products and processes;
2. training workers for the increasingly high-end manufacturing and service jobs called for in the new economies of the developed world; and
3. attracting more students from outside the state or region to attend college within the state than the number of students leaving the state to pursue other opportunities; that is, by being a net exporter of higher education.

Contributing Directly to the Development of New, Innovative, Knowledge-Driven, Export-Oriented Products and Processes

This contribution is most closely associated with research universities and especially with those whose faculty, laboratories, and graduates are associated with the development of knowledge-based, high value-added products such as biomedical engineering devices, pharmaceuticals, and new generations of transportation and tele-communications technologies. Most states at least aspire to their own version of a university- (or universities-) connected research park or industrial cluster, such as Silicone Valley in California, North Carolina's Research Triangle, or Boston's Route 128. These places are full of dynamic, innovative, knowledge-driven start-ups, fre-quently originating from faculty or recent graduates and maturing into established global producers and exporters. Such innovative, knowledge-driven, export-oriented products and processes require a critical mass of world-class scholars and students (mainly graduate and postdoctoral), principally in the so-called STEM fields of sci-ence, technology, engineering, and mathematics/computer science. In search of replicating these pockets of knowledge-based economic vitality, states have invested in research parks and technology incuba-tion centers designed to link their public (and sometimes also their private) universities with established or fledgling industries capital-izing on innovative (and generally patentable) products emerging from the university laboratories. These public-private partnerships thus combine the existing human and physical capital of the state's universities and university hospitals with additional state funding, federal funding, and private venture capital.

For example, one of the hot new areas of science and technol-ogy with presumed future application to innovative products, and therefore to enhanced global competitiveness, is nanoscience, which draws on research university science and engineering and is being supported by both state and federal governments. The National Insti-tute of Standards and Technology, an agency of the U.S. Department of Commerce, created the Center for Nanoscience and Technology. The National Science Foundation funded the Nanoscale Science and Engineering Center (NSEC), a collaboration among Harvard Univer-sity, the Massachusetts Institute of Technology, and the University of California at Santa Barbara, with participation from the Brookhav-en, Oak Ridge, and Sandia National Laboratories, in addition to three European universities. States and state research universities, with funding from the states, the federal government, and private in-dustry, are now moving in the same direction, forming, for example, the University of Wisconsin-Madison's Nanoscale Science and Engi-neering Center in Templated Synthesis and Assembly; the University of Georgia's Nanoscale Science and Engineering Center, and the State

University of New York at Albany's College of Nanoscale Science and Engineering (see Feldman, Freyer, & Lanahan, 2012; Schultz, 2012—chapters 4 and 5 of this volume—for an extended discussion of the economic impact of such centers).

Such examples of large-scale investments in global economic competitiveness (and there are many others), drawing on research university strengths in physical and biomedical science and engineering, have multiple sources of funding, including the universities' operating budgets, physical plants, endowments, and philanthropic capabilities, as well as new funding from state and federal governments, private industry, and venture capital. These investments are probably robust enough to withstand even a prolonged economic downturn at the state levels—more so even than the universities' core instructional budgets. At the same time, the inherent riskiness of the high knowledge–based final products, together with the likely continuation of considerable financial austerity in virtually all of the states, suggests that new ventures that depend on new state funding as well as on additional university budget reallocation will be increasingly difficult to sustain and are likely to be both fewer in number and more modest in scale in the foreseeable future.

To complicate matters further, the correlation between the scholarly eminence of a state's array of public and private research universities and its economic health is complex and not altogether clear. For example, Economic Modeling Specialists reported in 2011 on the states with largest presence of STEM-related jobs, and the recent changes in the number of these jobs. California, with the nation's largest and arguably most eminent public research university system, plus similarly prestigious private research universities such as Stanford, California Institute of Technology, and the University of Southern California, as well as by far the largest number of STEM-related jobs (e.g., computer specialists, engineers, life scientists, physical scientists, and technicians), saw a loss of some nineteen thousand of these jobs over the previous decade. At the same time, the greatest growth in such jobs were in states such as North Dakota, Alaska, Utah, Rhode Island, Arkansas, and West Virginia—none of which (with due respect for their fine public universities) would be cited by most observers either for their extraordinary concentrations of public research universities or, with the exception of North Dakota, their states' growing investments in these institutions.

Obviously, percentage increases are extremely sensitive to the base from which the increases are calculated, as well as the nature of the jobs themselves, and the presence of STEM-related jobs seems to be most heavily correlated with government research enterprises. Therefore, it is impossible to draw any conclusions from these comparisons about the impact either of research university reputations or of the changes in state financial support of their public universities on changes in state and regional economies. Nonetheless, such data reinforce the complex nature of state and regional economic health and the dependence of that health on such varied factors as the extent of extractable resources (especially oil and gas), the location of federal research and defense installations (largely a function of relative political power), and a wide array of state policies such as business and personal income tax rates and the *business-friendliness* of the regulatory climate—all quite independent of the states' relative financial support of their public research universities.

More importantly—and perhaps more ominously—the long-run academic strength of the nation's public research universities depends on far more than a handful of robust centers of state and federally supported applied science laboratories. Rather, it depends on sustained strength in the basic arts and science disciplines as well as the applied STEM fields, on strong undergraduate programs balanced with liberal arts and sciences as well as graduate and postgraduate programs in science and technology, and on a healthy academic profession that attracts a constant infusion of new recruits to the life of serious scholarship and teaching. The academic strength of the U.S. public research university as we enter the second decade of the twenty-first century has proven relatively resilient to the recent (post-2008) economic downturn, as well as to a decade or more of at best uncertain, and more likely declining, state funding. But the academic strength of the nation's top public universities is nonetheless fragile. And the continued withdrawal of this core state funding of the nation's public research universities—even if supplemented in part by steeply rising tuition fees, additional philanthropy, and the uneven success of a relatively small number of successful university-affiliated research parks and public-private partnerships—threatens the long-run capacity of the public research universities to restore the strength of their buffeted state and regional economies and the global competitiveness of the U.S. economy.

Training Workers for Globally Competitive Manufacturing and Service Jobs

The second way that colleges and universities contribute to their state and regional economies is by training workers for the increasingly high-end manufacturing and service jobs called for in the new economies of the modern world. At least anecdotally and journalistically, the last half of 2011 was full of stories of firms unable to find workers with the right skills—alongside stories of prolonged unemployment and unemployed workers desperately seeking work. The more effective training of workers for state and regional economies operating in an increasingly competitive global economy is associated not merely with the nation's public and private research universities, but perhaps even more with the bachelor's and sub-bachelor's degree institutions that train workers who are—or who ought to be—job ready for the new economy, whether in manufacturing, tourism, health, or other sectors of modern productive, competitive economies. Strengthening this function depends on considerably more than the financial health of the institutions. It requires curricular flexibility and more responsiveness to the needs of local employers, and accommodation to the needs of frequently underprepared and financially hard-pressed students. Training today's and tomorrow's workforce requires internships and other instructional partnerships with regional and local employers, as well as other reforms that may be challenged, but are not necessarily jeopardized, by state financial austerity.

However, state financial austerity is already having deleterious effects on the training of the modern workforce. In 2011, some community colleges actually had to turn away applicants—the numbers of which were increasing precisely because of the changing economy and the need for retraining—in spite of the public community college's traditional mission to accept all high school graduates. Rising tuition fees forced by static or declining state appropriations, even in public comprehensive and community colleges, threaten to force more students into part-time status, jeopardizing persistence and completion rates. And the loss of state funding and shrinking of college budgets makes the retraining of faculty and the reallocation of resources all the more difficult. If the current state budget–imposed financial austerity begins to be lifted in 2012 and beyond, permitting the states to at least maintain their shares of instructional costs, and if a more measured growth in tuition fees and enhanced philanthropy can provide needed improvements in instruction and accessibility, then the aforementioned reallocations and reforms in instruction can help public colleges and universities rise to the challenge of better preparing the workforce needed in the new globally competitive economy. But continued austerity of the nation's public colleges jeopardizes this function.

Attracting Students from Outside the State or Region

A third contribution by public colleges and universities to their state and regional economies is to attract more students from outside the state or region than are being sent out: that is, to be a net exporter of higher education. The economic impact of the state and regional colleges and universities is thus associated with student and family spending not only on tuition, but also on food, lodging, and other purchases made in the regional economy that create and sustain a myriad of local and regional business and jobs. Many colleges and universities estimate a part of their regional economic impact by calculating such spending and then applying some multiplier to infer a net economic impact. (Similar economic impact calculations are made for grants and contracts from outside the region, as well as for construction and other capital and equipment spending in the local economy.) The appropriate multipliers are a matter of considerable debate (discussed in chapter 3). However, there is clearly some impact of such expenditures on the regional economies. The question for this chapter is the likely net enrollment impact, if any, from the national and state economic downturn on the state and/or regional economy.

This enrollment impact may arise from eroded family financial circumstances resulting from the loss of family savings or the diminished chances of a second home mortgage, or from greater than anticipated tuition increases in turn precipitated by financial pressures on the institution, or from a reduction in federal or state grants or loan subsidies—any of which can lead to changes in enrollment behavior designed to reduce net family expenditures. The altered behavior may be to not enroll at all and instead to enter directly into the workforce—at a probable lower level of productivity and remuneration than would have been likely with a tertiary-level degree or certificate. More likely, the altered enrollment behavior in response to reduced family financial circumstances or to the loss of a student's own income will be to work additional hours in outside employment (if the outside employment continues to be an option), or to borrow more (although increasing student debts are becoming more worrisome), or to move back home with parents in order to lower expenses (whether moving home but remaining at the same college or university, or changing institutions from a high tuition private college to a lower tuition public college). Overall, the net economic impact of a prolonged economic downturn, considering only the effect on enrolment behavior, is likely to be slight but positive in the case of a region that has been a net importer of higher education and that stands to gain more returning students than it loses as a result of the tight economic times, and slight but negative on the net exporting regions that are likely to lose more students returning home to other regions or other states to save money.

From the standpoint of state and federal policies, the importance of public higher education to state and regional economies is arguably greater as a result of the first two contributions mentioned above—that is, developing new, innovative, and competitive products and process (largely from the research universities) and training the workforce of the new global economy (also a contribution of comprehensive and community colleges)—than from attempting to affect the net import or export of students from a state or region. Nevertheless, the net effect of reduced governmental support of higher education, especially the almost inevitable reductions in state support of public colleges and universities, is clearly likely to have a detrimental effect on the contributions these institutions can make to the economic recovery of our regions, our states, and to the nation as a whole.

We need to return to consideration of the economic contributions colleges and universities can make to their state and regional economies that need not be diminished by the possible prolonged financial austerity, even if there is damage to other, equally important goals of higher education, such as widening participation, improving persistence and completion, and creating a more attractive academic profession.

For example, faculty and staff allocation and reallocation decisions might be made in the direction of greater regional economic impact in spite of heightened institutional austerity and in spite of the inevitable losses that such reallocations inevitably have on other parts of the university. Such consequences—that is, possible gains in regional economic impact occurring in spite of the state and federal economic downturn and heightened institutional austerity—are very conjectural. However, such could be the case where the economic downturn leads to presidential and decanal decisions to reallocate resources in favor of programs and scholarly activities that seem more likely to attract more tuition-paying students, more fundable grants and contracts, or more regional philanthropy, and at the same time to downsize or shed programs and activities that have very low enrollments or are conspicuously non-grant producing, even if the losses to institutional reputation, faculty and staff morale, and the long-run scholarly quality of the institution may be compromised.

Less drastically, we can conjecture other activities and policies that might be undertaken to enhance a college's or university's regional economic impact and that should not be affected either way by prolonged economic downturns and institutional austerity. These might include, for example:

- updating and improving the curricula of those applied programs that avowedly seek to produce job-ready graduates;
- tilting new faculty and staff hiring and faculty promotion and retention policies to favor faculty likely to engage in activities with direct regional economic impact;
- investing in offices of technology transfer and patent encouragement that can recover operating costs from assessments on successful applications; and
- instituting local governmental, business, and industry advisory councils to advise on the kinds of academic degree and non-degree programs that are most needed—and taking such advice seriously.

In short, public colleges and universities need to strengthen the case for continued and restored funding based partly on the several critical roles these institutions make to regional and state economies as well as to the national economy. At the same time, there are ways for presidents and chancellors to sustain and even to enhance these contributions even if the financial austerity of the past decade, and especially since the Great Recession of 2008, continues—which seems, from the vantage point of early 2012, to be likely, if unfortunate.

REFERENCES

Delta Cost Project. (2010). *Trends in college spending 1999–2009.* Washington, DC: Delta Project on Postsecondary Costs, Productivity, and Accountability.

Delta Cost Project. (2010a). Extracts in key issue areas from *Trends in college spending, 1999–2009.* Washington, DC: Delta Project on Postsecondary Costs, Productivity, and Accountability.

Economic Modeling Specialists. (2011). States with largest presence of STEM-related jobs. Downloaded December 20, 2011 from http://www.economicmodeling.com/2011/09/20/where-are-stem-jobs-concentrated/.

Feldman, M. P., Freyer, A. M., and Lanahan, L. (2012). On the measurement of university research contributions to economic growth and innovation. In J. E. Lane & D. B. Johnstone (Eds.), *Universities and colleges as economic drivers.* Albany: State University of New York Press.

Grapevine. (2011). An annual compilation of state fiscal support for higher education. Downloaded October 20, 2011 from http://grapevine.illinoisstate.edu/.

Grapevine. (2011a). One-year (FY11–FY12), two-year (FY10–FY12), and five-year (FY07–FY12) percent changes in state fiscal support for higher education, by state and by source of fiscal support. Retrieved October 20, 2011, from http://grapevine.illinoisstate.edu/tables/index.htm.

Grapevine. (2011b). State support for higher education in Fiscal Year 2010–11, by state, per $1,000 in personal income and per capita. Retrieved October 20, 2011 from http://grapevine.illinoisstate.edu/tables/index.htm.

Johnstone, D. B. (2001). Higher education and those "out-of-control costs." In P. G. Altbach, P. J. Gumport, & D. B. Johnstone (Eds.),

In defense of American higher education (pp. 144–179). Baltimore: The Johns Hopkins University Press.

Schultz, L. I. (2012). University industry government collaboration for economic growth. In J. E. Lane & D. B. Johnstone (Eds.), *Universities and colleges as economic drivers*. Albany: State University of New York Press.

SHEEO (State Higher Education Executive Officers). (2011). *State higher education finance, FY2010*. Boulder, CO: Author.

Stripling, J. (2010, February 11). "Fading Stimulus Saved Colleges." *Inside Higher Ed*. Retrieved from http://www.insidehighered.com/news/2010/02/11/sheeo.

CONTRIBUTORS

ANTHONY P. CARNEVALE currently serves as director of the Georgetown University Center on Education and the Workforce. Between 1996 and 2006, Dr. Carnevale served as vice president for public leadership at the Educational Testing Service (ETS). While at ETS, he was appointed by President George W. Bush to serve on the White House Commission on Technology and Adult Education. Before joining ETS, Dr. Carnevale was director of human resource and employment studies at the Committee for Economic Development (CED), the nation's oldest business-sponsored policy research organization. While at CED, he was appointed by President Bill Clinton to chair the National Commission on Employment Policy. Dr. Carnevale founded and was president of the Institute for Workplace Learning (IWL) from 1983 to 1993. Prior to founding IWL, he served as director of political and government affairs for the American Federation of State, County, and Municipal Employees (AFSCME), the largest union in the AFL-CIO. Before joining AFSCME, he was a senior staff member in both houses of the U.S. Congress. Dr. Carnevale was appointed as the Majority Staff Director on the Public Financing Subcommittee of the House Committee on Government Operations. Dr. Carnevale received his BA from Colby College and his PhD in public finance economics from the Maxwell School at Syracuse University.

MARYANN P. FELDMAN is the S. K. Heninger Distinguished Chair in Public Policy at the University of North Carolina, Chapel Hill. Her research and teaching interests focus on the areas of innovation, the commercialization of academic research, and the factors that promote technological change and economic growth. A large part of her work concerns the geography of innovation—investigating the reasons why innovation clusters spatially and the mechanisms that support and sustain industrial clusters.

ALLAN FREYER is a public policy analyst at the N.C. Budget & Tax Center with a portfolio of policy research and advocacy work focusing on economic development, workforce development, and labor market issues. He has more than a decade of experience in federal, state, and local economic development policy, including service as a policy advisor to three members of the United States Congress and as an independent economic development consultant to nonprofits, universities, and state and local government agencies. Allan is also currently a third-year doctoral student in city and regional planning at the University of North Carolina, Chapel Hill, where his research agenda focuses on the role of innovative and traditional economic development practices in strengthening community bargaining position in the face of globally mobile capital. Allan has a Bachelor's degree in political science and history from Duke University and a Masters in city and regional planning from UNC-Chapel Hill.

THOMAS GAIS is director of the Nelson A. Rockefeller Institute of Government, the public policy research arm of the State University of New York. Gais has conducted research and written on federalism, program implementation, social policy, higher education and economic development, faith-based service delivery, state and local fiscal issues, performance management, campaign finance reforms, and interest groups. Selected recent publications include "The Social Safety Net, Health Care, and the Great Recession," in *The Oxford Handbook of State and Local Government Finance* (2012); "Stretched Net: The Retrenchment of State and Local Social Welfare Spending," *Publius* (2009); and "Federalism and the Executive Branch," in *The Executive Branch* (Oxford, 2005). Gais is currently writing a book on the U.S. safety net and the federal system. He received his PhD in political science from the University of Michigan.

JAMES JACOBS is the president of Macomb Community College. Prior to his appointment, he concurrently served as director for the Center for Workforce Development and Policy at the college, and as associate director, Community College Research Center (CCRC), Teachers

College, Columbia University. Jacobs earned his PhD from Princeton University and has more than forty years of experience at Macomb. He has taught social science, political science, and economics. He specializes in the areas of workforce skills and technology, economic development, worker retraining, and community college workforce development, and is widely published in these areas of expertise. In addition, Jacobs has conducted research, developed programs, and consulted on workforce development and community college issues at the national, state, and local levels. He is a past president of the National Council for Workforce Education, a national postsecondary organization of occupational education and workforce development specialists, and a member of the Manufacturing Extension Partnership Advisory Board of the National Institute of Standards and Technology and the National Assessment of Career and Technical Education. Jacobs is currently serving on the Governor's Talent Investment Board, which advises Michigan's governor on job creation, and talent development and retention. He is widely known for the Macomb County Economic Forecast, presented annually for more than thirty years for the coalition of the county's chambers of commerce. Jacobs serves on a number of local boards, including the Center for Automotive Research, Metropolitan Affairs Council, and the Detroit Institute of Arts.

D. BRUCE JOHNSTONE is Distinguished Service Professor Emeritus of Higher and Comparative Education at the State University of New York at Buffalo. His principal scholarship is in international comparative higher education finance, governance, and policy formation. He continues to direct the International Comparative Higher Education Finance and Accessibility Project, an examination into the worldwide shift of higher education costs from governments and taxpayers to parents and students. The project has been the principal single source of descriptive and theoretical work as well as ongoing research on tuition, financial assistance, and student loan policies worldwide. During a twenty-five-year administrative career prior to assuming his professorship at the University at Buffalo, Johnstone held posts of vice president for administration at the University of Pennsylvania (1976–79), president of the State University College of Buffalo (1979–88) and chancellor from 1988 to 1994 of the State University of New York—a system consisting at that time of some sixty-four campuses and more than 400,000 students. He has written or edited many books, monographs, articles, and book chapters. His books include *Financing Higher Education World Wide: Who Pays? Who Should Pay?* (Johns Hopkins); *Financing Higher Education: Cost-Sharing in International Perspective* (Sense Publishers); *Sharing the Costs of Higher Education: Student Financial Assistance in the United Kingdom, the Federal Republic of Germany, France, Sweden and the United States* (The College Board); *New Patterns for College Lending: Income Contingent Loans* (Teachers College Press); and several co-edited books on U.S. and international comparative higher education.

LAUREN LANAHAN is a graduate student in the Department of Public Policy at the University of North Carolina, Chapel Hill. Before coming to UNC-Chapel Hill, she worked at the National Science Foundation in the Social, Behavioral & Economic Sciences Directorate. She is currently a Kauffman Dissertation Fellow and serves as an editor for the *Journal of Science Policy and Governance*. Her research interests lie in science and technology policy and regional innovation as it pertains to economic development. For her dissertation research, she is examining state-initiated, R&D-based entrepreneurial activity among universities and firms.

JASON E. LANE is Director of Educational Studies and Senior Fellow at the Nelson A. Rockefeller Institute of Government, the public policy think tank of the State University of New York (SUNY). He is also an associate professor of educational administration and policy studies and a senior researcher with the Institute for Global Education Policy Studies at the University at Albany, SUNY, where he co-directs the Cross-Border Education Research Team (C-BERT). His research interests include government planning and policy, economic development, organizational leadership, and internationalization as related to higher education organizations. Lane has written more than thirty articles, book chapters, and policy reports. His books include *Organization and Governance in Higher Education* (Wiley Press), *Multi-National Colleges and Universities: Leadership and Administration of International Branch Campuses* (Jossey-Bass) and *Academic Leadership and Governance of Higher Education: A Guide for Trustees, Leaders, and Aspiring Leaders of Two- and Four-Year Institutions*

(Stylus Press). He has consulted and lectured in more than ten countries in Asia, Europe, the Middle East, and South America and his research has been cited in major media outlets including the Associated Press, *Boston Globe,* National Public Radio, *The Chronicle of Higher Education, Inside Higher Education,* and *University World News.* He serves on the board of the Comparative and International Education Society (CIES) and the Council for International Higher Education (CIHE) and is the publisher of www.globalhighered.org, a clearinghouse of scholarship and news about the movement of educational institutions across international borders.

PETER MCHENRY is assistant professor of economics and public policy at the College of William and Mary in Virginia. He was born into a U.S. Navy family in Norfolk, Va., and moved around the country as a kid. He earned a BS from Vanderbilt University and a PhD from Yale University, both in economics. His research focuses on workers, their skills, and schools. One of his articles measures how primary and secondary school characteristics such as class size influence students' earnings later in life. He also studies how people with more and less education make different migration decisions. McHenry teaches principles of microeconomics and is participating in an effort to revamp the course to enhance student learning. He also teaches labor economics to undergraduates and graduate students in the Thomas Jefferson Program in Public Policy at the College of William and Mary.

JASON OWEN-SMITH is currently director of both the Organizational Studies Program and the Barger Leadership Institute. He holds the Barger Leadership Institute Professorship of Organizational Studies and is an associate professor in both the Department of Sociology and the Organizational Studies Program at the University of Michigan. He is the recipient of a National Science Foundation Faculty Early Career Development (CAREER) Award and an Alfred P. Sloan Foundation Industries Studies Fellowship in biotechnology. In 2008 he received the University of Michigan's Henry Russel Award, which recognizes mid-career faculty for exceptional scholarship and conspicuous teaching ability. He received his MA and PhD degrees in sociology at the University of Arizona and a BA in sociology and philosophy from the New College of Florida.

TAYA L. OWENS researches topics of higher education governance, finance, and delivery through comparative analysis with the Nelson A. Rockefeller Institute of Government. She also collaborates with the Cross-Border Education Research Team at the University at Albany, SUNY. Her research is informed by experience analyzing large-scale state and federal databases to inform policymaking in the state of Tennessee as well as prior experience teaching at colleges in China, Ukraine, and Uzbekistan. She has served the Tennessee Higher Education Commission, the Tennessee General Assembly, the United States Peace Corps, and North Carolina public schools. Recently, she has focused her attention on international indicators of college completion, publishing on the topic in the *Journal of College Student Retention*. Taya is a doctoral student at University at Albany concentrating on educational policy while concurrently completing a certificate of demography with the Department of Sociology. She holds a BA in Spanish with a teacher's license from the University of North Carolina, Wilmington, and an MEd in international education policy and management from Peabody College, Vanderbilt University.

STEPHEN J. ROSE is a nationally recognized labor economist who has been doing innovative research and writing about social class in America for the last thirty years. His *Social Stratification in the United States* was originally published in 1978 and now is in its sixth edition. His recent book, *Rebound: Why America Will Emerge Stronger from the Financial Crisis,* addresses the causes of the financial crisis and the evolving structure of the U.S. economy over the last three decades. Rose has held senior positions at the Educational Testing Service, the U.S. Department of Labor, Joint Economic Committee of Congress, the National Commission for Employment Policy, and the Washington State Senate. His commentaries have appeared in the *New York Times, Washington Post, Wall Street Journal,* and other print and broadcast media. He has a BA from Princeton University and an MA and PhD in economics from The City University of New York.

ALLEN R. SANDERSON, a graduate of Brigham Young University and the University of Chicago, is a senior lecturer in economics at the University of Chicago. He came to Chicago from Princeton in 1984; served eight years as associate provost of the University; and has also been a senior research scientist at NORC. In addition to his popular sequence in introductory economics, he teaches a course on the economics of sports and an interdisciplinary team-taught course on "Sport, Society, and Science." He received the Quantrell Award for Excellence in Teaching at Chicago and the Thomas Jefferson Award for Teaching at the College of William and Mary. Mr. Sanderson is an oft-cited authority on sports economics issues, a contributor to op-ed pages on sports and non-sports topics in newspapers around the country and a frequent guest on national and Chicago-area television and radio programs. He writes a bimonthly column for *Chicago Life*. His most recent professional journal articles are on the political economy of Chicago's unsuccessful bid to host the 2016 Olympic Games (with Robert Baade); an essay on happiness and economic well-being, and an article on Milton Friedman at Chicago, both of which appeared in the *Milken Institute Review* in 2012. His latest newspaper and magazine columns have been on various aspects of football in American society, safety, labor markets in the United States and abroad, the intersection of economics and philanthropy, and how economists think about contemporary economic, political, and public policy problems.

LAURA I. SCHULTZ is an assistant professor of nanoeconomics at the University of Albany's College of Nanoscale Science and Engineering. Prior to joining CNSE, she worked with at the National Institute of Standards and Technology and Bureau of Economic Analysis developing metrics and methods to assess the impact of private and public R&D investment. Dr. Schultz's current research studies the transfer of emerging technologies from laboratory to market. Her recent research examines the role university-industry research centers have played in creating and commercializing nanotechnologies and their impacts on regional economies. In addition, she has tracked the emergence of nanotechnologies developed in industry with bibliometric techniques. Professor Schultz is actively engaged in entrepreneurship activities and training. She has actively mentored multiple university-based nanotechnology-related start-up companies in business plan development and commercialization strategy.

JOHN J. SIEGFRIED is Professor of Economics Emeritus at Vanderbilt University. He grew up on a farm near Allentown, Pennsylvania.

After graduating from Rensselaer Polytechnic Institute in 1967, he earned a Masters in economics from Penn State in 1968. He was on Vanderbilt's economics faculty since earning his PhD at the University of Wisconsin in 1972 until he retired in 2010. He has visited at Simon Fraser University, the University of Leeds, the University of Adelaide, and the Federal Trade Commission. He was on the senior staff of President Ford's Council of Economic Advisers. Siegfried chaired the Vanderbilt Economics Department from 1980 to 1986. Since 1997 he has been secretary-treasurer of the American Economic Association. His research has been in industrial organization, antitrust economics, economics of higher education, economics of sports, and the teaching of economics. He co-authored *Economic Challenges in Higher Education* (University of Chicago Press) in 1991. His latest (edited) book is *Better Living Through Economics* (Harvard University Press, 2010). Siegfried has been president of the Southern Economic Association and the Midwest Economics Association, and is on the board of directors of the National Bureau of Economic Research and the Council for Economic Education.

DAVID WRIGHT is director of urban and metropolitan studies at the University at Albany's Nelson A. Rockefeller Institute of Government. His research focuses on regional economic development and the effectiveness of place-based strategies and public partnerships in workforce development and neighborhood renewal. Wright co-led Institute research studies on the role of higher education in regional economic development nationally and in New York State. He was project director of the Roundtable on Religion and Social Welfare Policy, which examined the role, legality, and effectiveness of government partnerships with religious organizations in delivering public services. And he has directed national field studies examining the efficacy of workforce system one-stop services, the effectiveness of the Empowerment Zone/Enterprise Community program and the Neighborhood Preservation Initiative, and the consequences of welfare reform for affordable housing agencies. Wright is the author of *Taking Stock: The Bush Faith-Based Initiative and What Lies Ahead, Flip Side of the Underclass: Unexpected Images of Social Capital in Majority African American Neighborhoods,* and *It Takes a Neighborhood: Strategies to Prevent Urban Decline.* Prior to joining the

Institute, Mr. Wright served as deputy secretary to New York Governor Mario M. Cuomo for policy and program design.

NANCY L. ZIMPHER is the twelfth chancellor of the State University of New York by unanimous vote of the SUNY Board of Trustees. With more than 465,000 students, SUNY is the nation's largest comprehensive system of higher education. A nationally recognized leader, Chancellor Zimpher is known as an effective agent of change in education. She started her career as a teacher in a one-room schoolhouse in the Ozarks and has never lost her passion for providing accessible, quality education for every student. A former chair of the Association of Public and Land-Grant Universities, Dr. Zimpher now leads the national Coalition of Urban Serving Universities and co-chairs a national blue-ribbon panel on transforming teacher preparation. She serves on the board of CEOs for Cities, is a member of the Business-Higher Education Forum, and the board of governors of the New York Academy of Sciences. Prior to coming to SUNY, Dr. Zimpher served as president of the University of Cincinnati, chancellor of the University of Wisconsin-Milwaukee, and executive dean of the Professional Colleges and dean of the College of Education at The Ohio State University. She has authored or co-authored numerous books, monographs, and academic journal articles on teacher education, urban education, academic leadership, and school/university partnerships. Chancellor Zimpher holds a Bachelor's degree in English Education and Speech, a Master's degree in English Literature, and a PhD in Teacher Education and Higher Education Administration, all from The Ohio State University.

Index

Note numbers are indicated by a page number followed by *n*.

A

AAU. *See* American Association of Universities

Abu Dhabi, 12, 226, 230

African Development Bank, 230

American Academy for the Advancement of Science, 134–135

American Association of Community Colleges (AACC), 195–196

American Association of Universities (AAU), 17, 24–25*n*5

American Legislative Exchange Council, 24*n*2

American Recovery and Reinvestment Act of 2009, 278, 281

Anchor institution, xiv, 15

Antioch College, 67

APLU. *See* Association of Public Land Grant Universities

Apprenticeships, 45

Arizona State University, 92*n*16

Associate's degree, 187*n*5, 187*n*6
earnings, 181
lifetime earnings, 176
proportion of jobs by level of required education, 179

Association of Public Land Grant Universities (APLU), xiv, 221

Association of University Technology Managers (AUTM), 101–102, 149, 264–265

Athletics, 63–64, 73, 74, 76, 85–86

Auburn University, 83

Australia, 216, 221–222

Australian Council for Private Education and Training, 216

Australian Educational Services for Overseas Students Act (ESOS), 221–222

AUTM. *See* Association of University Technology Managers

B

Bachelor's degree, 187*n*6
earnings with, 181
lifetime earnings with, 176
median earnings by college major, 185
proportion of jobs by level of required education, 179
wage premium for employees with, 173

Bayh-Dole Act (1980), 92*n*18, 142, 239, 245, 247, 250, 264, 271*n*1

BHEF. *See* Business-Higher Education Forum

Bhutan, 12

Binghamton University (SUNY), 41

"Brain drain," 11

BrainKorea21 (BK21), 11

Brookhaven Labs, 285